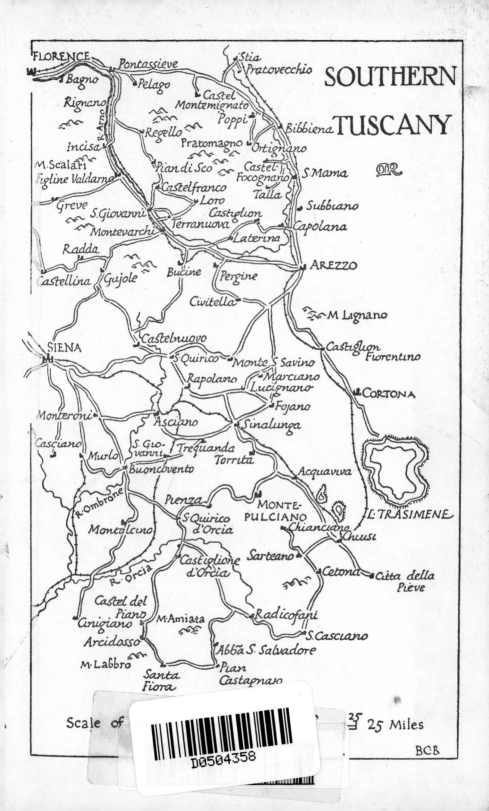

SOUTHERN

TUSCANY

FLORENCE
Bagno
Rignano
Incisa
M.Scalari
Figline Valdarno
Greve
Radda
Castellina
Pontassieve
Pelago
Regello
Pian di Sco
Castelfranco
S.Giovanni
Montevarchi
Gujole
Stia
Pratovecchio
Castel
Montemignato
Poppi
Pratomagno
Bibbiena
Ortignano
Castel-
Focognano
Talla
Loro
Castiglion
Terranuova
Laterina
Bucine
Pergine
Civitella
S.Mama
Subbiano
Capolana
AREZZO
M Lignano
SIENA
Castelnuovo
S.Quirico
Rapolano
Monteroni
Casciano
Murlo
S.Gio-
vanni
Buoncovento
R.Ombrone
Montalcino
R. Orcia
Castel del
Piano
Cinigiano
Arcidosso
M.Labbro
Santa
Fiora
Monte S Savino
Marciano
Lucignano
Fojano
Asciano
Sinalunga
Trequanda
Torrita
Pienza
S.Quirico
d'Orcia
Castiglione
d'Orcia
M.Amiata
Acquaviva
MONTE-
PULCIANO
Chianciano
Sarteano
Radicofani
Abbā S. Salvadore
Pian
Castagnaio
Castiglion
Fiorentino
CORTONA
L.TRASIMENE
Chiusi
Cetona
Citta della
Pieve
S.Casciano

Scale of
25 Miles

BCB

SIENA AND SOUTHERN TUSCANY

By the same author:

VENICE AND VENETIA

ASSISI AND UMBRIA REVISITED

ROME

FLORENCE

CITIES OF UMBRIA

COUNTRY WALKS ABOUT FLORENCE

THE VALLEY OF ARNO

A WAYFARER IN UNKNOWN TUSCANY

NAPLES AND SOUTHERN ITALY

CITIES OF SICILY

MILAN AND LOMBARDY

ROMAGNA AND THE MARCHES

RAVENNA

CITIES OF SPAIN

HIGHWAYS AND BYWAYS IN SOMERSET

HIGHWAYS AND BYWAYS IN WILTSHIRE

HIGHWAYS AND BYWAYS IN GLOUCESTERSHIRE

ENGLAND OF MY HEART

A GLIMPSE OF GREECE

THE COSMATI

IL DUOMO, Siena

SIENA AND SOUTHERN TUSCANY

BY

EDWARD HUTTON

*Cara e beata e benedetta Toscana, patria d'ogni
eleganza e d'ogni gentil costume e sede eterna
di civiltà*

LONDON
HOLLIS & CARTER
1955

MADE AND PRINTED IN GREAT BRITAIN
BY JARROLD AND SONS LTD, NORWICH
FOR HOLLIS AND CARTER LIMITED
25 ASHLEY PLACE, LONDON, SWI

TO

MY OLD FRIEND

F. F. MASON PERKINS

NOTE

I HAVE to thank a number of friends and especially Mr. F. F. Mason Perkins for various assistance in revising this book. I must also thank my friends Miss Mariano, Dr. Richard Offner and Signor Edgardo Mercanti of the Italian Institute in London for obtaining for me a number of photographs; and Mr. Dennis E. Rhodes, Mr. J. J. Dwyer and my son Mr. Peter Hutton for reading the proofs.

E. H.

CONTENTS

vii

LIST OF ILLUSTRATIONS

ix

*Acknowledgments for permission to reproduce these photographs are made to:
Anderson for Nos. V, VIII, IX, XI, XIV, XVI, XVII, XVIII, XIX,
XX and XXI: Alinari for Nos. IV, X, XV, XXIII, XXX, XXXII and
XXXIII; Azienda Autonima di Turismo for Nos. I, II, III, XII, XIII,
XXII, XXVI, XXVII, XXVIII, and XXIX: Foto-Enit-Roma for No.
VI; and Lombardi for No. XXV.*

INTRODUCTION

IN any journey through Southern Tuscany the traveller is wise who uses the old medieval highway, Via Francigena, from Empoli in Val d' Arno through Siena, Buonconvento and San Quirico to Radicofani on the confines of the Patrimony, for it is the backbone of the Sanese; by it whether from the North or from Rome the life of Europe passed into this great corner of Tuscany. It is a medieval highway, the way, as its name implies, of the Franks into Italy, one of the few things the Dark Age created; but both in its beginning and its ending it was dependent on Rome, for it was based in the north on the Via Aemilia, which it left at Parma, and it ended at the gate of the Eternal City. All the predatory Emperors traversed it and by it our forefathers came to Rome, so that in every old book of Italian travel from Richard Lassels in the seventeenth century to Nathaniel Hawthorne in the middle of the nineteenth, it has a part, and though for no other cause yet for this, it surely recommends itself. It fell into disuse with the advent of the railway but with the coming of the motor-car it has returned to life.

The motor-car, indeed, has changed everything, has made every journey short and many places easily accessible that once took a whole day to reach. But the motor-car if a good servant is a bad master, too often impatient of leaving the highroad for some rough and unmetalled lane, of stopping at some unregarded place with only one picture to be seen, and always eager to get to a fore-ordained destination. Let me give an example of what I mean with regard to a place not mentioned in the following pages.

Montepertuso is a Castello above Murlo, between Pompana and La Befa, on an almost inaccessible mountain, which can be approached from Buonconvento or from the station of Murlo on the Asciano-Grosseto line of railway. It possesses one picture of importance, a magnificent altarpiece, a triptych, by Benvenuto di Giovanni, signed, and painted in 1475, of Our Lady enthroned with her little Son. She is attired in a robe of rich tissue, her feet rest on a flowered carpet, four angels stand behind the gorgeous throne, and two others hold a crown over her head with its inscribed halo. In the side panels are full-length figures of

S. Catherine of Alexandria, a magnificent S. Michael, a Bishop in
cope and mitre and S. Ursula. Above in three pinnacles are Our
Lord in benediction and SS. Ansano and Lorenzo; below them
are two small rounds with the heads of prophets, and ten small
figures of saints adorn the pilasters of the frame. In the predella
are four—should be five—scenes from the life of the Virgin, one
being missing.

This picture, though a little hard and overcrowded, is one of
the most magnificently ornate in all Sienese painting, yet I have
never been able to persuade friends, whose guest I have been
when motoring, to make the journey to see it.

"What is there to see up there?"

"A wonderful picture," I answer.

"Only one?"

I admit only one.

"Well, if it were really important it would be in the gallery
in Siena."

"It used to be there—but has been returned to its native place."

"Ah well, they wouldn't have let it go if it had been any good.
Besides we shall soon need petrol and I am still uneasy about
that back tyre."

And so Montepertuso is refused and we go on to Montalcino,
Montepulciano or Pienza.[1]

It is true this magnificent altarpiece was till recently in the
gallery of Siena, but after a long law-suit Montepertuso won it
back. Who would not rejoice to know this? Who would not
make the long and difficult journey to see this splendour in its
own place, in the church and over the altar for which it was
painted in 1475?

And so it is that the motor-car gives you a somewhat different
country from that described in this book. For the secret of such
journeys as mine is to linger by the way, to remember that the
chance of passing along any road again is uncertain; to have no
fixed destination, but to stop where and when one is tired, to
put up for the night when a place takes one's fancy, or, as at
Montepertuso, when evening is come.

That is why I prefer even today to go on foot with the help of

[1] There is in fact more than one picture to be seen in the Pieve of San Michele in
Montepertuso, but the Andrea di Niccolò Assumption is of small importance. Also
at Murlo in the Pieve a Carli there is a Madonna and Child by Benvenuto di Giovanni
or Andrea di Niccolò.

the railway and above all never to be in a hurry. Tuscany is one of the few places left in the world where it is still natural to be happy. The pages which follow recount the fortunate wanderings of recent years and recall those, happier still, of former days.

1955   E. H.

CHAPTER I

CASTEL-FIORENTINO

CASTEL-FIORENTINO is, as you soon find if you are wise enough to be content to stay there, a busy and picturesque little country town, full of the life of the country, chaffering *contadini*, great, slowly moving oxen, and the happy laughter of children, which is the music of Tuscany. Originally set high on its fair hillside, it has run into the plain and mingled itself inextricably with its own *borgo*, that lies at the foot of the hill towards the railway and the sleepy Elsa. The whole place in its littleness and shadowy climbing ways is charming, and no one surely who has stayed there ever left the little inn in the lower town without regret.

But the lower town, in spite of its beautiful churches, Santa Verdiana, San Francesco, and Santa Chiara over the water, gives you no idea of the delight and ancientness that await you in the Castello, the true Castel-Fiorentino, which climbs the hill so precipitously and in the shadow of which the *borgo* lies.

The town gets its Florentine name, Repetti assures us, either from the fact that it was anciently under the civil and religious jurisdiction of the Bishops of Florence, or perhaps from the fact that it stood on the confines of the Florentine *contado*. But tradition, always the best guide, assures us that it was given to the place by the people themselves out of a devotion, very rare and strange, for Florence, their mistress, and that in recognition of their love the Republic granted them her own arms, the crimson lily in a field of silver, which the town bears to this day.

However that may be, Castel-Fiorentino was certainly not the creation of the Republic of Florence. She was already old in 1164, when we first hear of her as one of the feuds of the Conti Alberti, confirmed to them by Frederic I. But feud of the Alberti though she was, it was not they who ruled her, but the Bishops of Florence, and in 1215 we find Bishop Giovanni da Velletri compelling his *terrazzani* to build their houses no higher than thirteen *braccia*, though the *borghigiani* of San Lorenzo in Mugello

were allowed to build houses of fifteen. This seems to have been
a sore point with the Castel-Fiorentini seven hundred years ago.
In 1231, however, they obtained a certain relief in this as in other
matters from Bishop Ardingo, winning the right to elect their own
dispensers of Justice, provided always that the Bishop approved
their choice. In 1252 they seem to have elected their own Podestà.
They chose Forese di Buonaccorso Adimari, a Florentine magnate,
and no doubt this was a further blow to the jurisdiction of the
Bishop.

But the history of Castel-Fiorentino, in spite of the position of
the town in the Val d' Elsa, over the Via Francigena, the great
medieval highway to Rome, is without real importance. Only
twice, indeed, did it appear in any of those moving and dramatic
scenes that are so plentiful in the story of the thirteenth century
in Tuscany. The first of these occasions was by far the greater,
and is a good example of the little town's devotion to Florence.

On 27 September, 1190, the Emperor Frederic I died. It was
a moment for bold action, and Florence was great enough to
seize it. It was, however, the people of San Miniato al Tedesco,
in Val d' Arno, who gave the signal. They destroyed the fortress
held by the Germans under which they lived, and not long after
the walls of San Genesio. This was the first act in the great
movement that Florence now engineered for her own freedom and
that of Tuscany. At this moment, so unfortunate for the Empire,
she conceived and formed the Tuscan League, which was finally
arranged at San Genesio on 11 November, 1197, when the cities
of Lucca, Siena, and San Miniato, with the Bishop of Volterra,
swore to maintain it. The treaty thus made bound the signatories
to an alliance for their common defence against all enemies of
the League as well as to make no peace with "any Emperor, or
King, or Prince, or Duke, or Marquis" without the consent of
the League, and to attack all cities, towns, counts, and bishops
who refused to join the League when asked to do so. What did
this treaty mean? Certainly the independence of Tuscany, its
refusal to admit the claims of either Emperor or Pope. But it
meant much more than that. It meant the consolidation of their
contadi by the various cities, and the final ruin of the country
nobility: for the *castelli*, the towns, and small domains were only
to be admitted to the League as dependents of the legitimate
owners of the territories in which they stood. From this there

was but one exception, Poggibonsi, because she was claimed by many.

Two Rectors were appointed to govern the League, and, as it happens, they were solemnly sworn in at Sant' Ippolito di Castel-Fiorentino, the ancient *pieve*, now a mere chapel, about a mile from the Castello, on 4 December, 1197. The first of them was the Bishop of Volterra, and the other the Florentine Consul, Acerbo.

But Castel-Fiorentino was a feud of the Conti Alberti, and they had not yet joined the League, neither had their feuds of Certaldo and Mangone or their fortress of Semifonte. Yet Castel-Fiorentino, the last of Florentine towns, far in the *contado*, was the meeting-place of the League. Was it she who brought the Conti Alberti low? We read that Arezzo joined the League in December, the Count Guido gave his word in February 1198, and on the 7th of that same month Count Alberto also promised allegiance, but in signing the treaty with him Florence expressly reserved the right to attack the fort of Semifonte—that famous but ghostly fortress—and to procure the submission of the Alberti feuds of Certaldo and Mangone, "even by force if required". Thus Castel-Fiorentino bore her part in one of the few beneficent revolutions that Tuscany has suffered.

The second incident in the history of Italy in which the little town figures befell in 1260, and must have been to her an occasion of weeping. For Florence, her friend, was brought low; the Ghibellines of Siena, with their German allies and the Florentine exiles, had then "broken and put to rout the ancient Florentine people" at Montaperto, and Castel-Fiorentino was for a moment the meeting-place of the heads of the Ghibelline party.

In the fourteenth century Castel-Fiorentino figures somewhat more prominently. In 1312 she broke the contingent of Rupert of Flanders as it left the Emperor at Poggibonsi. In 1313 she was unsuccessfully besieged by Henry VII going to Siena, and in various years, notably in 1359, she was hard put to it; but on the whole her history was more peaceable than might be expected, since she was on the great highway.

Happy Castel-Fiorentino! She was able and content to till her fields always, as she does today, to tend her vineyards, to sow the corn under the olives, and to gather it in with songs, while the armies of Germany, the companies of adventure, the gay chivalry of France thundered by to destruction. Is not her story, which will never be told, one of those which should console us most in a world so busy about resounding tragedy? She has no history; but in her untold story the romance of Europe lies hid—the story of men like ourselves going up and down day by day about their business, labouring in the fields in a hard partnership with nature, chaffering in the market-place, rising at dawn, resting at midday, singing at evening, loving a little and weeping much— if we could but read it.

But if Castel-Fiorentino is without a history, if she never produced a great man or a great artist, she is by no means devoid of the consolation of beauty. She herself is as charming and picturesque as can be; her churches are spacious and full of light, and there, too, you may find many a picture of a rare and exquisite country grace that only her lovers have discovered.

Of her churches San Biagio, the old *pieve* in the Castello, has been chief since Sant' Ippolito, a mile away, fell into disuse. There, too, in the upper town is the Collegiata San Lorenzo, while in the lower town is San Francesco; and best of all Santa Verdiana, and across the river Santa Chiara, once a convent of Poor Clares, but now in the hands of the Osservanti.

On the morning of the day after I had the happiness to return to Italy—and it was a fine morning too—finding myself in Castel-Fiorentino, I set out to see what was to be seen, and the first thing I came upon was the church of San Francesco. And they told me the Government had closed it as no longer safe. This I learned chiefly from an old *contadina* who lived in the disused convent, and presently when we were friends she let me into the church.

San Francesco, as I knew, had originally been founded by the Franciscan friars who established themselves here in 1230. It is a fine church of a single nave, but neglect had allowed it to fall into a condition of disrepair that was really dangerous. In the choir I found Giottesque frescoes of the life of S. Francis as at Santa Croce in Florence, and opposite to them a Crucifixion of S. Peter as in the Roman altarpiece attributed to Giotto, and as at Assisi; and in a later niche a Madonna and Child, an early work by Bernardo Daddi.

In the nave are further spoiled frescoes. To the right of the west door is a damaged fresco of the SS. Trinità. On the right wall is S. Francis enthroned with the three virtues—Poverty, Obedience, and Chastity—and four angels, two of whom bear the insignia of the Passion. These lovely fragments, and they are very lovely, are by Cenno di Ser Francesco Cenni. Further, on the right, I found a fragment of a Madonna at Annunciation, and almost opposite to it on the left wall a fine head of S. Peter. Evidently the whole church was once covered with frescoes till they were hidden under the whitewash.

From San Francesco I passed on to the beautiful and spacious church of Santa Verdiana close by, standing over an early Christian chapel, now a crypt, dedicated to S. Antonio Abate. The great church was built long ago by the people of Castel-Fiorentino to their patron saint, S. Verdiana. Over the second altar to the left is a spoiled work by Granacci, a Madonna and Child with S. Sebastian and S. Francis. The church itself, indeed, holds very little that has any interest for us; but in the sacristies there are treasures. Here is a spoiled trecento picture of S. Verdiana between two snakes, probably by Giovanni del Biondo who painted an altarpiece here in 1360.[1] In the second, beside a Botticelliesque Pietà and a Crucifixion by some pupil of Ghirlandaio, is a most astonishing eikon, a Madonna perhaps by Taddeo Gaddi, colossal in size, which in its monumental weight and power one can only compare with the famous Giotto of the Florence Uffizi.

I spent the morning in these two churches, and then in the afternoon crossed the river to Santa Chiara, a charming and quiet convent founded in the thirteenth century by some Poor Clares from the Marches, to whom in 1278 the Contessa Beatrice di Capraja left a legacy of fifty lire. Today, however, the convent is in the occupation of the Friars Minor. It was one of them—jovial and fat—who, in answer to my call, came out of his siesta to show me the church. The church is delightful, filled with a country peace and scattered with sun and shade. Over an altar on the left I found one of those things I love best—a splendid Giottesque Crucifix, a magnificent thing into which the love and faith of the fourteenth century seem immediately to have passed. Over an altar on the opposite wall stands a picture of the Madonna and Child with saints, of the school of Vasari, a late

---

[1] Mr. Berenson attributes this panel to Taddeo di Bartolo, but with a query. In the *Rassegna d'Arte*, 1909, p. 161, it is attributed to the school of Duccio.

sixteenth-century work full of mastery and all the later mannerism, but curiously lacking in the assurance of peace.

Behind the high altar are two surprising figures of life-size carved in wood at the end of the fourteenth century and painted. They represent the Blessed Virgin Annunciate and S. Gabriel Archangel. To the delight of Fra Lorenzo, my guide, the arms of the Virgin moved, being flexibly jointed, as he showed me. But apart from this childishness, which he was so right to enjoy, the figures are fine of their kind; the Madonna, indeed, has the same rhythm as a French or English work in ivory of the thirteenth century.

The quiet beauty of the church, the eager chatter of Fra Lorenzo, caused me to linger here, and that was my good fortune. For just as I was about to leave, as I said farewell to Fra Lorenzo at the church door, a woman came towards us, and, greeting the friar, at once knelt down on the threshold, just under the lintel of the door, and prepared herself to be churched. With her came two ragged urchins and a little black dog. In the great shady nave the children played with the dog, quite at home, while Fra Lorenzo, excusing himself, went into the sacristy and brought forth a great taper, which he placed in the good woman's hand, and a large book, all in Latin, out of which he proceeded to read some prayers. I cannot tell you what a charming and old-world picture this made, recalling happier days. The children in the shadow playing with the little black dog; the good woman who had just brought forth a child kneeling in the sunshine, holding her taper carefully, on the threshold of the church; Fra Lorenzo in his stole, unctuous and sleek, reciting the Office—it was as though by some good fortune certain centuries had never happened, and we were back in those scarcely remembered days when everything could be accounted for, when there was still a unity in Europe, and we accepted the love of God and the offices of the Church as matters of course. Only I seemed to be out of the picture. And so quietly I slipped away without so much as "Thank you" to Fra Lorenzo, to whom I owed this consoling glimpse of life in Tuscany.

It was late in the afternoon when I climbed into the upper town, the real Castel-Fiorentino, and found the Collegiata San Lorenzo, a very old church, partly Lombard, where, over the second altar on the right, is a fine Ducciesque Madonna and

Child, much darkened. The church has, too, some good late pictures, but I did not linger, as I wished to see the sunset from the Castello.

I found it when I came to the platform before the *pieve* of San Biagio, where on the high altar is an early picture of the Madonna of surprising glory and tenderness.

Looking thence across the world in the most beautiful hour of the day, when in that level and golden light God seems still to bestow on the earth His benediction, I saw evening come from the mountains up Val d' Elsa. To the north the valley widened between the hills under Castelnuovo, at whose foot a little chapel, the Madonna della Tosse, as I knew, hid some frescoes by Benozzo Gozzoli. To the south the earth towered, breaking at last into the beauty that is San Gimignano delle Belle Torri, where every little hill seemed to be crowned with a city shining in the setting sun.

It is surprising that a place so lovely should never have expressed itself, should have produced no one to tell the world, in words, colour, or action, in the beauty of his work or the strength, sweetness, or perfection of his life, of the loveliness of his home. It is true there are the children. Indeed, one of them, a lad of twelve or thereabouts, had come up as I stood there thinking, and now waited beside me, looking up into my face or across the valley to where the sun had hidden itself already, behind a shoulder of the hills.

Presently I turned to him, and demanded, "Was there, then, no one born in this city who was ever famous?"

Now he answered, smiling up at me confidently, "*Ma sì, signore.*"

"What!" said I, "there was? You tell me there was? And who is this unknown and yet splendid personage who stands for Castel-Fiorentino? Eh?"

And he answered, looking down, a little baffled by my sharpness, "Signore, Santa Verdiana."

"Santa Verdiana," said I. "Santa Verdiana? And who may she be?"

"Signore, she is a great Saint, our Saint, the Saint of Castel-Fiorentino."

"Ha ha," said I; "I remember now, boy; you mean the little saint with the two snakes, the protector of the church down there?"

"*Sì*, signore."

"Was she of Castel-Fiorentino?"

"*Sì*, signore."

"Tell me, then." And I settled myself carefully on the wall, where I could see the glory of the sky, and prepared to listen.

"Signore, it was very long ago, if the signore will believe me, when that holy one, Santa Verdiana of Castel-Fiorentino, had the politeness to be born here in this town for the glory of us who live here and the edification of all Val d' Elsa. Signore, it was very long ago, but, nevertheless, we shall never forget it, any more than they of San Gimignano will forget their S. Fina, about whom, as Padre Bonifazio says, there is too much talk. Will the signore hear, then?"

I nodded.

"Signore, when Santa Verdiana was born here in Castel-Fiorentino her parents were very poor, yet in spite of this misfortune, always she was good and holy, and the saints talked with her. And so wise did she grow with hearing this talk, that if the signore will understand, every one here loved her, and a relation of her family who was rich, noble, and very powerful, seeing how good she was, made her the *padrona* of his family, and gave his whole house into her keeping. This when she was not yet very old. Now, as it happened, signore—and the signore knows such things were common in those days—while she governed the whole house of this rich man there was a famine in Val d' Elsa, and no one had enough, or even at last anything to eat. Only, as rich men do, being both wise and cunning—but cunning, signore, at least here in Castel-Fiorentino—the *padrone* of Santa Verdiana had known very well how to guard himself even in this, for he had in his house a great chest of beans laid by, and as such things grew more and more valuable, when they were worth their weight in gold, he sold them to a certain merchant of his acquaintance, who, as the signore may believe, having paid for them, was not slow in coming to fetch them. Signore, what do you think? Do you think that was a good bargain? Do you think that he filled his empty belly with those beans, and was able to sell the rest at a price of blood? If the signore were to think so, he would be mistaken—but how mistaken! For Santa Verdiana, signore, that little poor one, had long since given all those beans away to the poor of Castel-Fiorentino, since they were hungry.

"Well, the signore may believe me that when the *padrone* found that he had no beans to sell, and above all, when it occurred to him that the great price he had received must be given back, he was like a devil for rage. Signore, he bubbled over, he spat, tore his hair, and indeed behaved himself in a fashion unbecoming in one really well educated. But when Santa Verdiana saw how things were, for a whole night she gave herself to prayers; and behold, in the morning, the chest was as full as ever. Such is the power of God, as Fra Bonifazio says. Then, when she found that her prayers were heard, she called the *padrone* and said, 'Leave off being angry; Gesù Cristo has returned the beans you grudged Him.' And that she said because as the signore knows it is written in the Gospel.

"Now, when the *padrone* saw this thing and understood, you may believe he was astonished—astonished and proud, signore, he should have so great a wonder in his house; and so, altogether reckless in his pride, he went through Castel-Fiorentino telling every one of his good fortune, so that, to the great dismay and shame of Santa Verdiana, she found herself famous—an object, signore, of public veneration. In her great shame and fear of this which had befallen her, she made up her mind to flee away from Castel-Fiorentino, and to go on pilgrimage with some great ladies of this valley to San Giacomo di Compostella, very far off, signore. But we would only let her go when she promised at last to return as soon as she could. Now, of all that happened on that pilgrimage, as Padre Bonifazio says, we shall never know— no, signore, nor a half nor a quarter of it. But when she returned to this town, we met her in a fine procession; and as she wished, we built her a little cell looking into the church—it was called Sant' Antonio then—down there in the *borgo*, signore, now called Santa Verdiana. There, as the signore may suppose, she heard Mass every day; but before the cell was finished she went on pilgrimage to Rome; but of what befell on that journey, too, we shall never know anything.

"When she returned, she entered the cell we had built, and there she lived for thirty-four years, till she came to die there— sleeping in summer on the ground, and in winter on a plank with just a block of wood for a pillow.

"Now, signore, in dealing with saints you should always expect some wonder. So it was with Santa Verdiana. She had been in her cell perhaps four years, perhaps five, when, on the Feast of S. Antonio Abate, she heard the preacher describe what that patriarch endured from the presence of devils—devils, signore, who took the form of wild beasts—as the signore knows. So Santa Verdiana prayed that she might share the sufferings of that holy one, and it happened as she desired. For a few days after two magnificent and stupendous serpents came in at her little window, and there they remained for the rest of her life, eating out of her bowl, and lashing her with their tails, when, signore, she had nothing to give them. Now, one day the Bishop of Florence, a very great and most important personage, came to Castel-Fiorentino especially to pay Santa Verdiana a visit, and seeing, as he peeped through the window, the two serpents coiled up beside Santa Verdiana there in the cell, he immediately and hastily, without thinking twice about it, gave orders that they should be killed. But when Santa Verdiana heard it she wept bitterly and begged him to allow her to keep them as an exercise of her patience. What could he do, signore, but grant her this petition? And, indeed, these two serpents remained with her for thirty years, till the people of Castel-Fiorentino killed them, to her great sorrow and regret.

"And not long after a most important thing befell her and this town, namely this, that San Francesco of Assisi came here, and finding her made her a member of his Third Order.[1] And Fra Bonifazio says that that was the best and most important event in her life, but I think the serpents best of all—don't you, signore? Then she died.[2] That is all, signore. Would the signore like to see her?"

I said, I should very much like to see her.

So he led me a little way farther over the hill, till we came to a church by the wayside called San Pietro di Pisangoli, where there is a fine picture of the Madonna and Child by some pupil of Ghirlandaio. There we found a portrait of Santa Verdiana in the grey habit of the Third Order of S. Francis with S. Jerome.

It was quite dark when I came back into the town; all the lamps were lighted, and in the streets there was a going to and fro.

On the following morning I crossed the Elsa and made my way to the Oratory of the Madonna della Tosse, a mile or two northward, for the sake of Benozzo Gozzoli. Over the altar of this little

[1] This was in 1222.   [2] She died in 1242.

chapel there is a fresco by Benozzo of the Madonna and Child between SS. Peter, Catherine, Margaret, and Paul, with two angels at the sides and two above holding the curtain which is the background. In the *predella* is a Pietà. On the right of this is the Death of the Virgin with three donors and then the Assumption with the Apostles below kneeling round the empty tomb and S. Thomas reaching for Our Lady's girdle, which she vouchsafes him. These are charming, if late, works by the master, perhaps a little hard in execution.

After returning to the city in the afternoon, I went to the Chapel of the Visitation opposite San Francesco near the bridge over the Elsa, again for the sake of Benozzo. Most of these paintings have suffered and some have disappeared. The best preserved is the fresco of S. Joachim driven from the Temple. Over the altar something is left of a frescoed polyptych of the Madonna and Child enthroned with six saints. In the vault is a figure of Christ in a *mandorla*, the Doctors of the Church and the Evangelists. Fragments remain of an Annunciation, and a Presentation in the Temple. The Meeting at the Golden Gate is, however, in a good state, but the Nativity has almost disappeared. On the opposite wall is the Nativity of the Virgin, but not by Gozzoli.

I also visited the church of Santa Maria a Lungo Tuono, about a mile or a little more on the way to Castelnuovo, where I found a much damaged altarpiece dismantled and divided, of the Madonna enthroned giving her breast to her little Son and beside the throne four saints, S. Verdiana, S. Chiara, S. Antonio Abate, and an old and long-bearded figure which I was told was S. Francesco. Who the painter of this much damaged, but most interesting, altarpiece may have been I could not tell.

CHAPTER II

CERTALDO

LONG before one comes to Certaldo on its great hill over
the narrowing valley of the Elsa, which in fact it holds
and closes, the Castello shows, still very far off, a rugged
cluster of houses and towers against the sky. When at last one
finds oneself on the great road beside the river, at the foot of the
hill, it is to discover a town very like Castel-Fiorentino in this at
least, that the Castello, the walled and ancient town, is on the
hill and the modern *borgo* in the plain. But, as one soon realizes,
Certaldo is more splendid and more rugged than Castel-Fiorentino, though, as one sees her from the north, one has the worst
view of her, her true splendour looking southward.

Such of us who in the modern hurry stay here, perhaps, for a
few hours on the way to Siena or to Florence, come for Boccaccio's
sake, for he died here in the ancient house of his family still to
be seen in the Castello. But in fact Certaldo, with her picturesque
medieval ways, has much curious beauty of her own, a few
pictures, some narrow and ancient streets, certain old houses and
towers, the Palazzo Pubblico, the Casa di Boccaccio, and a
delicious countryside, besides the grave of that great and heroic
man, who has entranced the whole world with his stories, who
gave Homer back to us, and was the first defender of Dante
Alighieri, the devoted friend of Petrarch, the lover of Fiammetta;
who remained poor his whole life long for the sake of learning,
and who is indeed the most human and the most modest and
heroic spirit of the earliest Renaissance.

There is nothing at all to see in the modern township, the
borgo at the foot of the fruitful and beautiful hill on which Certaldo
stands. In the great empty Piazza before the church of Sant'
Andrea, founded on land left to the Augustinians of Florence by
Jacopo, Boccaccio's half-brother, in accordance with his will,
stands a poor modern statue of Certaldo's great son and bene-
factor. It is in the lofty Castello that what remains to be seen in
Certaldo is to be found.

If one turns to the left out of the Piazza and takes the steep way on the right called Costa degli Alberti, for Certaldo was a possession of that great house, one comes at last to the old and beautiful gate of the still walled Castello.

From the gate the main street mounts steeply on the left, past the old towered house of Boccaccio and the ancient church of SS. Michele e Jacopo, to the Palazzo Pubblico, the haggard fortress of the Alberti, with its coats of arms and beautiful with a few frescoes.

Then returning a little on the way, there is the church of SS. Michele e Jacopo, now the parish church of Certaldo, belonging to the Augustinians. Here in the single nave, on the left, is a large niche, perhaps for an altar, with a fresco of the Madonna and Child, and SS. Peter, John, and Verdiana, by Paolo di Giovanni Fei, and two charming angels by Pier Francesco Fiorentino. My interest in the place, however, was chiefly roused by the fact that it once held the tomb of Boccaccio, and still preserves a memorial of him—a fine bust high up between the first and second altars on the right, with several inscriptions. Here, then, within the shelter of his parish church till over a hundred years ago, Boccaccio lay in peace.

> Boccaccio to his parent earth bequeath'd
> His dust—and lies it not her great among,
> With many a sweet and solemn requiem breathed
> O'er him who form'd the Tuscan's siren tongue;
> That music in itself, whose sounds are song,
> The poetry of speech? No—even his tomb
> Uptorn must bear the hyæna bigots' wrong;
> No more amidst the meaner dead find room,
> Nor claim a passing sigh, because it told for *whom*!

The outrage which Byron refers to happened in 1783, when a new floor was built in SS. Michele e Jacopo. The "hyæna bigots" of Certaldo, finding it disgraceful that the author of so many merry tales should rest in holy ground, tore up the tomb, scattered the ashes, and flung the stone aside. This unfortunate and disgraceful outrage, exceptional in the annals of Italy, who has generally shown a touching devotion for the tombs of her great sons, was atoned for, in so far as was possible, by the principal person of the district, the Contessa Lenzioni, a daughter of the last branch of the house of Medici, ever famous for its generosity to and protection of artists and men of letters. This great and good lady rescued the tombstone of Boccaccio from the neglect in which it lay and found for it an honourable place in her own palace. She did more: the house in which Boccaccio had lived for many years, and in which he came at last to die, was as little respected as his tomb. This, too, she purchased, and devoted it to his memory. It stands a little lower down than and on the same side of the street as the church, and even contains a small Boccaccio museum. In a room upstairs, which the *custode* calls the studio of Boccaccio, are gathered a few of his relics, such as the stones of his broken tomb, a cabinet for MSS. said to have been his, and a curious sand clock. Here, too, are a few pictures. The house has a tower which commands an extensive view over the surrounding country, including Montajone and San Gimignano.

In the ancient house of his fathers Giovanni Boccaccio came to die in 1375. But Certaldo was not his birthplace, indeed he lived there, it seems, but little till the last years of his life. Sitting there, while the sunshine filled the room, I recalled his story.[1]

Giovanni Boccaccio was born in Paris, so he told Petrarch, in 1313. He was the son of Boccaccio di Chellino da Certaldo, a young Italian banker and money-lender at that time in Paris, and a certain Jeanne or Gianna, a Frenchwoman about whom we know nothing but what Boccaccio himself has told us in allegory in his *Filocolo*, save that it seems certain his father never married her. Their son, Giovanni, was brought to Italy when he was still a tiny child—at any rate his father was back in Tuscany, and in business in Florence, in 1318, where it seems Giovanni was brought up, *nel suo grembo*, as he says, in his father's house. Some have thought, among them the most learned student of his youth, Della Torre, that the hill on which he tells us his child-hood was passed, "a little hill strewn with seashells and dark with oaks", was that on which Certaldo stands, and that it was here his boyhood was spent. It seems more likely, however, that since he tells us he lived in his father's house—*nel suo grembo*, literally, in his lap—that it was rather in Florence, where we know his father to have been, than in Certaldo he spent his earliest years, and this belief is strengthened by the fact that he

[1] For a fully documented biographical and critical study of Boccaccio, see my *Giovanni Boccaccio* (Lane, 1909).

later devoted a book to the description of the country about
Florence between Fiesole and Settignano, which he greatly loved,
while he says nothing of Certaldo; and also by the fact that we
know his father had a house at Corbignano, under Settignano,
that is still standing, which came to him as part of the dowry
of his first wife, Margherita di Gian Donato de' Martoli, whom
he married almost immediately after his return to Tuscany between
1314 and 1318, and who, if we understand Boccaccio aright,
was the cause of the lad's sudden departure for Naples when,
as we think, he was still very young. It had been his father's
intention to bring Giovanni up to be a banker, but his early and
passionate dislike of business brought this to nothing, and, no
doubt to the delight of Margherita, his stepmother, whose son,
Francesco, was then about two years old, old Boccaccio presently
decided to apprentice Giovanni to a merchant in Naples.

But if he disliked banking and money-lending, trade, we may be
sure, was not more to his mind. He longed to be a poet, and the
gay life of Naples, which he describes so vividly for us, did not
encourage him to stick to his desk.

His education had been of the most meagre sort, consisting of
the mere rudiments of Latin and arithmetic. In Naples, however,
possibly among the sons of the Florentine merchants there, he
found a certain "Calmeta", who not only roused in him the desire
for culture, but was able to guide his first steps in those *conversazioni
astronomiche* of which he speaks so much. With him he pursued
his study in Grammar, Dialectic, and Rhetoric.

This new companionship was not, however, the only thing that
helped to strengthen his dislike of business. In 1327 he was
presented by his father, then on a visit to Naples as the representative of the great banking house of the Bardi, at the Court,
and one thing aiding another, before his father left Naples he had
told him he could not pursue his career, and in fact by 1329 we
find him engaged—not much more enthusiastically, it must be
admitted—in the study of Canon Law, for his father seems to
have insisted on a fixed profession.

But whatever his duties may have been at this time, neither
they nor his studies with Calmeta occupied all his time. He
entered with gusto into the gay life of the gayest city in Italy.
He speaks often of the beauty of the women in that splendour
of earth and sky and sea, and the beautiful names of two he

courted and loved, being in love with love, have come down to us, namely, Pampinea and Abrotonia, which we find in the *Filocolo*. Like Romeo, Boccaccio had his Rosaline. These were not profound passions, of course, but they proved nevertheless to be an introduction to love himself.

On entering Naples Boccaccio tells us he had had a vision of a beautiful lady who welcomed him with kisses.

This vision proved to be a prophecy of Fiammetta. This lady, about the same age as himself, but already married, was the illegitimate daughter of King Robert of Naples and a lady of French birth, the wife of the Conte d' Aquino. Boccaccio saw her first on Holy Saturday in the church of San Lorenzo of the Franciscans during Mass. He had gone to church, it seems, about ten o'clock, the fashionable hour of the day, rather to see the people than to attend the service, and there amid the throng he first caught sight of the woman who was so profoundly to influence his life and shape his work.

Fiammetta was tall and *slanciata*, and, as he tells us in a hundred different places, golden-haired and very beautiful. He watched her all through the service, and thought of nothing else for the rest of the day. Then on the morrow, which was Easter Day, he went again to San Lorenzo in the hope of seeing her, and she was there indeed, dressed finely in a green dress adorned with pearls. And at once he recognized her for the lady of his vision.

That meeting was the beginning of a new life for Giovanni. Yet when he learned that Fiammetta was, though illegitimate, a princess, he can have had but slender hopes of winning her love. Nevertheless he did not altogether despair, and we presently find him in her company telling her stories out of the French romances then so popular, and of the Trojans and Romans. At her request he seems to have set about composing a romance for her, which he completed later under the name of the *Filocolo*. He also wrote her many sonnets, hoping to win her, with all the *naïveté* of youth, with poetry. She allowed him to pay her court, and without giving him much encouragement no doubt enjoyed his homage. This courtship seems to have lasted some five years before an opportunity occurred which gave Giovanni what he so eagerly desired—the full possession of this disdainful beauty.

Those years so full of wild joy soon passed away, and Giovanni's troubles began. At first jealousy. Fiammetta, as he knew doubtless, was incapable of any stability in love, and he could never help looking at *altre donne*. He struggled against his fate, humiliated himself before her, heaped reproaches upon her and scorn, but it was useless; she was surrounded by admirers no more scrupulous than himself, and she, too, was in love with love.

But fate was not content with a single blow. Till then he had wanted for nothing; he had had a home of his own, and had been able to go to Court as he pleased and to enter fully into the gay life of Naples. Now suddenly poverty stared him in the face. His father, from whom all that was stable and good in his life had proceeded, was ruined, and before long, widowed and childless, summoned him home.

It cannot have been with any great content that Giovanni obeyed that call. It seemed to him, doubtless, that he was leaving everything that was worth having in Naples; but as it proved, it was in Florence he was to find, if not love, at least the fulfilment of his ambitions.

There in the next few years he wrote and completed the works of his youth—the *Filocolo*, the *Filostrato*, the *Teseide*, the *Ameto*, the *Amorosa Visione*, the *Fiammetta*, and the *Ninfale Fiesolano*, and somewhat in that sequence. Driven from Florence, it seems, by the revolution that disposed of the Duke of Athens, he seems to have returned to Naples, perhaps to look for Fiammetta, but the plague descended upon Italy with awful consequences in 1348. In that "black death" Fiammetta seems to have perished; we do not know whether it was Giovanni who closed her eyes. Within the next two years he lost his father and his second stepmother, his father's second wife, and was left as guardian of his half-brother, Jacopo.

He returned to Florence in 1350, to find Petrarch there on his way to Rome for the Jubilee, and this, his first meeting with the most famous man of his time, was to be full of good fortune for him.

In 1349 the Republic of Florence had founded a university, really with the intention of attracting strangers to herself, for she was half-depopulated by the plague. In 1351 Boccaccio was sent as ambassador to Padua to persuade Petrarch, whose father was a Florentine exile, to accept a chair in the university. Though he did not succeed in his mission, he cemented his friendship with the lover of Laura, and was evidently considered by the Republic as a good representative, for we find him serving as ambassador to Ludwig of Brandenburg, and three years later to Innocent VI in Avignon. About this time he finished the greatest of his works, the *Decamerone*. He was about forty years old then, and unmarried. Fiammetta was dead, and his relations with women had, it seems, always been casual. And it seems that about this time, in his forty-first year, he found himself taken by a very beautiful woman, a widow, who pretended to encourage him, perhaps because of his fame, provoked his advances, allowed him to write to her, and then, laughing at this middle-aged and obese lover, gave his letters to her young lover, who scattered them about Florence. In his exasperation he wrote the book called *Il Corbaccio*, the most cynical of his works, little more, in fact, than a passionate attack on woman. His "troubled spirit", as Petrarch wrote him, had declared itself.

In the spring of 1359 he went to Milan to meet Petrarch, and while there probably met Leon Pilatus, the Calabrian who passed for a Greek. This charlatan and rogue he invited to Florence, in the hope of learning Greek from him. For two years he gave him hospitality, and succeeded, with his assistance, in producing a Latin version of the *Iliad* and *Odyssey*, which Petrarch, who knew no Greek, was glad to borrow, and which, in fact, gave Homer back to the West.

During this labour a moral crisis, long threatened, of which the *Corbaccio* was a sign, overwhelmed him; in his fiftieth year he began to regret the irresponsibility of his past life.

It was in the midst of this dis-ease that a certain Gioacchino Ciani called upon him to warn him, as he intended to warn Petrarch, of the nearness of death. In doing this the monk—for he was a Carthusian—was but obeying the dying command of Beato Pietro Petroni, a Sienese, who had seen on his death-bed "the present, the past, and the future".

Already drawn towards a new life—a life which under the direction of the Church he was told would be without the consolations of literature—at the sudden intervention, as it seemed, of Heaven, Boccaccio did the wisest thing of his whole life—he asked for the advice of Petrarch. The letter which Petrarch wrote him takes its rank among the noblest of his works, and is indeed one of the most beautiful letters ever written. "You tell me,"

Right:
BOCCACCIO'S HOUSE,
Certaldo

Below: CERTALDO

SAN GIMIGNANO. LE BELLE TORRI

he says, "that this holy man had a vision of our Lord, and so
was able to discern all truth—a great sight for mortal eyes to see.
Great indeed, I agree with you, if genuine; but how often have
we not known this tale of a vision made a cloak for an imposture!
And having visited you this messenger proposed, I understand,
to go to Naples, thence to Gaul and Britain, and so to me. Well,
when he comes I will examine him closely; his looks, his demeanour,
his behaviour under questioning, and so forth, shall help me to
judge of his truthfulness. And the holy man on his death-bed
saw us two and a few others to whom he had a secret message,
which he charged this visitor of yours to give us; so, if I understand you rightly, runs the story. Well, the message to you is
twofold: you have not long to live, and you must give up poetry.
Hence your trouble, which I made my own while reading your
letter, but which I put away from me on thinking it over, as you
will do also. For if you will only give heed to me, or rather to
your own natural good sense, you will see that you have been
distressing yourself about a thing that should have pleased you.
Now if this message is really from the Lord it must be pure truth.
But is it from the Lord? or has its real author used the Lord's
name to give weight to his own saying? . . . What is there new in
all this? You knew, without his telling you, that you could not
have a long space of life before you. . . . Forsake the Muses, says
he. . . . Nay, I answer, when he bids you pluck sin from your
heart he speaks well and prudently; but why forsake learning, in
which you are no novice, but an expert, able to discern what to
choose and what to refuse? . . . Though unlettered men have
attained to holiness, no man was ever debarred from holiness by
letters. . . .

"But if, in spite of all this, you persist in your intention, and
if you must needs throw away not only your learning but the
poor instruments of it, then I thank you for giving me the refusal
of your books. I will buy your library if it must be sold, for I
would not that the books of so great a man should be dispersed
abroad and hawked about by unworthy hands. I will buy it and
unite it with my own; then some day this mood of yours will pass,
some day you will come back to your old devotion. Then you
shall make your home with me; you will find your books side by
side with mine, which are equally yours. Thenceforth we shall
share a common life and a common library, and when the survivor

of us is dead the books shall go to some place where they will be kept together and dutifully tended, in perpetual memory of us who owned them."

That noble letter, so sane in its piety, in some sort cured Boccaccio. We hear no more of the fanatic monk, and the books were never bought by Petrarch, for they were never sold.

Boccaccio's days of creation were, however, over. He retired to Certaldo to this house of his ancestors, and there read without ceasing the works of antiquity, annotating as he read. His learning became prodigious, and little by little he gathered his notes into the volumes we know as *De Montibus, Sylvis, Lacubus,* etc., a kind of dictionary of geography; the *De Casibus Virorum Illustrium,* which deals with the vanity of human affairs from Adam to Petrarch; the *De Claris Mulieribus,* which begins with Eve and comes down to Giovanna of Naples; and the *De Genealogiis Deorum Gentilium,* a cyclopædia of learning concerning mythology and a defence of poetry and poets.

In addition to all his other reading Boccaccio had never ceased to study the *Divine Comedy,* and in 1373 he was called from his retirement in Certaldo to lecture publicly on Dante's epic in Florence. He began to read on 23 October, 1373, in the church of Santo Stefano alla Badia, and continued on each day that was not a festival. He had got so far as the sixtieth *lezione,* when he was taken ill and had to cease. Really ill, he retired to Certaldo, where, utterly miserable and suffering much from his disease, but more from the ignorance of doctors, he groped about, far from Petrarch, looking for some certainty. He thought he might find it in the monastic life, and it was in a solitude almost as profound that he came to die at last on this hill in Val d' Elsa in the house of his ancestors—a magician, as was said, like Virgil or Ovid, by the folk of Naples and Sulmona, knowing all the secrets of nature. He must often have passed slowly, because of failing health, up and down the picturesque streets of this old town, which holds as many sudden peeps as Assisi; and at sunset, perhaps, he lingered by the gates as we do, for they are wonderfully placed for beauty. From his room he looked over a world as fair as any in Tuscany—a land of hills about a quiet valley where the olives are tossed to silver in the wind and the grapes are kissed by the sun into gold and purple,

where the corn whispers between the vines; till for him, too, at
last the grasshopper became a burden.

There, on 21 December, 1375, he died, and was buried, as he
had desired, above the quiet waters of the Elsa which puts all to
sleep. Here in this house of his in Certaldo today, it is part of our
heritage to remember him.

Not much remains to be seen in Certaldo. In the Palazzo
Pretorio, restored in 1893, the Cortile is picturesque, and there
are a few paintings. Among them is a Pietà by Giusto d' Andrea
(1484) and some frescoes by Pier Francesco Fiorentino. Just outside the city at Lucardo in the church of San Martino is a fine
altarpiece of the Virgin and Child enthroned between the Baptist,
S. Peter and two kneeling bishops, a work of the school of
Ghirlandaio. And farther along Via Francigena in a chapel
at Ponte dell' Agliena are frescoes of Tobias and the archangel
by Pier Francesco Fiorentino; and far better a Crucifixion and
the martyrdom of S. Sebastian, an Annunciation and figures of
saints and a Deposition by Benozzo Gozzoli. These were painted
in 1467 when Benozzo was also painting his masterpieces in the
Camposanto at Pisa, now lost to us.

CHAPTER III

SAN GIMIGNANO

CERTALDO, for all its narrow, winding ways and smiling country, holds little today that we can be sure Boccaccio saw. If we would know what a Tuscan hill town was like in the fourteenth century, we must go on foot or by carriage to San Gimignano delle Belle Torri, on the hills on the other side of the Elsa. There, it is true, we shall find no remembrance of Boccaccio, but we shall be treading in the footsteps of Dante, and we shall find there, too, the memory of one of those little saints who, as it seems, are only to be found in Tuscany. There are few refuges more secure from the rampant materialism of our time than San Gimignano.

To reach this towered hill city, that is a good way which leaves Certaldo by crossing the river, and so climbs over the hills. Just there at Cusano near the station of Barberino is a large villa of the Guicciardini. Behind the villa is the little church of San Biagio where over the altar is a picture of the Madonna and Child signed by Bartolo di Fredi. Then the city "of the beautiful towers" rises before you like a vision, and you come at last into her quiet and shadowy gates. That is a good way, but it is not the only one, or even the most frequented. For those who come from Siena will approach her from Poggibonsi, whence it is a drive of some seven *chilometri* to this strangely towered city, still walled on high, above the olives and the vines.

The road from Certaldo, which was the way I took, is as lovely as any in the world. You climb hill after hill between the olives and the vines, where the grain and the grapes grow together. Often you descend into delicious valleys where the vineyards are still with summer, and the silence is only broken by the far-away voice of some peasant singing *stornelli* and the *cicale* among the olives; often, too, you look back on Val d' Elsa, where Certaldo frowns on its steep hill over the river, till suddenly at a turning of the way San Gimignano rises before you on a lonely hill-top, girdled with the silver of the olives, the gold of the corn, with a mantle of vines, like a city out of a missal, crowned with

22

her trophy of thirteen towers. Over all that gay landscape, that quiet countryside, she alone still hovers like a sombre thought of the Middle Age; it is as though on that gay road some gaunt verse of Dante had come to you suddenly on the wind, at a turning of the way, and had changed the whole world in an instant.

Yet it is not anything too sombre or even too grave that you find as you enter her gates, those gates that she threatened to destroy—lest your motor-car should be compelled to wait drearily without and you yourself pass through her streets on foot! If Dante has trodden her ways she has surely forgotten it, and one is not surprised that the inscription in the Palazzo Pubblico, by which she has thought to remind herself of the honour, records the wrong date. For in spite of old age, in spite of poverty, in spite of the modern world that she seeks to placate, with too much condescension one thinks, San Gimignano is a joyful city; a city of fierce old towers, it is true, but also a city of singing voices, which, as it seems to me, those towers hear gladly: they do not frown, but rejoice in the sun. For, ancient as she is, she, in whose ears the verses of Cecco d' Angiolieri followed on the anathemas of Dante, can afford to greet one even today with a smile, it may be of welcome, it may be of tolerance.

She is very old. More than a thousand years, according to Luigi Pecori, her historian, have passed since she was founded in honour of S. Geminianus. Certainly so early as the eighth century there was a town here, crouched under a fortress castle, surrounded by the woods which gave her her second name, Castello della Selva. From that time, as we may suppose, and certainly in the tenth, eleventh, and twelfth centuries, she was subject to the Bishop of Volterra, till in 1199 we find her electing as Podestà Maghinardo Malavolti of Siena, no doubt to stand for her against the Bishop. For, as before, the *rettori* of the Bishop of Volterra had administered justice within her gates, so after 1199 the Podestà ruled the courts and presided at the meetings of her Council and led her armies in battle.

For all the cities of Tuscany the thirteenth century was a century of war, nor was San Gimignano an exception. Her position demanded it. Between Florence and Siena, she could not keep her independence and be at peace. When she had won her freedom from Volterra and forced the Signorotti of her *contado* to enter her gates, there were always these to watch and ward. Nor

did she escape the horror of faction and civil war any more than
her neighbours. Ghibelline as she was in the time of Frederic II,
there were Guelfs within her walls who only awaited an opportunity to seize the city. Their chance seemed to have come in
1246, when, finding the taxes on the churches a good excuse,
they rose, led by Guido Ardinghelli, and destroyed the towers of
the chief Ghibelline families, whose champions were the Salvucci.
It was the feud between these two houses that at last brought
San Gimignano into captivity. All through the thirteenth century
the city ran with the blood of the factions, and yet amid the
uproar little S. Fina passed by, thinking only of the love of God.

But San Gimignano was torn asunder. Now Guelf, now
Ghibelline, she suffered everything and gained nothing from any
one. In 1260 at Montaperto she was Guelf, and shared the defeat
and rout of the Florentines. In 1269 she was Ghibelline, and went
down with the Sienese before the Florentines at Colle. Thenceforth she followed the Guelf cause, in 1270 helping the Florentines
to destroy the Rocca of Poggibonsi, still obstinately Ghibelline.
There followed a peace, or sort of peace at least, of thirty years,
from 1270 to 1300.

It was then, on a May morning in the year 1300, that an
embassy from the allied cities of the Tuscan League came up the
long roads to San Gimignano, and when the gates were opened
Dante Alighieri, just thirty-five years old, rode into the town
with his company, with trumpeters gay with silver and gold, and
heralds all in scarlet and silver. In the great hall of the new
Palazzo del Comune he gave his message to the ancients of
San Gimignano: to wit, that a council was called of the League to
elect a captain of Tuscany, and that San Gimignano was invited to
send deputies.

That herald announced, too, the fourteenth century. The
Ghibellines were no more, in name at least. There remained the
broken Guelf party, irremediably split into Bianchi and Neri.
Again San Gimignano followed Florence; she was Black, and
went to the siege of Pistoia in 1305. She returned to look to her
own affairs. In 1308 war broke out between herself and Volterra,
and the whole country was laid waste, till the League, or at least
Florence, Siena, and Lucca, intervened. She followed Florence
and the League against Henry VII, who, being at Poggibonsi,
still ineffectually Ghibelline, threatened to fling down her towers

and walls, and actually burnt the *contado*. Then, in 1313, Henry died at Buonconvento.

It might seem that with the Ghibelline cause in utter ruin San Gimignano would have been at peace. It was, however, in the years following 1315, when Uguccione broke the Florentines at Montecatini, that she began to make an end of herself. Folgore, her poet, that fanatic Guelf, was, after all, but expressing the mood of his time when he refused to acknowledge God while the Ghibellines triumphed. It is written that "a house divided against itself cannot stand". It was so with San Gimignano, it was so with Italy. As in Florence, so in this little mountain city the trouble began with an attempt at tyranny. Trebaldo Baroncetti, one of the Guelf leaders, tried to make himself lord. It is true he was disposed of, but the factions would not be at peace. In 1332 the exiles, under the Ardinghelli, ravaged and burnt the *contado*, till the people of San Gimignano razed Camporbiano, in the Florentine territory, which had sheltered them. Florence demanded an explanation, and when this was not forthcoming she fitted out an expedition and imposed a fine on the Commune. Then San Gimignano asked for mercy. This was the beginning of the end. Where Florence had once had obedience she never brooked independence again. It was the Duke of Athens who first enslaved her, but she tore down his castle when Florence spewed him out. But she was ever at the mercy of her own factions, without whom the Ardinghelli, who would not give up hope of possessing her, would have been helpless. The end came with the plague in 1348. In debt to Florence, half depopulated, but still quarrelling, in 1349 she gave the government into the hands of Florence for three years. Even this did not sober her. In 1352 the Ardinghelli and the Salvucci set the whole city in uproar, and a year later Florence finally and for ever took over the government. Thus died the Commune of San Gimignano, because she would not be at peace.

By whatever gate one may enter the city one will scarcely pause on one's way through these silent streets full of shadows till one comes into the Piazza del Podestà, where on a great platform, reached by a noble flight of steps, the Collegiata stands with the Palazzo del Comune beside it, and the ancient Palazzo del Podestà, and the Chigi and Rognosa towers opposite to it closing the square. The whole place is deserted. A few beggars, a lounger here and there, an old woman spinning at a door, a few children playing on the steps—these and the sun are all that life has left the Piazza of San Gimignano which Dante trod as ambassador for the Florentine Republic. Only the past seems to remain here, magically embalmed for once by the indifference of men.

You enter the Palazzo del Comune beside the Collegiata. It is full of silence, your voice echoes in the narrow corridors, but no one answers. You come into the beautiful courtyard with its loggia and staircase: no one is there; and it is only after climbing that stairway and passing through many corridors that, quite by chance it seems, you find the ancient guardian of the place, who, with a sort of incredulous eagerness, leads you through those silent chambers that seem never to have heard the voices of today.

Your guide leads you first into the Sala di Dante, still used, you gather, by the Council of San Gimignano, but nothing modern, you feel sure, could ever be at home there under the majestic Maestà, a large fresco by Lippo Memmi, and the still older frieze representing a hunt, divided by coats of arms, that surrounds the chamber on three sides.

That fresco of Memmi's, the Madonna and Child enthroned, surrounded by angels and saints, S. Anthony Abbot, S. Fina, S. Gimignano, S. Agatha, S. John Baptist, S. Peter, S. Francis, and S. Nicholas, was the gift of Nello Tolomei, who kneels there before the Blessed Virgin. It was finished, as an inscription records, in 1317, which is very early for Lippo Memmi, and is no longer, as another inscription tells us, wholly Memmi's work, for in 1467 Benozzo Gozzoli restored it, adding three figures. This Maestà is perhaps the finest thing in San Gimignano. Dante never saw it, for he was here in the year 1300, seventeen years before Nello Tolomei, the Podestà, set Lippo Memmi—or was it his father?—to work. Dante's eyes have, however, looked upon the frieze painted in 1292, which, besides scenes of hunting and jousts, shows us Scolaio Ardinghelli settling a dispute between the Commune and the Church, which befell in 1290, when, on account of some taxes, the Bishop of Volterra placed the town under an interdict, and the people broke down the church door and forced a priest to say Mass whether he would or no. Nicholas IV appointed Bishop Scolaio Ardinghelli, it seems, to settle the quarrel, and he ordered this frieze from some Pisan painter, to celebrate the peace.

From the Sala di Dante your guide leads you upstairs into a set of rooms now devoted to the Pinacoteca, where among many ancient and some beautiful things are a polyptych of the Blessed Virgin with saints, with the Annunciation above, and a picture of S. Gimignano with scenes from his life by Taddeo di Bartolo; a Madonna in Glory, with SS. Gregory and Bernardo Tolomei, painted in 1512 by Pintoricchio; two small panels with eight scenes from the life of S. Fina, the golden-haired saint of San Gimignano, by Lorenzo di Niccolò, and two *tondi*, representing the Annunciation, by Filippino Lippi. Here, too, are two Madonnas with saints by Mainardi, and a Madonna between two kneeling saints, painted in 1477 by Pier Francesco Fiorentino; an altarpiece with S. Julian by the "Master of 1419", till lately ascribed by Mr. Berenson to ? Andrea di Giusto; a detached fresco of the Crucifixion by Benozzo Gozzoli; a Virgin and Child by Neri di Bicci; an early Sienese picture of the Madonna and Child and two great Tuscan Crucifixes of the thirteenth century, one with six scenes of the Passion, very dramatic, of the school of Coppo di Marcovaldo, perhaps the finest thing in the gallery. In the first room there are some recently restored frescoes, exotic scenes attributed most insecurely to Segna, a fine fourteenth-century bust of Guido Marabottini in coloured terra-cotta, and an Oriental carpet in the shape of a Greek cross.

From the Palazzo del Comune to the Collegiata, which heard the harsh voice of Savonarola when Florence was happily still deaf to him, is but a step, and you pass from one silence to another. This rather sombre but beautiful church of three naves is a building of the eleventh century that the fourteenth century has modified and restored, and to which the fifteenth century, by the hand of Giuliano da Maiano, has added a choir and two chapels. The naves, which are the oldest part of the church, are completely covered with Sienese frescoes of the fourteenth century, as so many churches must have been up and down Italy, yet this remains almost alone to tell us of what we have lost. On the left wall are the Old Testament scenes in three tiers, painted by Bartolo di Fredi in 1356; on the right are scenes from the New Testament, begun in 1380 by Barna of Siena, and finished by his pupil, Giovanni d' Asciano. These frescoes suffered badly

in the last war. The beautiful Agony in the Garden by Barna
and the Red Sea by Bartolo di Fredi win us by their simplicity,
but Barna's dramatic power is far superior to Bartolo's *naïveté*.
Here was the Bible of the unlettered *contadini* and the townsmen of medieval San Gimignano. About the west window
in 1393 Taddeo di Bartolo painted the Last Judgment, beneath
which Benozzo Gozzoli in 1466 painted the Martyrdom of S.
Sebastian, with our Lord and the Madonna appearing to him in
the heavens. That fresco commemorates the later pestilence of
1464, when the theologian of San Gimignano, Domenico Strambi,
an Augustinian, caused Benozzo to paint this picture, with its
decorations. Under it are two fourteenth-century statues of wood,
excellent Sienese work, of the Blessed Virgin and S. Gabriel
Archangel. Over the pillars of the nave Benozzo has painted
half-figures of angels.

It is not here, however, but at the eastern end of the right
aisle that I found the true shrine of San Gimignano—the shrine
of S. Fina. The chapel where the little saint lies is one of those
added to the church by Giuliano da Maiano in the fifteenth century, a delightful, charming work of the Renaissance. The
shrine itself, the altar, and the reliefs, however, are the work of
Giuliano's brother, Benedetto. They were finished in 1475. Above
the altar, in a *mandorla* of cherubim attended by two angels, the
Madonna sits enthroned with her little Son. Beneath, in the
beautiful reredos, are reliefs of scenes in the life of S. Fina—her
vision of S. Gregory, her death, and her appearance to an old
woman. On either side of the tabernacle are two angels in niches,
while two splendid winged angels kneel in prayer. Upon the
sarcophagus itself, splendidly carved, with naked *putti*, we read:

> Virginis ossa latent tumulo quem suspicis, hospes.
> Haec decus, exemplum, praesidiumque suis.
> Nomen Fina fuit; patria haec; miracula quaeris?
> Perlege quae paries vivaque signa docent.

Who was this S. Fina, "the example, the guardian of her fellow-
citizens", whose country was San Gimignano, and whose miracles
are set forth "on the wall and in the lifelike images"?

Fina de' Ciardi was born in 1238 of a poor yet noble family
of San Gimignano. Till she was ten years old she was the delight
of her father's house, bright as a ray of spring sunshine in the

dark rooms there, beautiful as a flower fallen from the gardens of
Paradise, happy as a little singing-bird at morning. But in 1248
she fell ill, one of the most dreadful diseases of the Middle Age
attacked her, and, thinking she was the innocent victim of God's
anger for that tremendous century, she chose to lie on a plank
of hard oak, refused a bed, and for five years offered herself to
God in expiation of sins she could not name. Fearfully tormented
by the devil, who appeared to her in his old form of a serpent,
eight days before her death she was comforted by a vision of
S. Gregory, who promised that on his feast day, 12 March, 1253,
she should join him in Paradise. And it happened as he said.
But when they would have buried her they found her body so
terribly mangled by disease that already the worms devoured it;
and when they would have lifted her from her plank they found
that her flesh adhered to it, and that indeed her body had died
before her soul had taken its departure. Scarcely had she gone,
when the devils, fearing doubtless her advocacy in heaven, "filled
the air with whirlwinds; but against them, moved by angel hands,
the bells of San Gimignano rang out in sweet confidence, so that
the whirlwinds were calmed and the storm stilled. And when
the people came to the house of S. Fina they found it full of the
most sweet fragrance as of Paradise itself, and lo, the room where
the holy body lay was filled with flowers"; and marvelling at
this, they presently went their way.

They went their way, but they did not forget, and two hundred
years later they built this shrine by the hands of Giuliano and
Benedetto da Maiano, and in 1477 employed Domenico
Ghirlandaio, the Florentine, and his pupil Mainardi to paint
on either side the chapel the story of her life, with saints and
prophets between. There on the right we see her awaiting death,
when S. Gregory appeared to her promising her Paradise; on
the left we see her funeral, when, incapable of not doing good,
she touched the hand of her old nurse, sick herself, and instantly
she was whole. Without, the angels ring the bells of San
Gimignano. S. Fina's body was brought to this chapel in October
1488, when it was consecrated: that was after Ghirlandaio had
finished his work, and the place was sweet and beautiful for her.

From the chapel of S. Fina I went into the choir, where hangs
a splendid picture, by Piero Pollaiuolo, of the Coronation of the
Blessed Virgin, signed and dated 1483, one of the most splendid

works of this rare master. Beside it hangs a charming but over-
sweet picture of the Madonna and Child with angels and saints,
by Benozzo Gozzoli, painted in 1466. And not far away is one
of the better works of Tamagni—a Madonna and Child.

In the sacristy close by is a fine bust of Onofrio di Pietro,
master of the works when Giuliano da Maiano built S. Fina's
shrine. The ciborium of marble is from the hand of Benedetto.
Here, too, is a Madonna and Child with saints, by Mainardi, the
pupil of Ghirlandaio.

The baptistery opens out of the left aisle. Here is a fine fresco
of the Annunciation by Mainardi, and an ancient font of Sienese
work, made indeed by Giovanni Cecchi in 1379, at the expense
of the Arte della Lana, whose arms it bears.

On leaving the old church at last with its fading frescoes and
half-forsaken shrine, I climbed up behind it to the Rocca for the
sake of the view over Val d' Elsa. Then I went on through the
streets, scarcely less quiet and scarcely less ancient. Tower after
tower comes into view over the roofs, and hides itself again;
palace after palace, that is called indifferently of the Salvucci, of
the Ardinghelli. In the Piazza della Cisterna the grass was
growing; the Torre Cinatti was crowned with wild flowers; now
and then, as down the Vicolo de' Becci, far-away views of the
world, the sweet hill country of Tuscany, recalled me for a moment
from the strangely silent streets of late summer.

But wherever one wanders in San Gimignano one always
returns to the Piazza. One leaves it at last by the Via di San
Matteo intent on seeing the church of Sant' Agostino. Just
before the gate one turns into a narrow street on the right that
presently brings one to the church. Built in the end of the
thirteenth century, Sant' Agostino is yet full of works of the
fifteenth. At the west end is the little chapel of S. Bartolo, a
saint who gave his life for others, and they lepers, at Cellole in the
year 1300. His marble shrine, the lovely work of Benedetto da
Maiano, is of the end of the fifteenth century. Above are the
three theological virtues—three panels representing the good
deeds of the saint, and an exquisite relief of the Madonna and
Child with two adoring angels. This is one of Benedetto's finest
works. All is enclosed in a marble arch carved with arabesques.
The three saints on the wall and the doctors on the ceiling are
works of Mainardi.

Close by on the south wall of the nave is a fresco of the Madonna and Child with saints, one of the best works of Pier Francesco Fiorentino. Above is a Pietà by Tamagni. I found Tamagni's work again over the next altar, where is a fresco of the Madonna and Child with angels, and SS. Nicholas, Roch, Paul the Hermit, and Anthony Abbot; and again, over the first altar on the north wall of the nave, where there is a cross beneath which kneels S. Chiara of Montefalco. Close by is a very fine fresco by Benozzo Gozzoli of S. Sebastiano protecting the town against the plague. It is to see Benozzo Gozzoli's work in the choir that one comes to Sant' Agostino, but as one passes to it one may notice the fresco by Mainardi, at the end of this north wall, of S. Gimignano blessing the magistrates of the town. Under that fresco lies Domenico Strambi, the Augustinian to whom San Gimignano owes so many of her treasures, for he was the patron of the Maiani and Pollaiuolo and Ghirlandaio, and it is to him are due these frescoes of Benozzo also.

Begun in 1463 and finished in 1465, these paintings which fill the choir with their radiance are the worthy companions of those Benozzo painted at Montefalco which tell the life of S. Francis. Here in Sant' Agostino is the life of S. Augustine. On the left he is leaving home for school, where later he is punished. Then at the age of nineteen he enters the University of Carthage, where, as he himself has told, he went too much in the way of the world till he found himself praying that so human prayer, "O God, make me chaste—but not yet." But from afar his mother was daily besieging Heaven on his behalf, so that at last he sets out across the sea for Italy, teaches philosophy in Rome, and at length comes to Milan, where S. Ambrose receives him. Him he hears, while S. Monica also recounts all her fears to the great Archbishop. To Augustine, reading in a fair garden, comes S. Ambrose, and taught by him, Augustine is baptized; and there are written the first words of the *Te Deum Laudamus*, that marvellous hymn of praise that S. Ambrose and he are said to have composed in antiphon. Later he teaches, and then in a vision sees a child pouring the sea into a hole he had dug in the sand. There follows S. Monica's death. Above in the lunettes are his ordination, his refutation of the heretics and vision of S. Jerome, his death and entry into Paradise.

Above in the vault are the four Evangelists, on the choir arch figures of saints—S. Gimignano, S. Bartolo, S. Nicholas and S. Nicholas of Tolentino, S. Catherine of Siena, S. Fina, S. Sebastian, and Tobit; and beneath these again are S. Bartolo washing the lepers' feet, an apparition of S. Nicholas of Tolentino, the martyrdom of S. Sebastian, and Tobit and the archangel. In a chapel to the right of the choir remains of frescoes of the life of the Blessed Virgin by Bartolo di Fredi will be found.

Of the other churches in San Gimignano, San Pietro is worth a visit, for it has a fresco by Barna—the Madonna a Spasso with the Bambino.

Many of the churches have been stripped of their pictures, several of which have been collected in the Museo d' Arte Sacra which is entered from the Torre della Prepositura. Here are two altarpieces by Benozzo Gozzoli, one from Sant' Andrea, a modest version of his picture in the Collegiata, only here the saints are SS. Prosper and Andrew; there are two angels with baskets of flowers and the donor with name inscribed. In the *predella* is a Crucifixion and the picture is signed and dated 1466. Here, too is an Assumption with angels by Luca di Tommè: SS. Bartholomew, Benedict and another saint; two pictures of the Madonna and Child by Mainardi (1502) and an early Sienese Madonna in half-figure. There is some fine goldsmiths' work, among which is S. Fina's crown and veil. A small Crucifix in wood by Giuliano da Maiano is also preserved here. In the chapel of S. Vittore below, there is a wooden Crucifix over the altar, of the fourteenth century(?). The Figure is clothed in the colubrium like the Volto Santo of Lucca. The two angels at the sides are by Benedetto da Maiano.

About a mile outside Porta San Giovanni stands the charming convent, founded in 1340 and enlarged in 1458, of Monte Oliveto. The little church of Santa Maria Assunta di Monte Oliveto in Barbiano has a fifteenth-century portico and a most harmonious campanile rising as it does over the olives and surrounded by a well-tended garden. It was from this church came the dismembered altarpiece by Luca di Tommè now in the Museo d' Arte Sacra. There remains in the cloister a fresco of the Crucifixion by Benozzo Gozzoli dated 1466.

Farther on, some two miles, I came to the village of Santa Lucia, where in the church is a fresco of the Crucifixion by Pier

Francesco Fiorentino and an altarpiece by Fra Paolino da Pistoia
(1525).

There are indeed many walks about San Gimignano if one is
content to linger there. Out of Porta San Matteo one may go in
twenty minutes to Casale where in the church of San Michele
there is a fine statue in wood of S. Antony Abbot of the fifteenth
century and an altarpiece by Balducci of the mystic Marriage of
S. Catherine.

Then there is Cellole. One climbs into it after passing the little
fourteenth-century Oratorio of San Biagio. The *pieve* of Cellole
is a fine Romanesque church of three naves divided by columns
with rudely sculptured capitals. The arcaded semicircular apse is
beautifully sculptured with pre-Romanesque design.

Or there is Castelvecchio some three miles away past San
Donato on the road to Volterra, with its ruined, towered Rocca
and Fortezza, its ruinous church of the twelfth century and
mighty walls half lost in an illimitable *macchia*, entirely deserted,
in a vast and lovely landscape with far-away lines of mountain.

But after all San Gimignano itself seemed to take up all my
days, its churches, ancient bastions, walls, and beautiful gates, its
narrow medieval ways like Via San Giovanni, its towers—how
many they be I can never be sure—its palaces and those great
archways like Arco de' Becci, Arco della Cancellaria, Arco della
Torre Grossa, the Piazza del Pozzo, the ruined façade of the old
church of the Gerosolimitani called San Francesco, a lovely
thing of the twelfth century or earlier; and then the fifteenth-
century Ospedale on the way out of Porta alle Fonti to the little
church there, and the great arched and pillared Fonti themselves,
where the women and girls still wash the household clothes. At
evening I would stroll to some spot just outside, such as Bigazzino
or Poggio or the Rocca, where from any of these one may have a
different view of the little towered city which has lingered here
from the Middle Ages so unbelievably that—seen thus against all
the gold of the sunset—one might be still in the museum looking
at some miniatured city, past which the Kings, led by a star, are on
their way to Bethlehem.

THE VINTAGE

The vintage has begun here at San Gimignano. The equinox of
autumn is over, the Pleiades have not yet set. On the roads the

heavy farm carts drawn by two oxen are already lumbering from the vineyards to the *fattoria*, each fully loaded with tubs. It is a festal time. Under the still powerful sun a strange enchantment has fallen on the countryside; silvery wreaths of haze girdle the far blue hills and lie along the valleys. The vineyards, till now so silent and empty, are echoing with laughter and sprinkled with happy people; men and women, boys and girls and children too, from neighbouring *poderi*, have come to help the ingathering, not for pay or wages but in expectation of similar assistance in their turn. The *contadino* provides these helpers with bread, fruit and thin wine through the long day. In the golden weather, amid the general happiness and the beauty and profusion of the hanging clusters, garlanded on high from maple to maple, one might almost fancy Dionysus himself with Silenus and his rout are but out of sight in some shady dell where the stream still trickles in its dry bed in spite of the summer drought.

> At parte ex alia florens volitabat Iacchus
> cum thiaso Satyrorum et Nysigenis Silenis
> te quaerens, Ariadna, tuoque incensus amore . . .[1]

Those gathering the sacred bunches bring up their baskets and empty them into wooden tubs and all the beauty is soon pounded into a pulp. These *bigoncie* are loaded on to the gaily-coloured ox-wagon, which when fully laden lumbers off to the *stanzone*. Here the grapes are crushed, alas, till every grape is broken up and then the pulpy mush is emptied into the fermenting vat, a vast open barrel holding perhaps 1,000, perhaps 2,000, gallons. The grapes here are still trodden by youths with naked legs—*nudata crura* as Virgil says, but this, the traditional custom, is no longer general.

What actually happens in this vast barrel? It seems that "when the grapes begin to ripen and the sugar is forming in the pulp, the spores of a certain plant which since the previous winter have been dormant in the soil of the vineyard, rise and spread over the skin of the grape. As soon as the skin is broken they are set free and multiply in millions. They seize on the sugar and devour it, converting it partly into alcohol, partly into carbonic acid gas. In the cool *fattoria* their work goes on without much energy and so for a first day or two there is but little outward sign of their activity; but

---

[1] Elsewhere youthful Bacchus was wandering with the rout of sàtyrs and the Nysa-born Sileni seeking thee Ariadne and fired with thy love. (Catullus LXIV, 251).

BRINGING HOME THE GRAIN

PORTA ALL' ARCO, Volterra

their own vital process develops the warmth that is best suited to their life and multiplication, and once the fermentation is well started the whole vat bubbles and seethes like a cauldron on a brisk fire. So fiercely does the 'boiling' progress, that the ferment which can hardly live at a temperature of more than 104 degrees is sometimes entirely paralysed by its own exuberant life and the wine, but partially fermented, retains a mawkish sweetness. If the fermentation goes on normally the transformation is complete in about a week and the wine is then ready to draw off into casks to cool and clear itself of floating matter." So I was taught; and such is the mystery of wine. This explanation is not perhaps very clear, but then a mystery cannot be explained and remain a mystery. Wine is a sacramental and must ever be considered as such.

Just before the vintage some of the best and ripest grapes have been selected and laid aside, to be preserved on canes until November or December, to *governare* the wine. This is a custom confined to Tuscany. These grapes are added in a state of fermentation to wine already made, thus setting up a second fermentation in the whole mass. The effect is to impart a slight sparkle to the wine, which is much appreciated here in the Sanese. The sparkle dies away after twelve months and is therefore only to be found in wine drunk during that period.

But the evening is come at last when all has been gathered in and the *fattore* has provided a feast in which we are all involved. Many are the courses and each course is traditional: *antipasti, minestra, lesso, pollo, piccione, stracotto, legumi* of variety, *dolci, frutta, caffè*—one after the other with many and various wines, black and red and golden and white, sparkling and still. Everyone talks at the top of his voice, the noise is deafening till old Ercole who has been *contadino* here since he was a child and his father and grandfather and great-grandfather before him, rises to propose the health of the *padrone* in the traditional and accustomed speech. . . .

Supper is over, the ancient peasant house now resounds with the music of a concertina and songs and jests and *stornelli*. Presently a fiddle and a mandolin or two join in, and dancing begins on the *aia*. In the moonlight I make my way back to the villa of my host, through the deserted *podere*, stripped of its wealth, where I should like to find a hedgehog, robber of the vines, carrying grapes on his spines. The ancients used to sacrifice the spoiler to Dionysus,

4

but why should he not glean his share of our riches? Unhappy urchin, he has a hard time between the ploughshare, the sickle and the dog of the sportsman. May he enjoy his plunder, black and white and pink, under the benediction of Madonna and her little Son in their shrine with its solitary lamp, beside the villa portal.

CHAPTER IV

VOLTERRA

THE road for Volterra—for it was thither I was bound that early October morning at dawn—descends from San Gimignano into the valley, and climbing again through the quiet and delicate country that marks all the Val d' Elsa, joins the high road from Colle at Castel San Gimignano—a village that is scarcely more than a ruined fortress. Thence the way lies over vast and barren downs tawny as a lion's hide, across an uplifted wilderness of sterile clay hills, past blue-grey chasms of volcanic *tufa*, till at evening "lordly Volaterrae" rears itself up threatening against the sky, haggard with loneliness and age like the dreadful spirit of this strange country so full of a sinister desolation. No traveller can, I think, approach this outraged stronghold of old time without a certain apprehension and anxiety. The way is lonely, precipitous, and threatening; and long before I climbed the last great hill into the city an eerie dread had seized my heart. As far as the eye could reach that barren and tortured world rolled away in billow after billow of grey earth scantily covered with a thin dead herbage that seemed to have been burned with fire. On either side the way vast cliffs rose over immense crevasses seamed and tortured into the shapes of ruined cities: yonder a dreadful tower set with broken turrets tottered on the edge of sheer nothing; here a tremendous gate led into darkness, there a breached wall yawned over an abyss. If there be such a thing as traveller's fear, it is here you will meet it, it is here it will make your heart a prize. As for me, I was horribly afraid, nor would any prayer I knew bring my soul back into my keeping. But then I came on foot.

And if the way was so full of fear, what of the lofty city that stood at the high summit of the narrow road winding between the precipices? It too was a city of dread—a city of bitterness, outraged and very old. Seven hundred years before the fall of Troy it had already suffered siege. Surrounded in those days by walls 40 feet high, 12 feet thick, and 8,000 yards in circumference, that have worn out three civilizations, and still in part remain,

Volterra was one of the greater cities of the Etruscan League. Like fortresses her gates were held impregnable. Enemy after enemy, army after army broke against those bastions of piled monoliths; she scattered them, and they were lost in the desolation in which she is still entrenched. From the lower valley of the Arno to the forgotten citadel of "sea-girt Populonia", which the Maremma has destroyed, she reigned supreme. She threatened Tarquinius Priscus, King of Rome; to her Scipio Africanus turned in his need when he would have broken Carthage, and she lent him sea-power, for she held the ports of the north, Luna and Pisa, as well as Populonia at the doors of Latium. Her sovereignty stretched over more than two thousand years, nor is there any record of her subjugation till Sulla, after a siege of two years, held her at the mercy of the City. Who knows what were her thoughts when that Rome whose birth she had seen, whose power she had known how to resist for so many ages, fell at last into the darkness? That her lordship grew in the time of the Lombards, that in the 450 years of the refounded Empire she still lived, though as its fief, her records prove. Then at the end of the Middle Age, as old as her own crumbling hills, she rose again on the verge of the new-made desert, desolate but free. It was her last brief resurrection. Little by little life forsook her, never to return. Nature had tired her out. Aloft above the silent Maremma, full of miasma and death, that had already swallowed up Populonia and many another city populous and strong, Volterra withered away. It was into a dead city that the Florentines marched when in 1361 they claimed to have subdued her.

The traveller who, forsaking the valley and its country towns in order to see Volterra, has had patience or perseverance enough to cross the solitude that surrounds her, might, in fact, have spared himself his journey: he will not see Volterra; what he will see is a vast gaunt ruin, the mighty debris of what was once a city.

Approaching her, as he must do, through a lonely desolation, he is in some sort prepared for those incredible ruins that await him: a vast wall thousands of years old that nothing but time or earthquake could have destroyed, a tunnelled gate like a primeval fortress, like the port of Thebes—massive stone set on massive stone without mortar or cement—

Piled by the hands of giants
For god-like kings of old. . . .

Encamped within these ruins he will find the debris of more
than one later civilization—Roman, Medieval, and Renaissance—
cheek by jowl with the fugitive and impermanent work of today.
Still enclosed and guarded by the wall of the Etruscans, and
entered by their gate, the shrunken medieval city of Volterra
awaits one amid the wreck of four different ages, like some fragment hidden in a crevice of the temples of Karnak.

Little by little as I wandered through those silent streets, those
lonely piazzas where today and yesterday have met, here in the
oldest graveyard of all, in an unlooked-for reconciliation, this at
least seemed certain, this at last I realized, that all things pass
away and nothing remaineth. What, I asked myself, could have
overthrown so tremendous a citadel, yet man has consumed it,
and even Rome has passed by here and left so little that the farthest
of her provinces more easily remembers her. Nor is it only
antiquity that is here in ruin. Be sure time has not done with
her; the medieval abbey is as desolate as the Etruscan wall.
For Volterra is set on the edge of the precipice; she clings, and
dizzily, to her rock over the abyss; little by little she is slipping,
falling, dropping stone by stone, church by church, flower by
flower, into nothingness, into that vast desolation that surrounds
her. You may see it through every arch, it haunts every byway
of the town, it greets you from Porta Menseri, from Porta San
Francesco, from Porta San Felice, and though Porta di Docciola
is hung with earth's loveliest garland, and the girls sing there at
the fountain, it too brings you to the brink, it too stares into open
nothingness. Death—if you would look upon it and know how it
lurks behind everything fair, noble, or venerable, you have but
to walk out of Porta Pisana for a short mile, and there, beyond
a more ancient gate, you look into the horrible depths of the very
pit where is hidden all that was once so strong. There, down there,
Volterra, what is left of Volterra, will lie soon, for her earth is
weary of the burden of her ruins.

You might think that a visit to such a tragic place in search
of beauty, in search of works of art, would certainly resolve itself
into just a pottering among the stones; and that whatever you
might bring to light would be, could, in fact, be, nothing but the

merest fragments. I don't know. What is all our "sightseeing"
then, our artistic enthusiasm, here in Italy at any rate, but a
patient search among the ruins for the beauties of an alien age?
Indeed, in most places even the search is spared us, and we by
so much the poorer. At least here in Volterra we may go quietly
and alone from ruin to ruin, from church to church, from piazza
to piazza, without too vulgar or noisy a curiosity. There is much
to see—and let us be thankful for it—that can never be labelled
or imprisoned in a museum; there is much even that the heart
must divine.

One at least of the dread problems of ancient Volterra is
brought very clearly before one by that great Piscina within the
Porta all' Arco, itself perhaps the most wonderful thing in the
city, between it and the Fortezza, which it is so difficult to get
permission to see. It is a great well, or reservoir, without which
no city, howsoever strong her walls, could avoid surrender. It was
the failure to obtain plentiful water that always troubled Siena,
and Volterra had provided herself with it in a situation even
more difficult centuries before Siena was anything but a negligible
stronghold of the hills. Whether that great cistern is the work of
the Etruscans, repaired and perhaps enlarged by the Romans, or
whether it is a contrivance of Rome, is difficult to decide. The
tremendous work of the Etruscans, however, is not far off, and
before attempting to explore the city itself every traveller should
pass out of the Porta all' Arco, and if he cannot make a complete
circuit of the ancient walls, which were some five miles in circumference, he should at least pass westward to Porta San Felice, still
outside the medieval city but within the Etruscan, continue his
way to Santa Chiara, and so to that horrible precipice, Le Balze,
by San Giusto, which is so surely swallowing Volterra itself.

There can be little anywhere else in Italy to compare for
antiquity with the spectacle offered by that brief walk. Thousands
of years have gone to the making of it, and these works, so
tremendous in their material features, are not less impressive in
their spiritual significance, for they were probably standing when
Troy fell, they were old when Romulus ploughed on the Palatine,
they have heard the words of the augur and watched him divine
the future in the face of the rising sun or the flight of a bird;
they have heard Pan piping in the woods and seen him desolate
upon the mountains; they have heard the wild chant of the

Bacchante when the grapes were purple in the waning summer, and watched the priest make Christ out of bread and wine in the early morning when our voices were hushed and the worshippers were few. They are part of the bulwarks of Europe; we built them when we were young and believed in the future, therefore we piled one mighty stone upon another that it should never be removed, and our faith was justified in our work. It is the earth that has grown weary of the weight we set upon it and, subsiding into that abyss, Le Balze, has brought down what nothing save earthquake has been able to destroy.

What those who built these walls believed, what they thought concerning life and death and the world in which they dwelt, we may discover, though but dimly, in the museum of the Palazzo Tagassi, the Museo Guarnacci, and better far at Tarquinia. Here in some fourteen rooms is arranged a collection of some six hundred cinerary urns dating from the second or third century B.C., the latest period of Etruscan art. The execution of the reliefs carved upon them is often feeble and even rudimentary, but the subjects are clear enough. Then, too, we were sorry to say farewell, and set forth on that long last journey with as good a heart as might be; we sacrificed to the gods, followed our brothers to the grave, and were weary at evening. That the men who carved these caskets for the ashes of their fellows were our brothers their work testifies, but indeed we know little more about them; we cannot read their language nor decipher their inscriptions. The best thing here, where all seems modern rather than ancient, is a bronze statuette, the Ombra della Sera, a strange masterpiece.

There is but little in Volterra today that bears witness to the Roman occupation that befell after Sulla's two years' siege: the Piscina perhaps, the inner façade of the Porta all' Arco, scarcely anything beside. But what Volterra owes to Rome is the establishment of the Catholic religion, and Volterra is not poor in Christian monuments. There is nothing here, of course, that can be claimed as due to the Empire, and in the tenth century Volterra, like the rest of Christendom, had fallen into decay; she owes her resurrection as a small encampment within her vast old walls to the Ottos. To this period nothing now remaining within the city strictly belongs, unless, indeed, it be certain arches or parts of arches, towers, and gates, but the ruined Badia beyond San Giusto, the ruined church of Santo Stefano outside the Porta

San Francesco, and the abbey of San Salvatore, are Romanesque buildings of the eleventh century.

Within the city the oldest building is the Duomo, which was consecrated in 1120 by Pope Calixtus II, and which was restored and enlarged by some builder of the Pisan school, certain authorities say by Nicola Pisano himself, in 1254. Though it was spoiled in the sixteenth century by the restorations and works of Ricciarelli, a nephew of Daniele da Volterra, the Duomo is still interesting, its façade being wholly of thirteenth-century work, save the doorway of black and white marble, which may be later. Within, the church is a spacious Latin cross, and it holds several works of art which are worth more than a passing glance.

The most ancient of these is the beautiful pulpit, a splendid work of the Pisan school, consisting of a four-sided rostrum, supported by four granite pillars standing on the backs of crouching lions. Each side of the rostrum is filled with a fine relief of the early thirteenth century, that in front shows the Last Supper, with Judas crouched at the feet of Christ, who gives him the sop, while behind him lurks the dragon, the ancient enemy of God and man; at the sides are the Salutation and the Annunciation, and at the back the Sacrifice of Isaac. To the right and left of the western doors are some further reliefs, fourteenth-century works of much charm, representing the legend of SS. Regolo and Ottaviano. These tender and lovely things deserve more attention than they are ever likely to get. But the Duomo is rich in sculpture. On either side the high altar, on two exquisite twisted columns, two angels by Mino da Fiesole kneel. It is to Raffaele Cioli, a sixteenth-century master, we owe the beautiful sarcophagus with attendant angels where S. Ottaviano sleeps.

And then, if the Duomo is rich in marbles, it has some astonishing works, too, both in terra-cotta and in wood. Perhaps the finest of these is the glazed bust of Pope S. Linus, the immediate successor of S. Peter, over the side door, made by Andrea della Robbia, but the S. Sebastian, a work of his school, is not to be passed over, nor a fresco by Gozzoli for background; a Presepio group, and the Adoration of the Magi, are two fine works by the master. In wood—and wooden statues and groups are always rare and always expressive—is an inpressive twelfth-century Deposition. But all the woodwork—the choir-stalls, the splendid work in the sacristy especially—and the metal reliquaries of the fifteenth and sixteenth centuries, a crucifix of silver, and such, should be carefully examined. They are part of the fragile charm of Volterra.

Of pictures the Duomo can now make no boast. Those she has are charming but of little real importance or beauty. The polyptych, painted in 1411 by Taddeo di Bartolo, which used to adorn the Oratorio di San Carlo, is now in the Museum; there remains the Annunciation which Luca Signorelli painted in 1491, the Nativity of Benvenuto di Giovanni, and a small triptych with an Annunciation, the Madonna and Child, and the Crucifixion within, and without S. Peter and S. Paul by Tamagni, and a picture of the Annunciation by Albertinelli (1497).

The Baptistery, an octagonal building of the thirteenth century, stands opposite the cathedral. The arch over the high altar is the sixteenth-century work of Balsimelli da Settignano, while the octagonal font, like the building in which it stands, is the work of Andrea Sansovino. The splendid tabernacle of marble, about which angels kneel in adoration, is the beautiful work of Mino da Fiesole. Close by the Campanile is the Opera del Duomo with some good goldsmithery.

These two buildings, fine and rich as they are, by no means stand alone in Volterra. Every church, and there are many, is full of interest. There is San Lino, for instance, built in the fifteenth century, which contains a good tomb of the scholar Raffaele Maffei, with a recumbent statue by Lorenzo Stagi. There is San Francesco, a thirteenth-century church rebuilt in 1623, which possesses a relief of the Assumption by a pupil of Andrea della Robbia. Out of it one passes into a little chapel of the Holy Cross, built in 1315, in almost perfect preservation and covered with frescoes, for the most part by Cenni di Francesco. There on the walls one sees scenes from the life of the Virgin, with the Massacre of the Innocents, the Invention of the Cross. The whole chapel is still an example of what such a place as this was in the fifteenth century. A fresco of the Circumcision by Signorelli remains here, but repainted by Sodoma.

Again, in San Pietro one finds two of those wooden statues, an Annunciation, like those at Castel-Fiorentino and San Gimignano; and in San Michele, over whose door is a Madonna and Child of the thirteenth century, a fine thing in a niche, perhaps by Giovanni della Robbia.

It is pleasant on an afternoon, too, to stroll out of Porta a Selci, and in some half-mile to come to the convent of San Girolamo, for it is full of beautiful things, and is itself, with its shady loggia, one of the most charming buildings about this harsh old city. There I found a great polychrome terra-cotta relief by Giovanni della Robbia of the Last Judgment, beneath which are three *predelle*— the Annunciation, the Nativity, and the Adoration of the Magi. There, too, are several of those delightful country pictures that so often delight one in Tuscany—Madonna and her little Son with S. Francis and five other saints, by Giusto d' Andrea, and, better still, a wonderful golden Annunciation by Benvenuto di Giovanni, where Madonna sits, very tall, upright, and full of grace, girdled with cherubim, while S. Gabriel Archangel, crowned with olive, fallen on one knee, repeats his message, S. Michael standing on one side thrusting at the dragon, S. Catherine on the other with her palm of martyrdom, and in the sky God the Father, in the midst of cherubs and musical angels, blesses the scene. Beneath, the donor kneels praying to the Madonna.

There are the churches of Sant' Agostino and Sant' Antonio, each of which possesses an altarpiece by Taddeo di Bartolo, among other pictures.

But if, indeed, one is to consider pictures here, one must do so in the Pinacoteca, whither so many—too many—have been taken out of the churches. The gallery of Volterra is to be found in the Palazzo dei Priori, a great palace with a two-storied tower close to the cathedral in the Piazza Maggiore. Begun in 1208, and completed in 1257, the Palazzo dei Priori is very like the Palazzo Vecchio of Florence, while its tower reminds one both of that at Florence and of the Mangia of Siena.

In the Pinacoteca the Florentine school is represented chiefly by the work of Ghirlandaio and Carli. Ghirlandaio's picture, a large and curious altarpiece, the Redeemer in Glory, where our Lord is enthroned upon the cherubim, an open book, inscribed with the Alpha and Omega, in His left hand, while His right is raised in blessing. On either side an angel kneels in heaven in adoration. Beneath, in a smiling landscape of river, hill, and valley, stand SS. Benedict and Romuald, and beside them kneel SS. Attinia and Greciniana. In the right-hand corner of the picture is the donor, a Camaldolese, in prayer. This important work comes from the Badia, to which it was given by Lorenzo de' Medici.

Raffaele dei Carli is represented here by an altarpiece of the Madonna, saints, and angels—an early work Mr. Berenson says. One finds his hand again in the Anticamera here, in a fresco of the Madonna and Child.

Coming now to the Sienese pictures, one turns first to the Adoration of the Shepherds by Benvenuto di Giovanni, a charming altarpiece, where above God leans from heaven amid a crowd of singing angels to bless our world, the Holy Dove descends through the darkness, and Christ Himself, a little child, lies at His mother's feet beside the careful ox in the rude stall. Far away in the winter fields an angel tells the glad tidings to the shepherds who are come to worship Him. Beneath this simple loveliness were four *predelle* scenes of the life of the Virgin—her Birth, her Presentation in the Temple, her Marriage, and her Assumption. They are now separated from the picture and three small *tondi* have taken their place. This large work was painted in 1466, as was the lovely Sassetta-like Annunciation in San Girolamo.

An earlier painter, Taddeo di Bartolo, is represented here by a polyptych of the Madonna and Child with saints. There are two works by Signorelli in the Municipio, two of them in the Museo, and all were painted in 1491. The Madonna and Child with saints comes from San Francesco, while the S. Girolamo, a fresco on the first landing of the staircase, is still in its own place.

But these strong or tender works, for all their beauty, have, in fact, little in common with Volterra. Day by day as one goes to and fro in the narrow streets, in the continual shadow of those frowning palaces and medieval towers, or at evening watches the sunset across the horror of the Balze, one realizes that Volterra has little in common with Tuscany—the Tuscany of Giotto, of Fra Lippo Lippi, of Botticelli, of Sassetta and Sano di Pietro. Etruscan still, she towers over that bitter desolation of which she seems to be the final and complete expression, the last monument of a civilization titanic and incredible that forms one of the tremendous and hidden foundations of our own. In spite of that medieval town, which is so impressive and insistent in that naked corner of the ancient city where one dwells, one's final thought of her is as of something more elemental than that, less complicated and more absolute. She has grown amid that bitter landscape which surrounds her till she has become a part of it, till in herself she has summed it up. As my eyes pass slowly from the vast height at which I seem to stand over that desolate world to the far-away sea and the dark and jagged outline of the mountains of Elba and Capraja, I am conscious only of emptiness, a negation of life, as in some landscape in the Inferno over which the sun never rises, or where, if it rises, it has no kingdom, no effect. And as I leave her at last and go on my way, I turn and gaze back on the ruined city, out of whose wonderful debris she soars like some zodiacal beast, a terrific sign against the sky. And it is as just that, for it was my last sight of her, that I shall always remember her—a monstrous sign in heaven, the bitter, the monstrous emblem of Death up-reared over an abyss in loneliness and desolation.

CHAPTER V

COLLE, POGGIBONSI, SAN LUCCHESE, STAGGIA, MONTERIGGIONI, AND BADIA A ISOLA

As I came down from the desolate great hills over which Volterra reigns an Acheronian monarch, little by little the sun began to shine again with its old splendour, Elsa was golden with light; the vineyards and the olive gardens seemed full of joy; little by little I lifted up my heart. Towards the end of my journey, I went off the road to the south to visit the splendid Vallombrosan abbey church of Santa Maria a Coneo. This is a Romanesque building of the twelfth century with single nave and transept and three apses at the eastern end, under an octagonal cupola. It has a triple arched entry. The parish church here of SS. Ippolito e Cassiano is also of the twelfth century. It had three naves and apses, now reduced to two, divided by columns of black and white marble with fine sculptured capitals. I left these Romanesque churches with regret and went on my way past Le Grazie, a small Renaissance sanctuary with frescoes of the school of Benozzo Gozzoli. At Colle di Val d' Elsa, where I came at evening, I found the streets thronged and happy with people.

Set on a long and lofty ridge with a modern town at its foot, Colle Alto, the old hill city, is one of the heroic *castelli* of this valley which led indeed to Siena, but which was so largely in the power of the Florentines. That stone signed with blood, which, as Villani tells us, was the foundation of Colle, is at least significant of her history, since her position here in Val d' Elsa, close to Poggibonsi, on the frontiers of Florence and Siena, always thrust upon her that difficult and dangerous choice: would she follow the Sienese or the Florentines?

The cities that lay behind me in the valley—Castel-Fiorentino, Certaldo, and San Gimignano—when the time came for them to lose what independence they had been able to win from the nobles or the bishop who had received them from the Empire or the Church, had, in fact, but little choice: the power of Florence was already so great that they found themselves already within her *contado*. It was different with Colle, Poggibonsi, and Staggia. These three little towns, the first two more especially, grew up actually upon the frontier, the continually disputed frontier, of the two great rival States of Tuscany. And until in the end of the thirteenth century Florence finally disposed of Ghibelline Siena, the territory that lay between these little hill towns was a continual battle-field.

As might be expected, Staggia and Poggibonsi, lying so near to Siena, sided with her, while on that account Colle leaned to the side of Florence. Not that any one of the three cared more for Florence than for Siena, but that since Poggibonsi, for instance, had chosen, or had been compelled to choose, one side, Colle perforce chose the other, for in those days, the nearer the neighbour the greater the enemy.

On a larger scale one sees this in action throughout Tuscany in the Middle Age. Pisa is Ghibelline, therefore Lucca is Guelf; Florence is Guelf, therefore Pistoia and Arezzo are Ghibelline. It was not that any one of them was eager for the cause of Emperor or Pope, but that all were passionate in defence of their own independence, and sought to use the great quarrel in their own behalf. Such was the birth of nationalism; but no one understood it. Even to Dante the condition of affairs was incomprehensible. Confused in inevitable nostalgia, he cursed the cities of his fatherland, and dreaming of the Empire, welcomed into Italy a barbarian king.

As it was with the greater cities, so it was with such *castelli* as Colle, Poggibonsi, and Staggia: with this difference, however, that whereas the greater cities were in fact independent, and only in theory at any time dependent upon the Empire or the Holy See, the smaller towns were continually and actually at the mercy of their greater neighbours, and were compelled to change their colour with the victory or defeat of these in a quarrel not their own.

Colle, which had always leaned to Florence because Poggibonsi stood for Siena, had fallen to the Ghibellines after Montaperto in 1260. It was in 1269 that she was forced to decide once and for all, so that in that year just for a moment her history becomes vivid, as she looked down from her ridge on the battle that avenged Montaperto and finally decided the fortunes of Tuscany.

The battle of Montaperto, fought and won by the Sienese and the Florentine Ghibellines in 1260, had seemed doubtless once and for all to dispose of the Guelf cause and the power of Florence. In that fight, which dyed the Arbia red with blood, "was routed and destroyed the ancient people of Florence," more than 2,500 were slain, and over 1,500 "of the best of the People of Florence" led into captivity. Siena seemed to have the hegemony of Tuscany in her hands. And no doubt, had she followed the advice of her leader, Provenzano Salvani, and razed Florence to the ground, she might have looked forward to a century of lordship. But Farinata degli Uberti at Empoli was too strong for the lord of Siena. The man who in his fiery sepulchre seemed to Dante to hold hell itself in scorn was not likely to be beaten by an impetuous Sienese. Alone in the assembly at Empoli, where the fate of Florence was debated, he forbade the decision that would have destroyed her. He had his way, and by that act secured the lordship of his city and the overthrow of Siena. In the year of the great victory Siena may well have thought she could afford to be generous; that again but proved her unfitness to rule. Politics know no generosity; to spare your enemy when your own life is at stake is weakness. So it proved with Siena. Six years after the battle, in 1266, the Ghibelline cause and the city of Siena received a staggering blow in the death of Manfred. In that same year a second Popolo rose in Florence, and the Conte Guido Novello, untractably Ghibelline, with his friends was expelled the city, the Guelfs were restored, and their enemies sent into exile. Two years later Corradino was taken at Tagliacozzo, and King Charles, more ruthless than the Sienese, in the same year, struck off his head in Naples. Where was the Ghibelline cause now? In fact, it was dead. It was but its ghost that startled Italy when Henry VII crossed the Alps—a ghost finally laid at Buonconvento in 1313.

Now in the year 1267, when Manfred was dead, Charles of Naples and the Florentines had taken Poggibonsi from the Sienese, and with it Colle. It was in June 1269 that Provenzano Salvani, Governor of Siena, thought the time had come to reclaim them. In this, too, he showed the Sienese failing—a lack of judgment.

"In the year of Christ 1269," writes Giovanni Villani,[1] "in the month of June, the Sienese, whereof M. Provenzano Salvani, of

---

[1] G. Villani, *Cronica*, Lib. vii, cap. 31.

Siena, was governor, with Count Guido Novello, the German and Spanish troops, and the Ghibelline refugees from Florence and other cities of Tuscany, and with the forces of the Pisans to the number of 1,400 horse and 8,000 foot, marched upon the stronghold of Colle di Val d' Elsa, which was under the lordship of the Florentines; and this they did because the Florentines had come in May with an army to destroy Poggibonizzi. And when they had encamped at the Abbey of Spugnole,[1] and the news was come to Florence on Friday evening, on Saturday morning M. Giambertaldo, vicar of King Charles for the League of Tuscany, departed from Florence with his troops which he then had with him in Florence: to wit, 400 French horse; and sounding the bell and being followed by the Guelfs of Florence on horse and on foot, he came with his cavalry to Colle on Sunday evening; and there were about 800 horsemen or less, with but few of the people, forasmuch as they could not reach Colle so speedily as the horsemen. It came to pass on the following Monday morning, the day of S. Barnabas, in June, the Sienese, hearing that the horsemen had come from Florence, broke up their camp near the said abbey and withdrew to a safe place. M. Giambertaldo, seeing the camp in motion, without awaiting more men, passed the bridge with his horse, and marshalled his troops, with the cavalry of Florence and such of the people as had arrived, together with them of Colle (who by reason of the sudden coming of the Florentines were not duly arrayed either with captains of the host or with the standard of the commonwealth); and M. Giambertaldo took the standard of the commonwealth of Florence and requested of the horsemen of Florence, amongst whom were representatives of all the Guelf houses, that one of them should take it; but none advanced to take it, whether from cowardice[2] or through jealousy one of the other; and after they had been a long time in suspense, M. Aldobrandini, of the house of Pazzi, boldly stepped forward and said, 'I take it to the honour of God and the victory of our commonwealth'; wherefore he was much commended for his boldness. And straightway he advanced, and all the horsemen followed him and struck boldly into the ranks of the Sienese; and albeit it was not held to be very nice and prudent leadership, yet, as it pleased God, these

---

[1] The Badia di Spugnole stood at the foot of the hill of Colle, on the left bank of the river.

[2] Probably they remembered the fate of the standard at Montaperto, and the effect of its fall on the battle.

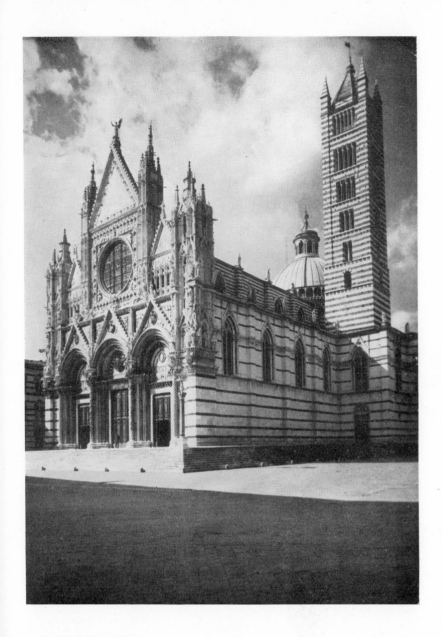

IL DUOMO, Siena

IL DUOMO: interior, Siena

bold and courageous folk, with good success, broke up and defeated the Sienese and their allies, which numbered well-nigh twice as many horse and a great number of foot, whereof many were slain and taken; and if on the Florentine side the foot had arrived and had been at the battle, scarce one of the Sienese would have escaped. Count Guido Novello fled, and M. Provenzano Salvani, lord and commander of the host of the Sienese, was taken prisoner; and they cut off his head and carried it through all the camp aloft on a lance. And thus was indeed fulfilled the prophecy and revelation made to him by the Devil in an incantation, though he never understood it. For having invoked him to learn how he would fare in that expedition, he made a lying answer and said, 'Thou wilt go up and fight; thou shalt conquer, not in battle shalt thou die, and thy head shall be highest in the field.' And he thought he had the victory by these words, and hoped to remain lord over all, for he did not put the comma in the right place, and detect the fraud thus, 'Thou shalt conquer not, in battle shalt thou die'. . . ."

Such is Villani's account; it agrees in the main with the Sienese version, but is sparing in detail. It seems that Provenzano Salvani was taken prisoner and after the battle Cavolino Tolomei, a Sienese exile, his personal enemy, stole in disguise through the trenches in search of him, and when he had found him, suddenly stabbed him to the heart, and cutting off his head, placed it on his lance, and so rode through the camp.

Cavolino Tolomei was not the only Sienese exile who rejoiced in the defeat of his countrymen. Sapia, a lady of Siena, watched the battle from a tower near the field, and prayed for the victory of Florence. Her confession is in the thirteenth *Purgatorio*:

> I' fui Sanese, rispose, e con questi
> altri rimondo quì la vita ria,
> lagrimando a Colui che sè ne presti.
> Savia non fui, avvegna che Sapia
> fossi chiamata. . . .
> Erano i cittadin miei presso a Colle
> in campo giunti co' loro avversari;
> ed io pregai Iddio di quel ch' e' volle.
> Rotti fur quivi, e volti negli amari

passi di fuga; e veggendo la caccia,
letizia presi a tutt' altre dispari;
tanto ch' i' volsi 'n su l' ardita faccia,
gridando a Dio: Omai più non ti temo. . . .[1]

Montaperto was avenged. In that vengeance the Ghibelline cause was killed, and the battle of Colle ended the age-long wars between Florence and Siena. For not long after, the Florentines restored the Sienese exiles and drove out the Ghibellines, and there was peace between the commonwealths, which, according to Villani, "remained ever after friends and allies".

Lingering in Colle, today so full of a country quiet, one scarcely suspects it of so momentous an action as that terrific battle proved to be. Decay, repose if you will, has fallen upon it with an infinite grace, and one passes up its steep ways, through the formidable Porta Volterrana, through a street of still picturesque palaces, including one by Antonio da Sangallo the Younger and the house of Arnolfo di Cambio, in and out of many churches, with an ever-fresh delight in the smiling, gay aspect of the little city so wonderfully overlooking the quiet valley. Here and there I passed a monument in those narrow ways, now and then a tabernacle made lovely by the work of some dead painter for the comfort of men dead and gone these many years. In the Via Venti Settembre it is perhaps Pietro di Domenico who charms one with a fresco of the Adoration of the Magi, in the Via Gozzina and the Via Santa Lucia it is Pier Francesco Fiorentino, first with a fresco of the Madonna and Child between two bishops, and again with a fresco of the Annunciation.

And the churches are serene and full of light; each possesses something to give one pleasure. In the Duomo, for instance, I found a fine pulpit set on four ancient marble columns; in Sant' Agostino, over the first altar on the right, a picture of the Madonna and Child, by Taddeo di Bartolo, and a little farther on, over the third altar, a fine Pietà painted in 1521 by Ridolfo Ghirlandaio; while in the Conservatorio di San Pietro I came upon the work of Giovanni di Paolo in a picture of the Circumcision; and in the

---

[1] I was, the spirit answered, of Siena; here I cleanse away with these the evil life, weeping to Him that He lend Himself to us. Sapient I was not though Sapia I was named . . . My townsmen hard by Colle were joined in battle with their foes, and seeing the rout of my countrymen, I was seized with joy exceeding all other: so that I lifted up my impudent face and cried to God: "Now I fear Thee no more." *Purgatorio* XIII, 106 et seq.

Palazzo Antico del Comune two works by Pier Francesco Fiorentino—an altarpiece of the Madonna and Child and four saints
complete with *predella*, and a Madonna and Child, S. Bernardino,
S. Antony Abbot, S. Mary Magdalen, and S. Catherine.

But charming as Colle is, and convenient for the wayfarer, she
did not hold me long from the road that leads to Poggibonsi in
whose mere name laughter seemed hid.

Poggibonsi, indeed, is but five miles away, and I found her one
evening like a ghost on her hill over the whispering poplars. This
apparition, however, proved to be the Castello, the town itself—
—to which I came presently—lying on a low hill close to the road
and the railway in the valley. There I found a good inn, the
"Aquila", which I had not done at Colle, and I was content.

History has little or nothing to do with the town of Poggibonsi;
where it touches her it is concerned only with the beautiful
Castello, which, after the battle of Colle, the Florentines destroyed:
for Poggibonsi still clung to the bankrupt cause of the Empire:
she was the friend of Siena.

And today, save her own country beauty, she has really
nothing to offer us. I wandered through her gay and noisy streets,
passed in and out of her churches, and climbed in a long afternoon
up to the Castello; I found nothing save a few country frescoes, but
in San Lorenzo there is a picture by Neri di Bicci, one of his best
works, of S. Nicholas of Tolentino and two small donors, and in the
Collegiata a large picture, aloft behind the high altar, of the
Resurrection, attributed to Tamagni. The font is of the fourteenth century. And then at Cedda, about an hour away to the east,
there is a church of San Pietro, Romanesque, with a magnificent
apse which I remember very well. But that was not for me
today.

So presently I set out where the road led towards Siena. It was
still quite early; the stillness of the hours about the sunrise had not
yet been broken. The whole valley was asleep, till slowly the pure,
cold dawn, wrapped in a grey mantle, stole down from the hills
through the woods into the vineyards and the gardens of olives.
I was marching along thus in the earliest morning, humming and
talking to myself, on the way to Siena, when suddenly the road
forked, and I found myself standing before a great and old church
beside a convent, around which a few poor houses were set.

Now before the church stood a peasant of perhaps thirty years,

and he gave me good day. Presently, when we had spoken of the
fine autumn the gods had vouchsafed us mortals, and he had told
me his name was Beppino and I had told him mine in English and
in Italian, a little bell began to ring, and we went into the church
together, I a little in advance.

And so we heard Mass—a low Mass said swiftly in the early light
by a little friar of S. Francis who presently came towards us, for,
save a child who served him and two old women, we were all his
congregation. He greeted Beppino, who introduced me, and then
I asked him the name of this place and the dedication of the church,
what fame it had and what relics, and why it was set there at a
turning of the way not two miles out of Poggibonsi.

The last question he could not resolve, but the rest was easy.
First, he told me that the name of the convent and of the place
was San Lucchese; then that it was famous on account of that very
saint, who, as I doubtless knew, was a great servant of God, and,
moreover, a Franciscan of the Third Order; and, thirdly, that the
relics they had were his, and that I should see them.

We saw them, and when that was finished he proceeded to
discover other treasures to us, but the Noli Me Tangere by
Raffaele del Garbo was destroyed in the war, the Fei fresco
damaged, but a Madonna and saints by some disciple of the
Robbia, remains. Frescoes, too, I saw by Bartolo di Fredi, of
S. Nicholas of Bari throwing the bags of gold through the window
of the house of the three girls he wished to save from dishonour—
the original Father Christmas; and opposite this a Crucifixion of
S. Andrew and, above, a frescoed triptych. When I had looked
on all this, Frate Nicola led us both into the convent, placed bread
and wine before us, and began his tale.

"You must know, signore, and thou, Beppino, that this church
and convent were built by the Franciscans of the Observance, to
which Order I also—a little poor devil—belong, and that it stands
here on this hill on the site of an abbey of Benedictines called
Poggiomarturi. It was here in this very place that the Emperor
Henry VII encamped when he retired from that unfortunate siege
of Florence, of which you have heard, signore, and thou hast not,
O Beppino; and in memory of this the place was called Poggio
Imperiale. Also you must know that Cosimo I, the Grand Duke,
later fortified it also. These are things doubtless to lend it some
little fame, but its glory, signore, has nothing to do with emperors

or dukes, or even with Benedictines—its glory is due to our most Holy Founder, S. Francesco, and to that *gran servo di Dio*, S. Lucchese, who loved him.

"This S. Lucchese, signore, or more properly S. Lucesio, was born, as our records tell us, in the Castello of San Casciano, in the *contado* of Florence; others have it otherwise, but it is no matter at all, for wherever he was born it was here he lived and here he died on the 28th day of April, 1260. That was a wonderful year, as doubtless the signore knows. Many wonderful things befell in it, but none, I can assure the signore—none half so wonderful as those which accompanied the death of S. Lucchese.

"S. Lucchese was born, signore, in the end of the twelfth century of very honourable ancestors, and, as it happened, in the flower of his age he fell in with a maid of the best manners and disposition, whom he married; her name was Buonadonna, whence she was called Buona or Bona. By her he had several children, whom he brought up in the fear of God. But in process of time a certain personage in the town where he dwelt was moved by a most fierce hatred against him, so that our S. Lucchese found it best to depart from his own place and to come to Poggibonsi, where, indeed, he had some property.

"Signore and Beppino, our S. Lucchese was, as you might expect, a very good Guelf, and, having lost much of his substance in the cause, he decided here in Poggibonsi to open a little shop of *mercanzia mista*, but especially of provisions and food, which he was able to buy cheaply and to resell to great advantage, O Beppino, wherefore he made much money and grew rich.

"Now, with all respect for the signore, who is doubtless as charitable as he is rich and powerful, riches are a great snare even to the most well disposed, and often a curse in disguise. For what is the comfort of the body in comparison with the safety and peace of the soul? Out of all comparison nothing. Well, riches, as ever, proved a snare also to S. Lucchese. He coveted more and more, cut down his charities, and hoarded everything he could scrape up, like any peasant, O Beppino, or like any Jew. Then, signore and Beppino, came repentance. He wept bitterly for his sin, and to remedy the evil he had done he determined to dispense all he had in charity, not waiting for his death, but immediately at that moment, O signore, reserving only a very small portion with which to buy a little *orticello*, a little garden plot for his sustenance and that of his wife, with whose consent he finally proposed to retire from the world. Just then, as God willed, S. Francesco himself, who dazzled the angels, came by, and S. Lucchese, moved by God, sought him out and desired from him the habit of a Tertiary of our Order, and, indeed, signore, he was the first that ever received it, for all this befell in 1221. No long time after his wife Bona followed his example, and determined to live a solitary life, so, separating herself from her husband, not without tears, she entered the Third Order also.

"But S. Lucchese, O signore, was not content to give all that he had to the poor; naked as he was of this world's goods, Beppino, he tramped all through the countryside begging alms from the faithful that he might spend them on the *poveri*, and specially on the sick, many of whom he would succour or take to the hospitals, carrying them thither when they were helpless on a little ass he had, bidding them bear all their miseries for the love of God. Also, each year in summer-time he would carry himself to the Maremma, where, as the signore doubtless knows, owing to the malignity of the air at that season, many are sick and many die. To these he brought such succour as he had, and presently returned to his hermitage.

"Now, having given away everything for the love of God, he was in grievous want, and when his wife found him thus she feared for him and besought him with tears to spare himself, for indeed they loved one another very well. Going secretly to the cupboard, she found it bare, even of bread, and turned to upbraid him; but as it chanced just then, signore and Beppino, there was a knock at the door, and when S. Lucchese opened it, behold a poor and old man seeking food. Then S. Lucchese bade his wife bring some food, but she, knowing the cupboard to be bare, laughed at him half in tears. Nevertheless, to please him when he bade her go again, she went, and, opening the cupboard, found it full of bread. And, marvelling greatly, she brought it to him; and ever after was as eager as he in her gifts, and rested not from charity.

"Twice at least each week the Blessed Lucchese with the greatest devotion received the most holy Sacraments of Penance and of the Eucharist, and because many times, after receiving the Bread of the angels, he went into ecstasies, he hid himself; nevertheless he was privily observed while kneeling in prayer to be lifted from the ground two or three *braccia* by unseen hands, and so to taste the delights of Paradise.

"So the fame of his sanctity was noised abroad that one day a certain priest, one Rainuccio, came to visit him, and, entering into his garden, saw that he had sown there certain onions, Beppino, and wishing to transplant some of them to his own garden this priest asked leave of the Blessed Lucchese, who readily gave it, so that he took all but a few, Beppino, and these few Rainuccio begged him to bless. After some persuasion, with a certain reluctance S. Lucchese made over them the sign of the Cross, to please the priest; who, returning on the day following, found to his amazement that the onions had been replenished, O signore and Beppino, so that they were as many as before, but that they now grew in the form of the holy sign of our salvation. And this miracle being published in these parts—to the great displeasure of the saint, who begged the priest to say nothing of it—caused the folk hereabout to venerate him more than ever.

"Well, signore, about this time the blessed wife of this most blessed servant of God and brother of our Order fell sick, for she was growing old and had long been ailing. Therefore, S. Lucchese proposed to visit her and to be present with her when she received the Holy Sacraments. And so it happened that as she received our Blessed Lord even in that hour he prophesied in this wise: 'My most dear companion,' says he to her, 'we have already abandoned the riches of this world together in order to serve our Lord in Heaven, and He will presently grant us the grace to depart still together to rejoice in Paradise. In this expectation I also have taken these same Sacraments that I have watched you receive.' So saying, he made the sign of the Cross over her, and, kneeling beside her, took her in his arms and tenderly kissed her; and thus they remained a long time, signore, till many having entered in and watched them for some time, the parish priest spoke to them, and, getting no answer, touched the Blessed Lucchese on the shoulder: and behold! he was dead, and his wife with him, even as he had said. All this befell, signore and Beppino, on the 28th day of April, 1260, and on that day we keep the feast here in this church, which was built in their honour."

"Well," said I, after a properly long minute, "I thank you for your story."

"But as to the onions . . ." said Beppino.

No one spoke. Only the frate rolled a grave eye over Beppino, that summed him up from head to foot.

"I was thinking of the onions," said Beppino again a little hurriedly. "It seems to me, messer frate, that this holy man, of whom you have had the politeness to tell us, may well have sown them too profusely, as one is apt to do if one is thinking of other things, as in my case, girls, as in his, saints in Paradise. It comes to the same thing, does it not, signore? I mean it has the same effect. Thus, since he had sown these onions too thick, when the *prete* took away the greater part of them—and we know how natural that was—this Blessed San Lucchese transplanted the rest, as one who loves onions and knows them will never omit to do, and he planted them in the shape of the Holy Cross to please his fancy. Now it runs in my head that when the priest returned with a guilty conscience, signore—for had he not taken as many as he could carry?—he jumped to the conclusion, when he saw the ground all planted out, in that holy shape, too, that the Blessed Angel guardian of S. Lucchese had got even with the devil for once. Therefore he raised that hue and cry, deceived by his own evil heart. And it is easy to understand the distress of S. Lucchese when that old rooster, thinking he had happened on a wonder, went crowing through the *paese*—for he was a very honest man, and he could not expose religion when once it had committed itself to that tale. So, signore, he shouldered the miracle."

"But," said I, hastily, seeing that the frate had long had the fidgets, "but what then of the bread that was there and not there? And then, again, what of the ecstasies, the lifting from the ground, the prophecies?"

"The signore says well," said the little frate in a terrible voice, low and a little shaky; "what of the bread, Beppino, that was not there, what of the ecstasies and the lifting, Beppino?"

Beppino was in no way disturbed: he looked across the valley to the far hills. Then he spoke. "In the matter of bread," said he, "I am no expert; ecstasies, messere, I confess I know nothing of, nor of such lifting or prophecies as you describe. These may all be as they may be; *but onions I know!* . . ."

Beppino left me at the gates of Staggia, some five *chilometri* up the valley, where he had business. Here I was truly across the

Sienese frontier, of which this old and broken fortress had been one of the guards. A walled village about a *rocca*, Staggia is a ruin; what remains of life is to be found in the plain at the foot of the hill on which the old *rocca* stands, beside which passes the Roman road and the torrent that takes its name from the fortress.

Staggia is an ancient lordship and stronghold of those nobles, descended, as some say, from the Contessa Matilda, who took the surname de' Franzesi. They ruled in Staggia from 994 certainly till 1227, when the people of the place united themselves by a public act dated 10 August to the Commune of Poggibonsi, and from that time Staggia and her district remained a part of that commune. Before that, however, in 1156, and again in 1174, Staggia had been in the thick of the quarrels between Florence and Siena, and had been able to give a good account of herself. But today she is of little account, her picturesque ruins tell no tale, nor has she much to offer in the way of entertainment. Only in her Pieve di Santa Maria one may see a fine picture, a panel painted in oil, from the hand of Piero Pollaiuolo, according to Mr. Berenson after a drawing by his brother Antonio, of the Communion of S. Mary Magdalen. It is a very strange picture. In a wild landscape of rocks the Magdalen, her long hair about her body, is borne up by four cherubs while a fifth communicates her.

From this poor place I set out on the road again that led me still up the valley of the Staggia, ever nearer to Siena. It was not quite midday when I set out, and though the valley was delicious to look upon and cooler than the hills, it was yet very hot. So I did not go up to Sant' Antonio al Bosco on the hills to the west, where in the church there used to be a magnificent picture by Luca di Tommè of the Virgin and Child, a majestic thing though not altogether in a good state. When some years ago I came this way I was told the picture had been stolen, then recovered, but it was not back in its own place. Where is it now? Has it returned to Sant' Antonio? I ought to have gone to see. But I stuck to the road, with the promise of Siena in my heart at evening. So I marched, in silence, till after some seven *chilometri* of dust and sun the towers of Monteriggioni rose before me across a bend of the torrent crowning an isolated hill.

More beautiful than Staggia, Monteriggioni has yet much the same character; it is a walled village, half-deserted now, close to

Via Francigena. Nothing is known of its origin or whence it had its name. One would, however, certainly not be far wrong to say that it was built by the Sienese to guard their northern approach. Andrea Dei even says that it was first fortified by the Sienese in the year 1219, the same year, he says, in which the façade of the Duomo of Siena was completed. However that may be, long before that it was a fortress, and sixteen years before, it suffered siege.

In 1254 it was ably defended, and successfully resisted the Florentines when they attacked Siena and destroyed Poggibonsi for the first time. After Montaperto it was fortified again, and more strongly, by Siena, and it was then Dante saw it "crowned with towers",[1] so that he likens that abyss "turreted with giants", which he describes in the thirty-first *Inferno*, to this great Castello.

So strong was it that in 1266, owing to the general insecurity of the countryside, the people of Badia a Isola and of the places round were invited by the Nine of Siena to enter, or at least to live under the Castello. Though it seems to have escaped the fate of Poggibonsi in 1269, it fell into the grasp of Florence at last some three hundred years later, on 25 August, 1554, when the Marchese di Marignano, commandant-general of the Imperial and Medicean army, took it on his way to Siena.

Now, as it happened, it was here in Monteriggioni that my plan of walking into Siena at nightfall came to nothing. For I was determined to see once more that abbey hard by, now fallen to a mere parish church, which conserved even yet certain pictures beyond price. I set out.

I found the abbey, Badia a Isola, some two miles away to the west of Monteriggioni. It is very ancient, most worthy of a visit, and possesses, as I knew of old, three fine pictures of the school of Siena. It gets its name, as you might suppose, from the nature of the country hereabouts, on the lower flanks of Monte Maggio, where a little lake formed, so that the abbey was often called not only Badia a Isola, but Badia del Lago. Founded in 1001 by the Contessa Ava, daughter of Conte Zanobi, and widow of Ildebrando dei Franzesi di Staggia, near her Castello of Borgonuovo, with the consent of her sons, Tegrimo and Benzo, it was enriched from time to time by this illustrious clan. Many popes confirmed it in its growing power and wealth, and we see the fruit of these

---

[1] Cf. Aquarone, *Dante in Siena* (Città di Castello, 1889), cap. iv, pp. 64–9.

concessions, gifts, and favours in the baronial dominion which the Benedictines exercised in those early centuries over the territory of their churches, towns and *castelli* in the country between Siena and Poggibonsi. In 1221 Corrado, Bishop of Spira and Legate of Frederic II, on behalf of the Empire confirmed to them in feud all these possessions in a diploma of 28 December.

For some two hundred years they seem to have flourished, till in 1446, owing to the growing unhealthiness of the district, caused no doubt by the continual wars, the monks of San Salvatore, for the Badia was dedicated to our Saviour, were reunited by a Brief of Eugenius IV with those of their Order at Sant' Eugenio, some two miles to the south of Siena.

Their church, with the annexed San Rufiniano, was continued as a parish church and baptistery, which it remains to this day. It is a building of three naves upheld by columns, and in the sacristy is the tomb of the founder, Contessa Ava, with her bust on a column of granite. In the church itself I found the pictures I had come to see. The great polyptych by Sano di Pietro was as wonderful as ever and as great a glory as seen from the doorway; the altarpiece of the Virgin and Child by some follower of Duccio[1] as mysterious, the Taddeo di Bartolo fresco of the Madonna and Child with saints and angels was charming and tender, his medallions of saints, too, under the arch to the right of the portal; only the imposing work attributed to Vecchietta failed to impress and convince me. And I thanked God these masterpieces were still here where they belonged and had not been carried off to a museum.

All this was very well worth coming to see, but it effectually prevented my reaching Siena afoot that night. Perhaps I lingered too long amid this country loveliness in one of the sweetest and quietest byways of Tuscany. However that may be, it was not to Monteriggioni I returned, but over the hills to the station of Castellina, and so, though I reached Siena at evening, it was by train in the company of a host of poor people, who made me welcome and joined with me in praise of the incomparable city we all loved—*Sena Vetus, Civitas Virginis.*

---

[1] Mr. Berenson attributes this picture to the Master of the Rucellai Madonna in Santa Maria Novella in Florence, Mr. Perkins to a close pupil of Duccio.

CHAPTER VI

SIENA

I THINK perhaps there is nothing in the world quite like Siena, no other place, at any rate, that has just her piercing beauty, her quality of joy, of passion, of sheer loveliness. It is true that in Florence you will find a clear, intellectual beauty, virile and full of light; that in Assisi, that little supra-terrestrial city in Umbria, a mysterious charm—is it the beauty of holiness?—will discover itself to you in the memory of a love, touching and still faintly immortal, pathetically reminding you of itself like the fragrance of a wild flower, on that rude mountain-side; but in Siena you have something more than these, something more strange if not less human—how shall I say?—you have everything that the heart can desire: a situation lofty and noble, an aspect splendid and yet ethereal, a history brave, impetuous, and unfortunate, a people still living yet still unspoiled by strangers. Yes, Siena set so firmly on her triune hill, towers there even today with a gesture of joy, radiant and beautiful, caught about by her vineyards as with a kirtle of green, girdled with silver and gold—the silver of her olives mixed with the gold of her corn.

It is thus she always seems to me when I come to her, it is thus I always remember her from afar, a place of happiness, of welcome, a fortress still, it is true, but without a threat—a fortress dismantled, in the hands of invincible peace, where every tower has become a dwelling-house, every bastion a garden, every bulwark a shady walk, where the gates are open wide that the children may run in and out.

Come to her any summer morning from Florence, where a kind of surliness in the people might seem to bear witness to an Etruscan origin, and she will win you at once. A certain sparkle and sweet glitter in the light, even without the gates, lifts up your heart, and long before you have passed half-way down Via Trieste[1] the charm of the place has fallen upon you almost in spite of yourself, unreasonably, too, for you will never be able to decide just what it is that has caught you, to define in what her delight consists. Is it

[1] The old Via Cavour renamed Via Trieste after the 1914 War.

in her aspect of conscious life, her individuality, her aloofness, the city climbing upward, built as it were in the shape of a star, creeping up to the Cathedral, and sharply divided from the country which the walls scarcely thrust back? Is it in the architecture, the sheer beauty of form and colouring of the city itself? Or is it in the people, their speech so pure that any other sounds like a dialect, their manners, their noble bearing, their fine courtesy, so that you discern in them at once the aristocracy of Italy? Or is it in the beauty of the women? Those pale, wilful, sweet ladies who pass and repass up and down Via Trieste in the twilight with a mother or a husband or a sturdy little maid for company and protection. Or is it in the laughter of the children, so fresh and so delicious in the cool green of the Lizza, which you may hear any golden morning and can never forget, since it is the one thing which reminds you of home? It is perhaps all these things together and a thousand beside which your heart takes note of though you be all unaware.

The modern spirit, a mean utilitarianism, has stolen away the universal beauty of Rome, is even now overthrowing Venice, and is rebuilding and ruining Florence; but Siena it has not really touched, she remains perfectly herself. Perhaps it is in that we find a good part of our delight. No noisy trams rush through her beautiful medieval streets, which are still lined with palaces, splendid and severe; not separated from the lesser houses, but joined to them with only here and there an opening through which you see a vista of steep, lofty narrow way, under an arch perhaps, that leads suddenly and swiftly down into the valley, or winds slowly uphill, where the wind rushes madly to and fro or sighs wearily in the darkness, where the sun rarely peeps. And these streets that tunnel and climb and wind so narrowly and steeply through the city are at once lively and quiet—lively by reason of the children who play in them, the women who gossip at their shadowy doorways, the pedlars and hawkers who cry their wares between these ancient echoing walls. The only traffic that passed up and down these paved, narrow, twisting, climbing ways was, till recently (when of course the motor-car has changed everything), the *barocci* of the charcoal merchants, the asses of the woodmen laden with wood from the mountains, or the great wagons drawn by drowsy white oxen, whose horns almost touch the houses on either side the narrow ways as they draw slowly home the burden of wine from the vineyard. Yes, they are quiet enough even today, only never silent, echoing every now and then with the musical cries of pedlars above the voices of many women, mixed with the laughter, the inarticulate cries of babies, of children. And in and out of these narrow ways, now hidden by a tower or shut out by a high roof, the sun looks down and the shadows advance and recede, and over all, between the tall houses, is a strip of soft blue sky.

It is much the same with the great street lined with little shops —the chief street of Siena, which runs quite through the city, entering at the Porta Camollia and leaving by the Porta Romana, the Via Francigena, indeed, though within the walls it is called by various names, of which the chief is now Via Trieste.

Here the sweet noises of life, so individual in the narrow, steep ways, are mingled together and broken for the first time. You come into this clamour on your way from Porta Camollia, at the *trivio* the Croce del Travaglio. A mere vague murmur at the first it waxes louder and louder, resolving itself at last into the hum of many voices, till, before the Loggia di Mercanzia, where a great crowd conducts its business in the street, you come really into the midst of it, and are surprised when, having pushed your way through these busy, cheerful people, in less than twenty yards you find yourself alone again on that paved way, between the tall, sober palaces, almost in silence.

But though it be in her streets—those narrow, lofty byways— that Siena is still living and to be found, it is not in them that she has set her pride. All the nobility, the impetuous ardour and valour of Siena, for the most part unrepresented or at least largely invisible in her streets, is to be found in the Campo—that beautiful piazza, shaped like a shell, before which stands the rosy Palazzo Pubblico, over which rises the loftiest tower in Tuscany, Il Mangia. This is the true centre of the city; and in its light, its fantastic and lovely shape, in the dizzy and noble height of its tower, all that is most characteristic of Siena might seem to be hidden and expressed. Yet that palace, that piazza, that tower stand less conspicuous in any view of Siena from the walls than the Cathedral, which, set on a spur of one of the three hills on which Siena stands, shines like some precious casket or tabernacle far over the countryside—the capitol of the city of the Virgin.

Nothing in Siena becomes her so well, or so certainly sums her up as her Cathedral, into which, in its aloofness, its pride, its distinction, its beauty and broken ambition, the history of the city seems to have passed. It is set perfectly in a great, silent space, a miracle of light. It is true its façade is disappointing, but it is something more than a barn before which a miracle has been performed, as Orvieto is. Look at it from the Lizza: the long, exquisite line of the aisles broken by the columned transept, and the great octagon over it. Enter and be comforted by the distinction of its colouring, the strength and majesty of its Romanesque, the nobility of its lantern over the crossing. It is here and in those lean friars' churches, San Domenico and San Francesco, that you will learn what Siena is, her true aspect—there and in the altarpieces of Duccio, the frescoes of Simone Martini and the Lorenzetti. For in the strangely ardent, almost hysterical beauty of Siena there is something Byzantine, an exquisite finish, an elaborate ornament which belong to the earliest painters of miniatures. Often at evening, looking on her from Santa Barbara when the world is so quiet, and in the dim valleys and on the clear hillsides the grey olives are a mist of silver, the cypresses very still and black against the blue and gold of the sky, suddenly she has seemed to me, piled up so closely, house over house, church over church, tower over tower, culminating in that almost visionary Duomo, like a city out of a missal—one of those exquisite, unreal places past which the Magi came to Bethlehem—the very city at whose gate S. Anne waited for Joachim, in whose valleys Christ was baptized by John, against whose battlements of old was set the Crucifixion.

For there is an element not altogether explicable in Siena—an element of strangeness, of wonder, which we must confess we do not wholly understand. As she stands there on her triune hill, dreaming of the Middle Age, she seems more than a city, more than the work of man; she expresses something that is hidden from us, that we can only guess at dimly as we gaze over her profound valleys across the garden of her *contado* to the desert on whose verge she stands.

It is just that, perhaps, which day by day as you abide with her comes at last to impress you most, to mix with your every thought of her and in some dim way seems to have informed her with itself: she stands on the edge of the wilderness and looks all day long across a vast desolation to the faint, far-away outline of a great mountain—the most beautiful mountain in Tuscany, Mont' Amiata.

It is this spectacle, so profound, moving, and expressive, that little by little grows into your heart as you pass up and down the steep, winding, narrow streets, from church to church, from palace to palace, from sanctuary to sanctuary: the smiling, gay persuasive loveliness of Siena is set against the solemnity of that beautiful mountain, against the barren loneliness of that desert, out of whose virile and mysterious beauty she has sprung up like a rare and delicate flower. It is this contrast which, as it seems to me, lends her half her charm. On the verge of that vast country of channelled rock and wrinkled clay, where the sun is without pity and no bird sings, she seems more human in her beauty than in fact she is. For, with all her happiness and joy, she is aware of the loneliness that is about her; she never forgets the bitterness of the desert or the silence of the mountains on which she must look all day long. You will find them not only in herself, in the city we see today, but in everything she has done. For in her story, as in her work—the great altarpiece of Duccio, for instance, the lovely spellbound Maestà of Simone Martini, the flowerlike panels of Sassetta, her vast, cold Duomo, her dizzy Mangia tower, there is that element of strangeness without which, it is true, there is no excellent beauty, but which here seems to be their chief characteristic. How sensitive they are to that silent country out of which they are sprung! They have understood the mystery of that desert, and have drawn from its lean strength a certain curious sweetness.

Nor is it only in material things such as these that we find that strangeness which is so characteristic of her, but in her history also and in those who made it; above all, in her saints and in that religion which, with her alone in Tuscany, was mystical. Consider then such an action, almost religious in itself, as the battle of Montaperto and all that led up to it—the strange self-abnegation, self-accusation, and love, the ardent belief which, in fact, caused the miracle; consider the wild prayers for as miraculous a deliverance from Charles V; consider S. Catherine and S. Bernardino; but chiefly consider that adoration of the Blessed Virgin in which the whole city expressed itself, which compelled every gentleman to place his hands between Hers and to swear allegiance, and which inspired an impassioned loyalty in every man, woman, and child.

MAESTÀ (detail), Duccio. Opera del Duomo, Siena

BIRTH OF THE VIRGIN (detail), Pietro Lorenzetti.
Opera del Duomo, Siena

In all this there is an element of insanity, something strange and unconfined, out of proportion, as it were, with anything but that vast waste country of barren clay and rock which is stretched out before her, across which the eternal mountains shine.

In summer, half veiled in heat, invisible at noon, beautiful only at evening, you may miss its true character and meaning. But watch it on a dark or threatening day, a day of storm or wind, when it surges against every gate and is uptossed by every bastion. It is as though that masculine and voracious wilderness, more barren and more unharvested than the sea, had hurled itself against the city, and would have consumed her but for the protection of Her she still invokes, in whom for so many ages she has found safety and peace.

CHAPTER VII

THE STORY OF SIENA

T HE story of Siena, as we examine it now, would seem to resolve itself into the narrative of a struggle waged by a great hill town against forces greater than itself, against forces that from the beginning were too strong for it. These forces, so certainly antagonistic to the real establishment of Siena as the great power in Tuscany, were of two kinds—the one geographical and the other political, more or less deriving from the first. Set as she was, upon a goodly hill, the last westward spur of the Chiana range, in the very heart of Tuscany, Siena was from the first a lonely city; lonely not only in that she had, and could have, no near neighbours, but geographically lonely, too, in that the country which surrounded her was very distant from the sea and provided no natural highway, such as a river, by which she might reach the world—on the contrary, the nature of the country in itself cut her off from every part of Italy. To the south lay a vast desert of rock and clay in which nothing would grow or prosper; to the west lay the Maremma, a loneliness of swamp and death; while to the north lay difficult ranges of hills and to the east the wide Chiana marsh. This loneliness in the earliest Middle Age was somewhat mitigated, it is true, by the coming of that great road, Via Francigena, which united Cisalpine Gaul with Rome; but, on the other hand, nothing was done then—very little was done till today—to provide against the most serious of all the drawbacks from which the city suffered, the want of water— not merely the lack of a great river such as the Arno, which was crudely navigable certainly so far as Signa—but the want of water for industrial purposes. Thus from the beginning nature herself had handicapped Siena beyond hope in the race for the headship of Tuscany. Nor was the other force which prohibited her victory less formidable. Something has already been said of the psychological and spiritual influence of the landscape, of the world in which it stands, on the city itself; its action upon the people of Siena was not less profound. Impetuous, easily cast down, as easily uplifted, without persistence or that unconscious and almost brutal strength, characteristic of every people destined for dominion, Siena was from the first at the mercy of her great and cruel antagonist, Florence, the favourite of nature, who had been given everything Siena lacked—a magnificent position in Val d' Arno between three mountain passes; easily rendered impregnable; a splendid navigable river within reach; a race without aristocratic prejudices, cunning, formidable, and persistent.

From the first, then, there was no doubt as to which of these two cities would in the end dominate Tuscany, and perhaps hold the balance of power in Italy; their story but confirms our logic.

Thus Siena is a city of the Middle Age. Her great period, if that can be called great in which so little was achieved, and which was always on the verge of disaster, is the thirteenth century. After that time her geography, her civil discord, a shameful foreign policy, an unimaginable disaster brought her to nothing.

Her romantic story, more fascinating, certainly more sympathetic, than that of her great rival, invites us to inquire into her origin, if so be we may find there the causes of her decadence, though, in fact, they are writ large enough for all to see in the strange and beautiful country in which she lies. Her origin, however, is hidden from us. The oldest chronicler who speaks of her is our John of Salisbury, who asserts that she was founded by a Briton, a certain Brennus, captain of the Senones, having provided a camp here for his sick and wounded soldiers.[1] This legend, however, fantastic as it is, does not explain the Sienese badge of the wolf and the twins, which first appears, indeed, in the thirteenth century. Some legend older than any we now possess connecting Siena with Rome there must have been, but whatever it was archaeology does not support it. On the contrary, if it assures us of anything, it is of the Etruscan origin of Sena Vetus, for a small Etruscan necropolis has been uncovered near the Porta Camollia, and so far as we may know it seems probable that it was not till 90 B.C. that the Sienese were granted by the *Lex Julia* citizenship of Rome. Even if this much be true, it would prove no more than the existence of a community, probably on the hill called Castel Vecchio, in the later days of the Roman Republic.

[1] This story, and others more vague but of a like nature, have been eagerly accepted by the Florentine chroniclers, who gladly asserted that Siena owed her origin to an infirm and foreign folk (cf. Villani, Lib. i, cap. lvi). The legends of Siena's Roman origin belong to the Renaissance.

What is certain, however, is that it was Augustus who, in 29 B.C., established Sena as a Roman colony. Of her condition under the Empire we know little. It is legend which tells us, without much authority, that it was S. Ansano who converted her to Christianity. Before the fifth century, however, she certainly received a bishop and became the capital of a see. That she was ruined with the advent of the Dark Ages seems certain; at any rate, we hear nothing of her till Rotharis, King of the Longobards, restored her bishopric in the seventh century; later there followed what was probably her first quarrel with one of her sister cities, Arezzo, which was not finally decided till fifty years later, after the restoration of the Empire.

That restoration confirmed, if it did not establish, the power of the Bishop in Siena, as in other cities, and at the same time feudalism, that marvellous and logical theory of political and economic life, began to take the place of the independent, anarchic allodial system. Feudal castles held by Imperial nobles sprang up in the *contado*, holding the road to Rome and the ways to the sea, and all who passed by paid tribute. Nor was the property of the city itself exempt. Indeed, a continual war was waged by the nobles the one upon another, and thus the whole country was kept in a condition of fear and insecurity. This state of affairs in some sort explains the power of the Bishops in all the Tuscan and Umbrian cities. For the citizens, untrained to war, townsmen as they were, anxious for trade, could do nothing against these nobles, who, in such aeries as the Aldobrandeschi possessed in Santa Fiora, were answerable to no one, and entirely safe and invincible. Thus it was to the Church, and first to the spiritual power of the Church, that the citizens looked for protection and redress. So things developed through the ninth and tenth centuries, till in the eleventh we find the Emperor eager to acknowledge the temporal dominion of the Sienese Bishop; nor does it seem that he was sorry to find a power strong enough to curb his unruly barons, whom he was powerless to keep in order. In this way the Bishop gradually became a tenant *in capite* of the Empire, and, in fact, wielded, beside his spiritual power, a very considerable temporal weapon also. Thus the Bishop as a temporal lord owed a new allegiance to the Emperor as well as his ancient and original allegiance to the Pope. As temporal lord he superseded the Count, the earlier representative of the Crown in Siena, and ruled

absolutely within the walls of the city. This rule was good for
Siena; it protected the people from spoliation at the hands of the
nobles of the surrounding country and at the hands of the hordes of
Barbarians that were continually marching through Italy. It
failed at last because ultimately the Bishop was dependent for
armed force on a part at any rate of the people. This party, the
milites, the fighting-men, forced him to admit them to a part in
the government. Consuls arose, their representatives, who at first
shared the government with the Bishop, and at length superseded
him as he had superseded the Counts.

Thus rose the Commune, at first a completely aristocratic State,
but modified little by little till the party opposed to the *milites*, the
populus, obtained a real part in it. But even before that the super-
session of the Bishop was certain. An opportunity soon offered
itself. A quarrel about the jurisdiction of a monastery in the
contado which was dependent on a convent in Florence, and which
the Sienese wished to see placed under the rule of Vallombrosa,
was the ostensible cause of the final rupture with the Bishop and
the Church. The Consuls went so far in 1169 as to try to compel
the clergy to acknowledge the antipope when Alexander III
would not grant their request. But the real reason of this rupture
was jealousy of Florence. The Emperor had already in 1158
acknowledged the existence of the Commune, and had protected
it. And we may see perhaps the first expression of the Ghibellinism
of the Commune in its breaking with the Church, and gladly
becoming the great feud of the Empire in the heart of Tuscany.

The allegiance of Siena directly to the Emperor does not seem
to have been given without an attempt on the part of the Church
party to prevent it. In 1185 we find the city divided, and on the
advent of Frederic the Church party, in a moment of tumult, shut
the gates against him, and defeated him in the battle of Rosario.
A year later peace was re-established, and the Commune undertook to pay an annual tribute, while it gained a full recognition of
its right to elect Consuls, to issue money, and to tax its citizens and
its vassals in the *contado*. Among the first works of the Commune
was that of gradually forcing the nobles of the *contado* to come into
the city. Thus began the allegiance of Siena to the Emperor—an
allegiance strengthened in 1209 by the visit of Otho IV to the city,
when all the privileges of the Commune were confirmed.

In the first years of the thirteenth century, therefore, we see the

Commune firmly established, allied with the Emperor for their common good, but in fact his vassal owing him allegiance. For Siena had become nothing less than a feudatory of the Italian kingdom; her relation to the Emperor was the same as that of the dukes and marquises of Germany; she was his tenant *in capite*, while the nobles of her *contado*, submitted to her suzerainty, were *arrere* vassals. Indeed, the relation of the *contado* to Siena was as substantially feudal as was her relation to the Emperor.

But the history of Siena in the thirteenth century is the history of her rivalry with Florence, in which for a brief moment she gained the advantage, only to be finally beaten in the fight for supremacy before the century's end. The struggle has little or nothing to do with the claims of Pope or Emperor; it has absolutely nothing to do with any struggle between the aristocracy and democracy; it is primarily an economic struggle, in which Siena, starting with a seeming advantage, was betrayed from the beginning by nature, by her geographical position, and the character of her people.

Like most of the great wars, this small but famous combat was a fight for commerce. At the opening of the thirteenth century the Sienese were perhaps the chief bankers of Italy. When the Commune forced the nobles of the *contado* into the city they had devoted themselves to the formation of commercial companies of adventure. They dealt in money chiefly, but also engaged in the Eastern trade and established houses in England and France. They were the bankers of the Holy See, and in return the Church helped them to collect their debts. It is, then, as the determined commercial rivals of Siena that we see the Florentines time after time, from the end of the twelfth century till their final victory at Colle, attack Siena. On the other hand, all the policy of Siena was devoted to the protection and development of what she possessed. She sought to subdue the great feudatories of the *contado* in order to ensure the safety of the roads to Rome, to the north, to the sea. Florence opposed her and supported or encouraged the feudatories in order that she might herself dominate these roads. For this cause she would not permit Siena to establish herself in Montepulciano and Montalcino to the south, or in Staggia or Poggibonsi to the north. Florence herself tried to hold the Chiana valley, and supported the Aldobrandeschi in their struggle with Siena in the Maremma.

We shall see when we come to examine the region to the south of Siena between Asciano and Mont' Amiata how favourable that desert region of low clay hills was to that robber nobility which Siena sought to vanquish for the sake of her trade. Yet she beat them, and her victory was used with wisdom and moderation; but it achieved little more than to unmask the real enemy who stood behind these chieftains; whom she could never destroy.

It is thus that all through the first half of the thirteenth century we see Siena fighting with the nobles of the *contado*, reducing them to impotence, and in their place establishing her own power. This great work can never have been more than half done, for she was always compelled to consider and nearly always to come to terms with Florence. From the first she fought a losing battle; Montaperto, that resounding victory, after all has no importance—it was but an incident.

In the first year of the thirteenth century Siena was forced by her rival to give up all hope of domination in the Val d' Elsa, for Florence seized Semifonte, the strongest fortress in that region; in return, Siena was allowed the right to take Montalcino if she could. No doubt she sacrificed the north in the hope of finally securing the south. If any such hope was in her, she was woefully deceived. With Montalcino in her hands, she tried to occupy Montepulciano. Florence immediately refused to permit this, at the same time laying claim to Tornano, a fortress less than nine miles north-east of Siena. The whole quarrel was submitted to the decision of the Podestà of Poggibonsi, who so far favoured Florence that he deprived the Sienese of any rights they had in Poggibonsi, and brought the Florentine frontier within six miles of Siena on the north. Florence immediately allied herself with Montepulciano. Siena appealed to the Tuscan League, to which both she and Florence belonged. The League decided that Montepulciano belonged to Siena; Florence promptly repudiated the decision. War followed in 1207, and Siena was signally beaten at Montalto. Before peace was signed in 1208, Siena was forced to renounce the rights she claimed in Poggibonsi and those she had been awarded in Montepulciano. There followed fifteen years of peace, which saw the prosperity of Siena wonderfully increased, in spite of her loss of territory. Frederic II befriended her and established Poggibonsi as an Imperial stronghold, at the head of the

Val d' Elsa, similar to San Miniato at its mouth. Florence, meanwhile, was at war with Pisa, and Siena seized the opportunity to
consolidate her power to the south, humbling the Aldobrandeschi
and taking Grosseto from them, thus establishing herself in the
Val di Merse and the Val di Ombrone.

This seemed so like success, that in 1228 Siena made another
attempt to bring Montepulciano under her rule. But the time was
unfortunate; Frederic II had just abandoned the Crusade, and
when he returned to it, nevertheless the Pope cursed him. This
set all Italy by the ears, and revived the old quarrel, and Orvieto,
in secret treaty with Florence, renewed an old alliance with
Montepulciano. In the war which followed, success at first still
favoured Siena, but presently Aldobrandino Aldobrandeschi
forsook her, and she seems to have lost heart. At any rate, the
Florentines were able to destroy very many of her fortresses and to
burn and spoil her *contado* up to her very walls, taking at last Porta
Camollia by surprise and entering the city as far as San Pietro della
Ragione, and, according to the Florentine chronicler, "had they
not been pitiful, they might have destroyed all Siena with fire
and sword".

Then Siena, in her great danger, put aside the private quarrels
that distracted the State, and beat back the Florentines. Nevertheless, she lost Montalcino and any chance she had of bringing
Montepulciano under her sway. Yet two years later she took the
place, avenged herself on Orvieto, and made a new compact with
Montalcino. But Florence was not to be denied. In 1233 she
stirred up the people of Montalcino to revolt; she once more
ravaged the *contado*, and this time for two years. Siena was reduced
to starvation. By 1235, in spite of the capture of Campiglia
d' Orcia, on the slope of Mont' Amiata, a very redoubtable piece of
work, Siena was ready for peace at any price. It was granted on
condition of a renunciation of lordship in Montepulciano and
restoration to Orvieto of all that had been taken from her, and
among other things a dissolution of an alliance made during the
war with Poggibonsi.

Siena was in the dust, but she was still alive; her commerce
remained to her, and, as so often happens after a defeat, she
reformed her constitution, setting up now the famous Council of
the Twenty-Four—half nobles, half *popolani*—under which she was
to attain her greatest triumph.

The new Government enjoyed a long peace of fifteen years. In June 1240 Frederic II visited the city, and was joyfully received, but his exactions daunted the people, and Provenzano Salvani, the greatest of the Sienese, who now comes on the scene, went so far as to bid them not to invite ruin for the sake of the Emperor, but to use him for their own advantage. Ten years later Frederic was dead, and the Ghibelline cause, which had seemed so prosperous, was in jeopardy. Indeed, in a moment the whole position had been changed, or rather, the development which had been taking place was suddenly obvious to all. Florence seized her opportunity, and, thinking to free herself from Pisa, whose port had been necessary to her, she made a compact with Guglielmo Aldobrandeschi for a free passage of goods through his dominions to the Maremma port of Talamone. Pisa, thinking her prosperity to be threatened, agreed with Siena, Pistoia, and Arezzo, while Florence answered by calling Genoa, Lucca, and Orvieto to her aid.

War broke out in the autumn of 1251. The Sienese armies were beaten, and Pisa submitted. The result, however, was fortunate for Siena in this, for the Florentines, with Porto Pisano open to them, gave up all thought of Talamone.

The peace of 1254 thus secured was, however, but a truce. In September of that very year Manfred, Frederic's natural son, who had sworn allegiance to Innocent IV, revolted. Gathering his Moslems, he made war in Apulia, and recovered that province for himself. In the midst of the successes of his enemy Innocent died.

At first it seemed as though the new peace of Tuscany would not be broken. In July 1255 the envoys of Florence and Siena met and concluded an "eternal amity", which, as it happened, lasted scarcely three years. By this peace the two cities swore, among other things, not to harbour one another's exiles; but when, in 1258, the Ghibellines were expelled from Florence, Siena took them in. From that moment war was merely a question of opportunity.

Preparations to meet it were made during the ensuing year both in Siena and in Florence. In the spring of 1259 Siena sent ambassadors to Manfred for his assistance. He agreed to send help, and in December Giordano of Anglano, cousin of the King, entered Siena with his knights, to be joined later by a troop of German horse. Florence meanwhile engineered a revolt in the Maremma. Grosseto and her sister cities rebelled, but with the help of the German horse, Siena was able to compel surrender. Then Florence decided upon immediate action. It is impossible to deny that she was threatened. Manfred's troops in Siena forced her to make war. She set forth some thirty thousand strong with the *carroccio*, but the vast body of troops moved slowly, and a month elapsed before it came in sight of Siena. There followed some doubtful skirmishes, in which the German troops of the Sienese seem to have suffered badly. Then the Florentines marched away. The Sienese, having been reinforced by Manfred, prosecuted the war. They tried to seize Montalcino. So the Florentines set out again in August with contingents from Prato, Volterra, San Gimignano, and Bologna, by way of Val di Pesa, and pitched camp not far from the castle of Montaperto in Val d' Arbia.

From Pieve Asciata ambassadors had been dispatched to Siena with an insolent ultimatum. They arrived in Siena on 2 September, and they found the Council of the Twenty-Four in session in the church of San Cristofano in Piazza Tolomei. "Without making any reverence or obeisance," they delivered their message:[1] "We will that this city be forthwith dismantled and that all the walls shall be levelled with the ground that we may enter and depart at our pleasure. . . . And further we will to place a Signoria in every Terzo of Siena at our pleasure; in like manner to build forthwith a strong fortress in Camporegi and to garrison and provision it and to maintain the same for our magnificent and potent Commune of Florence; and this right quickly without any delay. As for you, if ye do not do all that we have commanded you, ye may await with certainty to be besieged. . . ."

The Twenty-Four replied, without boasting, in the following manner: "We have heard and understood that which ye have demanded, and we bid you return to the captain and to the commissaries of your Commune and to say unto them that we will give them answer face to face."

The chronicler continues: "Now the citizens of Siena had heard of the cruel demand of the Florentines . . . and all the city was moved. All the people left their dwellings and came to San

[1] I use the splendid translation here and in what follows of William Heywood. See *Palio and Ponte* (1904), pp. 25 et seq., and "La sconfitta di Montaperto secondo il MS. di Niccolò di Giovanni di Francesco Ventura," in *Miscellanea Storica Sanese* (Siena, 1844).

Cristofano; and so great was the multitude of the people in Piazza Tolomei and through all the streets that scarcely were they able to contain them.

"And when they beheld this, the Twenty-Four who ruled and governed the city of Siena forthwith assembled a council; and it was proposed to make a syndic who should have full pre-eminence and power and should embody in his own person the authority which belonged to the whole body of the citizens collectively; and that he should be empowered to give, grant, sell, and pledge Siena and its *contado* as to him might seem advisable.

"As if inspired by God, the said councillors by common consent chose for syndic a man of perfect and good life and of the best qualities which at that time could be found in Siena, by name Buonaguida Luccari. To him was given full and free authority and power, as much as had the whole body of the city, as is said above. And while this man was being elected syndic our spiritual father, Misser the Bishop, caused the bell to be rung to call together the clergy of Siena, priests, canons, and friars, and all the religious orders in the church of the Duomo of Siena. And all the clergy being gathered together as you have heard, Misser the Bishop spake briefly to those clerics who were there and said: '*Tantum est ministri Virginis Dei*,' &c. . . .

"Now while Misser the Bishop was making procession with his clergy in the Duomo, God by reason of the prayers of the clergy and of all good people who prayed to Him throughout the city—God, moved to compassion by the prayers of His Mother, suddenly put it in the heart of the syndic, namely, Buonaguida to rise and speak as follows. Now he spake in so loud a voice that he was heard by those citizens who were without in the Piazza San Cristofano. 'As you Signori of Siena know, we have prayed the protection of King Manfred; now it appears to me that we should give ourselves, our goods and our persons, the city and the *contado* to the Queen of Life Eternal; that is, to our Lady Mother the Virgin Mary. To make this gift, may it please you all to bear me company.'

"As soon as he had said these words, Buonaguida stripped himself to his shirt, and barefooted and bareheaded, with a rope around his neck, came forth into the presence of all those citizens, and in his shirt betook himself towards the Duomo. And all the people who were there followed him; and those whom he met upon his way went with him; and for the most part they were bare-footed and without their cloaks, and no man had anything over his head. And he went barefooted, repeating over and over: 'Glorious Virgin Mary, Queen of Heaven, aid us in our great need, that we may be delivered out of the hand of our enemies the Florentines—these lions who wish to devour us.' And all the people said: 'Madonna, Queen of Heaven, we entreat thy compassion.' And so they reached the Duomo.

"And Misser the Bishop went through the Duomo in procession. At the high altar, before our Lady, he began to sing *Te Deum Laudamus* in a loud voice. And as he began Buonaguida reached the door of the Duomo, with the people following him, and commenced to cry with a loud voice, '*Misericordia*'—the said Buonaguida and all the people—'*Misericordia*'. At which cry Misser the Bishop turned himself about with all the clergy and came to meet the said Buonaguida. When they were come together each man made reverence, and Buonaguida fell upon his face upon the ground. Misser the Bishop raised him up and gave him the kiss of peace; and so all those citizens kissed one another on the mouth. And this was at the lowest part of the choir of the Duomo.

"Then, holding one another by the hand, Misser the Bishop and Buonaguida went to the altar before our Mother the Virgin Mary, and kneeled down with great crying and continual tears. This Buonaguida remained stretched out upon the ground, and all the people and women with very great weeping and sobbing waited for the space of a quarter of an hour. Then Buonaguida alone raised himself upon his feet and stood erect before our Mother the Virgin Mary, and spake many wise and discreet words, among which were these: 'Gracious Virgin, Queen of Heaven, Mother of Sinners, to thee I, a miserable sinner, give, grant, and recommend this city and the *contado* of Siena. And I pray thee, Mother of Heaven, that thou wilt be pleased to accept it, although to one so powerful as thou art it is but a little gift. And likewise I pray and supplicate thee to guard, free, and defend our city from the hands of our enemies, the Florentines, and from whomsoever may desire to injure us or to bring upon us anguish and destruction.'

"These words being said, Misser the Bishop ascended into the pulpit and preached a very beautiful sermon, teaching the people of unity and exhorting them to love one another, to forgive those who had done them wrong, and to confess and communicate.

And he entreated them to unite to place this city and their persons under the protection of the glorious Virgin Mary, and to go with him and with his clergy in procession.

"And in this procession, before them all, was carried the carven crucifix which stands in the Duomo, above the altar of S. Jacomo Interciso, beside the campanile.[1] Next followed all the monks and friars, and then came a canopy, and under the canopy was our Mother the Virgin Mary. Hard by was Misser the Bishop, and he was barefooted, and at his side was Buonaguida in his shirt and with a rope about his neck, as you have heard. Then followed all the canons of the Duomo, barefooted and bareheaded. They went singing holy psalms and litanies and prayers. And behind them came all the people, barefooted and uncovered, and all the women barefooted, and many with their hair dishevelled . . . saying *Paternosters* and *Ave Marias* and other prayers. . . .

"So they went in procession to San Cristofano and into the Campo, and returned to the Duomo, where they remained to confess and to receive the Sacrament, and to make peace one with another. And he who was the most injured sought out his enemy to make with him perfect and good accord. . . .

"Now these things befell on Thursday, the 2nd day of September. And nearly all night long the people thronged to confess and to make peace one with another. . . . And when morning was come the Twenty-Four who ruled and governed Siena sent three criers—into every Terzo one—proclaiming and crying: 'Valorous citizens, make ready! Arm yourselves! Take your perfect armour; and let each man in the name of our Mother the Virgin Mary follow his proper banner, ever recommending himself to God and to His Mother.'

"And hardly was the proclamation finished when all the citizens flew to arms. The father did not wait for the son, nor one brother for another; and so they went towards the Porta San Viene.[2] And thither came all the standard-bearers. The first was that of San Martino, first for reverence for the Saint, and also because that Terzo was near to the gate. The second was that of the City, with a very great army of people and well equipped. The third was the royal banner of Camollia, which represented the mantle of our Mother the Virgin Mary, and was all white and shining, fair and

[1] The Crucifix is said to be that which is today over the altar of the first chapel in the north transept.
[2] i.e. Porta Pispini.

pure. Behind that banner came a great multitude of people, citizens, foot-soldiers, and horsemen; and with this company were many priests and friars, and some with weapons and some without, to aid and comfort the troops; and all were of good will, of one mind, and of one purpose, and well disposed against our enemies the Florentines, who with such vehemence had demanded things unrighteous and contrary to reason.

"Now, all the men having gone forth, those devout women who remained in Siena, together with Misser the Bishop and the clergy, commenced betimes on Friday morning a solemn procession with all the relics which were in the Duomo and in all the churches of Siena. . . . Thus they went all Friday, and all that day they fasted. When even was come they returned to the Duomo, and there they all knelt, and so remained while Misser the Bishop said litanies, with many prayers to the honour and glory of God and of His and our Mother. . . .

"And now we have told of Misser the Bishop, our spiritual father, and of the devout citizens and women, how they besought God and His Mother, Saint Mary, to give victory to the city of Siena and to its people, we will speak of the ordered legions of the army.

"The day commenced to break; and it was that blessed day, Friday, the 3rd of September, in the year aforesaid; so being drawn up in battle array they began their march towards the Bozzone. Ever the squadrons kept close together, that of the Captain of the Commune of Siena and that of Messer the Count Giordano. . . .[1] All went calling on the name of our Lord God and of His Mother the Virgin Mary, and to her they ever commended themselves, beseeching her to give them help and strength and courage and power against these wicked and perfidious Florentines. Thus praying they came to the foot of a hill which is called Poggio de' Ripoli, which hill was over against the camp of the Florentines."

That night the Sienese watched and prayed, and in the darkness there was seen over the Sienese camp as it were the mantle of the Blessed Virgin Mary for a sign of her protection. The battle broke with the daylight, and resulted, as we know, in the complete victory of the Sienese and their German allies—a victory they owed in large part to the Florentine Ghibelline, Bocca degli Abati,

---

[1] The Chronicle says little of the Germans, yet it was in a large degree to them and to the treason of Bocca degli Abati that the Sienese owed their victory.

"that traitor Messer Bocca degli Abati", as Villani calls him, who struck Jacopo della Narda, who bore the Florentine standard, with his sword and cut off the hand with which he held the standard, and killed him.[1] "And this done," Villani tells us, "the horsemen and people beholding the standard fallen, and that there were traitors among them, and that they were so strongly assailed by the Germans, in a short time were put to flight. . . . Thus was abased the proud arrogance of the ungrateful and proud people of Florence." "It was astonishing to see," writes the Sienese chronicler, "the great butchery that they made of those dogs of Florentines. . . . And the slaughter ever increased, and so furious was the press that if one fell to earth he might by no means regain his feet again, but was trampled to death."

The account of dead and wounded varies. The Sienese tell us 10,000 were slain, and 20,000 were taken. Villani says 2,500 fell and 1,500 were captured. It is a matter of little consequence. Siena had won, and by her victory had once more raised the Ghibelline cause in Tuscany; her *contado* was hers to take, Florence itself was at her mercy.

Her triumph was shortlived. With incredible vacillation and weakness she allowed one strong man, in the Council at Empoli that followed the battle, to force her to spare Florence, which, if she had had a statesman worthy of the name, or a tradition worth following, would have been razed to the ground. Her opportunity had come, but she did not dare to seize it. She spared Florence, and in less than ten years the lily blossomed amid her ruin. She claimed dominion, and having too often failed in war, now that the Germans had given her victory she proved unworthy of it. Montaperto was but the splendid herald of an end too little glorious.

The battle of Montaperto ensured the immediate triumph of Ghibellinism throughout Tuscany; from every city the Guelfs were expelled, even from Lucca, and so far as Siena was concerned the treaty signed in November compelled Florence to renounce all her claims to Montalcino, Montepulciano, Campiglia, Staggia, and Poggibonsi, which Siena secured for herself. Her triumph, like the triumph of Ghibellinism generally, was but shortlived. In 1261, and again in 1262, the Pope excommunicated

[1] When Dante finds Bocca degli Abati frozen in the ice among the traitors in the Inferno, he kicks him in the face—he says accidentally.

her, and the withdrawal of papal patronage, though only partial, was a great and a shrewd blow to her predominance. Misfortunes showered upon her. In 1266 Manfred was killed at Benevento; in 1268 Corradino, the last of the Hohenstaufen, was taken at Tagliacozzo and executed in Naples. The Ghibelline cause was dead; the battle of Colle in the following year, when Florence avenged Montaperto, was but its funeral; and when Henry VII, Dante's Emperor, entered Italy in 1310 it was but its ghost that walked. That ghost, however, Siena was unable to greet. After Colle—was it to save her banks?—she had become Guelf, thus riveting the chains Florence had put upon her; while for the admirable government of the Twenty-Four she substituted the oligarchy of the Nine in its many forms. In vain Ambrogio Lorenzetti painted his frescoes representing the ideals of Good Government and the consequences of Bad Government in the Hall of the Nine.

Meantime wealth had increased vastly, and the hired armies marched about seeking employment. Then in 1348 the Black Death fell upon Siena. After that appalling catastrophe the Nine went down, and were replaced by that cynical jest the Government of the Twelve. For near seventy years then, Siena had been governed by a rich middle class;[1] she now entered on the second stage of democratic government—she fell into the hands of the small tradesmen. This befell in 1355, and the final stage was achieved in 1368, when the artisans, the *popolo minuto*, acquired a part in the government. Faction grew stronger every day, the Companies of Adventure became more and more intolerable, and at last commercial depression fell upon the city. Democracy had done its work. Siena was ruined and utterly weak, and it is now the Despot appears, in the form of Pandolfo Petrucci who rules her, save for a brief moment under the threat of Cesare Borgia, from 1487 to 1512 when he died at San Quirico. His progeny follow him; so that when at last Siena fell finally into the hands of Duke Cosimo de' Medici she was helpless and all her protest was an hysterical, if heroic, siege and flight, and almost painless weeping.[2]

What is, then, chiefly worth our notice during the fourteenth

---

[1] It was then Cecco d' Angiolieri (d. 1313) sang of "la donna, la taverna e 'l dado" and Folgore da San Gimignano (d. c. 1316) showed us in his fourteen sonnets her "brigata nobile e cortese".

[2] In 1561 Duke Cosimo made his triumphal entry into Siena. He became Grand Duke of Tuscany in 1569. Bargagli, the Sienese *novelliere*, in the Introduction to his *Trattenimenti*, has a detailed and pathetic account of the siege.

PALAZZO PUBBLICO AND THE MANGIA TOWER, Siena

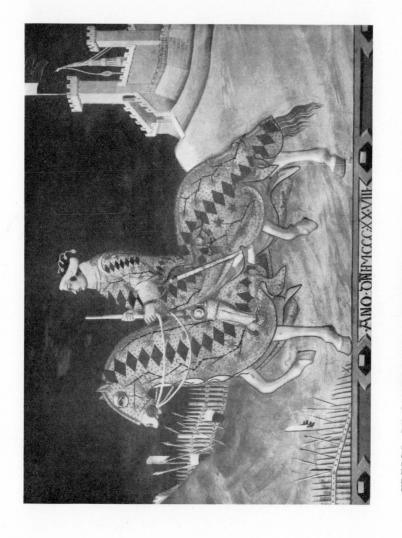

FRESCO OF GUIDORICCIO DA FOGLIANO, Simone Martini.
Palazzo Pubblico, Siena

and fifteenth centuries, is not the political decadence but the renaissance of the arts of architecture and sculpture and painting which the wealth and luxury of the merchants made possible. It is to that one should devote attention when thinking of these two centuries in Siena.

Nor should it be forgotten that it was in these years that Siena produced three great personages whose influence radiated far beyond the Sanese and indeed beyond Italy: Bernardo Tolomei the founder of the Olivetan Order, S. Caterina Benincasa the Dominican tertiary who brought the Pope back to Rome from Avignon; and S. Bernardino who helped to re-establish the Order of Friars Minor.

CHAPTER VIII

SIENA

THE PIAZZA DEL CAMPO AND THE PALAZZO PUBBLICO

WHAT the Piazza Signoria is to Florence, that, and something more, the Piazza del Campo is to Siena: it is at once the most beautiful and the most characteristic thing in the city. However one approaches it—and since it is set at the junction of the three hills on which Siena lies there are many ways of approach—it is always suddenly, with surprise, one looks across that vast and beautiful space shaped like an open fan, enclosed on all sides by palaces, and radiating as it were from what one is often tempted, there at least, to proclaim the most beautiful palace in Tuscany, the Palazzo Pubblico, with its marvellous bell-tower soaring adventurously into the blue sky.

This piazza so spacious in form, so strange in its colour and loveliness, is, as it always has been, the heart of Siena. For work or for play, for council or for pleasure, in time of foreign war or civil riot, here the Sienese have always assembled. It was the market-place, the true piazza, the universal meeting-place of the city. But today it is almost deserted. One by one it has lost its uses till now but one remains to it: it is still a playground when on 2 July the feast of the Visitation and on 16 August the morrow of the feast of the Assumption of the Blessed Virgin, the Palio is run there over the sanded bricks round the central space enclosed by the great pavement.

Then, indeed, one may see the Piazza in all its glory, almost as it must have been when, as Boccaccio tells us, Dante Alighieri "lay with his breast upon a bench" outside one of the little shops—it was an apothecary's—reading an ancient book which had just been placed in his hand, and heard nothing of the great tournament that "was begun and carried through there", as now, with "a mighty din . . . and dances of fair ladies and sundry sports of youth".

But the Piazza is older far than Dante, as is the Palio. It was here on the day of our Lady of August, in 1224, after the fall of

Grosseto, that "the Sienese for joy of the victory held high festival and lighted bonfires and closed the shops", while in 1260, after the Ghibelline victory of Montaperto, the men of Montalcino made there their submission before the *carroccio*, and were "accepted as subjects of the Magnificent Commune of Siena". And it is Dante himself who shows us the proud Provenzano Salvani there begging for alms to ransom his friend—*Per trovar l' amico suo di pena.*

There, too, later were set up the gambling booths "walled with branches", while in May 1425 S. Bernardino preached there in the presence of the Signoria to a congregation of some forty thousand persons. And when Siena was dying it was there were held those splendid tournaments and jousts that were in fact her funeral games.

Nor is it only of such peaceful scenes as these that the Piazza has been a witness. It has seen much bloodshed and infinite cruelty. To name but two occasions: in October 1285 the Sienese mob lynched five poor wretches there, and hanged other fifty-six "between Arbia and Bozzone"—this in the Guelf and Ghibelline quarrel. But even so short a time ago as the year 1799 nineteen Jews, men and women, were burned alive there at the suggestion of certain Aretine priests, and with the help of the French Tree of Liberty that had been set up before the Fonte Gaia a few months before.

But always, first and till yesterday, the Piazza was the market-place of the city; it began as just that, and it only ceased to fulfil this function in the year 1884.

Thus the Piazza del Campo was the heart of Siena in which the whole life of the city, civil and religious, in war and in peace, was gathered and expressed: it is a heart that has almost ceased to beat.

A quietness, but seldom broken now, fills the Piazza with an exquisite peace. It is the only silent place, I think, in a city full of little human noises beyond any other in Tuscany: the clang of metal on metal, the hammers of the coppersmiths that wake you so early, the plaintive cries high up among the old houses of innumerable swifts, the shouts of hawkers, the shrill voices of children, the songs and laughter and endless loud, free talk of a Latin people not yet quite dominated by the stupefying thunder of machines. And so to pass from any one of the narrow, echoing streets of the city into this beautiful desert is always to be suddenly alone—alone, and yet not alone, for out of this silence, actually golden for once, where the sun seems to be enthroned, comes the voice of old Siena telling her wonderful tale.

It is with that tragedy in your heart that you turn at last to the Palazzo Pubblico. It is a building of the thirteenth and early fourteenth centuries, added to in the fifteenth and again in the seventeenth, and its material is a beautiful and rich-coloured brick relieved in the window shafts by white marble. It is the first two stories of the central building which belong to the thirteenth and fourteenth centuries, the upper story and the two wings being additions. Decorated with the Balzana, the black and white shield of Siena, in the midst of the façade are the arms of Grand Duke Cosimo, whose lordship was the end of Siena as a free Republic. Above is the beautiful monogram of Christ, set there by S. Bernardino; while over the door to the right is a statue, very small, of S. Ansano, a patron of the city, since he converted it in the fourth century, and beneath, on either side, the Lion of the People, the Wolf of Rome, which we find again on a pillar close by, marking the door as that of the Governors of the Republic as against that of the Podestà.

On the other side of the palace, to the left of the main portal, is a building like a fine portico—in fact, a chapel—the Cappella della Piazza, set up by the Commune in fulfilment of a vow made in the Black Death of 1348, in which some eighty thousand persons perished, and from which Siena never really recovered. Begun in 1352, it was finished, not easily, in 1376. About a century later, however, Antonio Federighi altered it, adding the whole of the upper structure with the frieze. The statues of the Apostles, only six of which were ever executed, are work, however, of the earlier time, and in their poverty of execution serve to remind us into what a state of decadence the plague had thrown the city.

Above the chapel soars the Torre, which was begun ten years before the Black Death, and was still unfinished when that awful pestilence depopulated the city. Begun by Minuccio and Francesco di Rinaldo of Perugia, it was continued by Agostino di Giovanni, while Lippo Memmi, the brother-in-law of Simone Martini, is said to have designed the crown.

There is something in the Torre del Mangia[1] that is peculiarly

---

[1] It is probably so called on account of the mechanical figure which used to strike the bells at the summit.

Sienese. We are reminded of something fearless, daring, even hysterical, as though into this one perfectly expressive thing the very soul of Siena had passed—that soul which, mystical as it was beyond that of any other Tuscan city, was so often boastful and unstable, so that it too easily came to naught. Something of all this we find almost everywhere in the city, and especially perhaps in the great unfulfilled boast of the Duomo, but nowhere so subtilely and completely expressed as in this rose-coloured tower soaring over the roofs of Siena.

It is at the other extremity of the façade, by the second door, that one enters the ground floor of the palace. Within are the remains of fourteenth-century frescoes, and on the ceiling, more than that, a fine figure of our Lord among cherubim, surrounded by the four Evangelists, from the hand of Bartolo di Fredi. Leaving this threshold, one is led by the *custode* through various rooms. One sees a fresco of the Resurrection by Sodoma—and that will not detain us. Then in the Sala di Biccherna, where the Provveditori, as the officials who presided in Biccherna—the Exchequer, as we might say—were called, we see one of the finest works of Sano di Pietro—surely his favourite subject, too, the Coronation of the Virgin. Painted in 1445, this fresco, so splendidly decorative, was contrived by Sano over the work of an earlier master, Lippo Vanni, whose signature still remains. Nor, as it happens even so, is the work altogether Sano's, for Domenico di Bartolo is said to have painted some of the chief figures. Close by is another work of Sano's, a figure of S. Bernardino of Siena. And just without the chamber is another, a damaged fresco of S. Pietro Alessandrino, Beato Ambrogio Sansedoni, and Beato Andrea Gallerani. And it is to Sano's work again one comes—a head of S. Catherine—after passing through the Sala dei Matrimoni.

In the Sala di Anagrafe close by is a splendid work of Vecchietta, a fresco, his finest work in Siena, of the Madonna of Mercy guarding with her cloak the people of the city, who kneel about her feet. Above is a world of angels, and to the right S. Martin divides his cloak with the beggar by the way.

To reach the upper floors of the palace it is necessary to return to the Piazza and to re-enter by the last door, beyond that by which one has come out and so climb to the *piano grande*.

Immediately on the right is the great Sala delle Balestre or del Mappamondo, which holds Simone Martini's magnificent

Maestà of the Virgin and Child enthroned under a splendid canopy upheld by SS. Peter, Paul, and the two SS. John, in the midst of a choir of saints and angels. Before the Madonna, Siena, her own city, kneels in the person of its patron saints, Ansano, Vittore, Crescenzio, and Savino, and the whole fresco is enclosed in a border of medallions and shields bearing the arms of the Commune and people.

This vast and glorious illumination is at once like a tapestry and a huge miniature. It was painted in 1315, and restored by Simone himself, probably in 1320, when he renewed eight of the heads of the principal figures: to wit, S. Ansano, the two angels offering flowers, S. Crescenzio, S. Catherine, the saintly woman opposite to her, and the Virgin and Child. It has in parts been restored at various later times, but substantially remains the very beautiful work of the most subtle of Sienese painters.

The mastery foreshadowed in this great work has been achieved in the splendid equestrian portrait of Guidoriccio da Fogliano by the same artist on the opposite wall. It seems to have been finished before it was begun, so certain is it of itself and so confident in every gesture are that horse and its rider. Guidoriccio, the "Captain of war in Siena", is riding out of the Sienese camp to the siege of Montemassi. In the background we see one of those *Battifolle*, those strange ramparts and towers of wood which in those days were constructed for the siege of a town. But that is merely a curiosity of archaeology. What strikes one most in this splendid work is the immortal gesture of life which it expresses as surely as any work by Titian or Velasquez could do. Nor is it without a certain dramatic quality, poetical and beautiful—that imposing figure so full of almost regal dignity thrown against the dark sky, its irresistible advance, its proud gesture of absolute command and certainty. And with this, like a true Sienese, Simone has contrived that his work should not be merely realistic but perfectly decorative: even here, if you will, you have but a pattern of colours on the wall, a sudden glance of light, a miraculous gift of the sun.

Under this portrait hangs the so-called Guido da Siena, a Madonna which bears the date 1221. The picture is perhaps less genuine than the signature, which has excited numberless suspicions. On either side of it are frescoes by Sodoma of two of the patrons of Siena—S. Ansano, baptizing the Sienese, and S. Vittore, and the Blessed Bernardo Tolomei, who founded the

Olivetan congregation. Happily they are among his better and more virile works, and do not disgust us in the presence of Simone.

On the long side wall are two almost anonymous battle-scenes in monochrome. The finer, to the left, represents the victory of the Sienese at Torrita in 1363, when Messer Ceccolo degli Orsini of Rome, in command of the Sienese, attacked against the orders of the magistrates. The other shows us the battle of Poggio Imperiale, near Poggibonsi, fought more than a hundred years later, in 1479, when Siena, after the failure of the Pazzi conspiracy, sided with the Pope and the King of Naples against Florence and Milan, and won this victory under the Duke of Calabria. Here too are frescoes by Vecchietta and Sano, full-length figures of S. Catherine and S. Bernardino.

Leaving the Sala delle Balestre one passes into the Sala dei Nove, the Hall of the Nine, or, as it was later called, the Sala della Pace. And here one is in the presence of Ambrogio Lorenzetti's famous frescoes, completed in 1339, which cover three of its walls. It is with the results of Good and of Bad Government that he deals. The best preserved of these works is that opposite the window; unhappily a door cuts off a part of its right corner.

Above, high up on the left, is a half-figure of Wisdom hovering, crowned and wearing a veil. In her left hand is a red book, in her right she holds a huge balance, whose beam rests on the head of Justice, who looks up into the eyes of Wisdom as though for inspiration. In the scales to the left is a winged angel, who bends to decapitate a kneeling man, and places a crown on the head of one who prays. From the scale to the right another angel leans and dips one hand into a box held by a kneeling figure, while he gives a lance and a sword to another, kneeling too. This obscure and confused allegory would appear to express distributive Justice inspired by Wisdom dealing out death to the wicked and benediction to the good; while commutative Justice aids one with money and another with weapons. It matters little, perhaps, what the meaning may be. One is consoled for one's dullness by delight in that figure of Justice, one of the finest efforts of Sienese art.

But I have not half described the picture. Beneath the figure of Justice sits Concord, scarcely less noble, holding in her left hand two cords, which are tied around the waists of the angels in the scales. One is red, the other white. These cords she passes to a small personage near by, who hands them on to his neighbour, who does the like, a procession of twenty-four persons being thus formed, which advances to the vast throne on the right whereon is seated the Commune of Siena—a splendid figure of a man in middle age, who holds in the right hand a sceptre, in the left a seal or disk bearing the image of the Blessed Virgin, the Protectress and Liege Lady of the city. Above the throne hover figures of Faith, Hope, and Charity, and to its right and left are seated those marvellous figures of Prudence, Fortitude, Peace, Magnanimity, Temperance, and Legal Justice: Peace being indeed, as she is, the most lovely of them all. Beneath the throne are the Wolf and Romulus and Remus, and armed men on foot and horseback and others offering tribute, and again others bound in fetters. The allegory would seem to suggest that if Justice inspired by Wisdom be followed she will induce Concord, which in her turn will lead men to live in fellowship under the benign sway of the Commune of Siena, supported by Prudence, Fortitude, Peace, and their sisters.

And this lesson is emphasized in the two frescoes to right and left. That on the right shows the effect of Good Government. In the city all is gay and prosperous; girls dance the *rigoletto*, knights and their fair ladies ride joyfully through the streets, while without is a smiling countryside full of happiness, and peasants who bring their produce to the city gate. Over all abides Security, with a scroll and a gallows.

On the left wall are the effects of Bad Government, under the monstrous figure of Tyranny, whose left foot rests on a goat. Above are Greed, Pride, and Vainglory; and beside them Fraud, Treason, Cruelty, Fury, Division, and War. Beneath, Justice is cast down and bound, while in the city murder and rapine walk the streets, and without the fields are bare; and over all abides Fear half-naked, a drawn sword in her hand.

The allegory here is sufficiently obvious. It is a pity that the decorative value of these frescoes is not so fine as the detail which their didactic purpose demanded.

To reach the chapel it is necessary first to return to the Sala del Mappamondo, out of which it opens. It is for the sake of Taddeo di Bartolo one comes here, who began to paint in the chapel in 1407. The work in the antechapel—those allegorical frescoes— was done seven years later. The frescoes in the chapel itself consist of the figures of various saints and of four scenes from the life of the Blessed Virgin—her Farewell, her Death, her Funeral, and her Assumption. In the last, which is the best of his works here, against the glow of the sunset is the city of Siena in all her delicate beauty.

Taddeo di Bartolo was born in 1363. The pupil of Bartolo di Fredi, he was at twenty-two years of age employed in the Duomo, but his best work in Siena was not done till at over forty years of age he began these frescoes, and painted in 1409 the great Annunciation now in the Pinacoteca, and in 1413 the polyptych of the Osservanza, finishing both the latter while he was engaged on the frescoes in the chapel and antechapel here in the Palazzo Pubblico. Between his employment in 1385 in the Duomo and his work here, begun in 1407, he had been something of a traveller. In 1390 he was in Pisa, in 1393 in Genoa, in 1395 in Pisa again, where, indeed, he remained for some years, painting in San Francesco. In 1400 and 1401, however, he was in Montepulciano at work on the Last Judgment in the Duomo there, where he contrived his great reredos, consisting of the Annunciation, the Coronation, and the Assumption of the Blessed Virgin. In 1403 he went to Perugia, after briefly visiting Siena, where he worked in San Francesco and Sant' Agostino, and, according to Vasari, in San Domenico, where he painted some frescoes of the life of S. Catherine. He had, therefore, seen something of the world and of the art of Tuscany when, in 1405, he returned to his native city and two years later began to work in the chapel of the Palazzo Pubblico.

Passing from the chapel through the Sala dei Cardinali, where hang a panel of the Virgin and Child with angels by Cozzarelli, dated 1484, and two pictures of the life of S. Bernardino by Francesco di Giorgio, one comes to the sala della Balia, which Spinello Aretino in his old age, with the assistance of his son, painted with scenes from the life of the Sienese Pope, Alexander III. It was Caterino Corsino, Operaio of the Duomo of Siena, who in 1404 persuaded Spinello Aretino to forsake Arezzo and to come to Siena to work there. The work of foreign artists is so rare in Siena that one cannot but notice these frescoes. Spinello and his son Parri arrived in Siena in October 1404, and laboured there till the end of the summer of 1405. For eleven months they worked in the Duomo, but nothing is left to us of all their labour. They returned to Florence, but two years later, in March 1407-8, they returned to Siena to paint these frescoes of

the Sala di Balia, in company with Martino di Bartolommeo, who
worked on the ceiling.

Spinello's frescoes, in painting which he was doubtless much
assisted by his son, are concerned really with the heroic story of
the Venetian campaign against Frederic Barbarossa: in this
campaign legend assigns to Orlando Bandinelli, later Pope
Alexander III, an heroic share. So successful are these frescoes in
composition, colour, and movement that they may stand as the
masterpiece of a man who was not the least among the followers
of Giotto. And, in fact, where else in work of that time shall we
find the living splendour of the scene representing a naval fight,
or the grace of that in which the Pope arms the Doge surrounded
by his guard, or the triumphant joy of that in which we see the
victorious Pope, his mule led by the humbled Emperor?

From the Sala di Balia one enters a corridor, where at the end is
that unique thing, a fresco by Neroccio—of the Virgin and Child
enthroned.

Hence one climbs to the top floor of the palace, where after all
the best of all awaits one—not the ruined fresco of the Virgin and
Child there by Ambrogio Lorenzetti, or the fragments, lovely
enough, of Jacopo della Quercia's fountain, but the very world
itself, the vast *contado* of Siena, hill and valley and desert stretching
away to where, in the evening mist maybe, the pure, serene
outline of Mont' Amiata rises into the sky on the verge of the
Patrimony, on the confines of Umbria, on the road to Rome. He
who has once seen that majesty will never forget it. It seems to
seal every one of the days one spends in Siena, or in the little cities
to the south that were once her vassals. From here you may count
them all: only you will not. You will look only at that mountain
whose crest, shaped like the crescent moon, bears as of right the
symbol of Mary, and in silence you will await the sunset. And as
the bells once more, as of old, ring the Angelus, you will be
reminded that Siena is the Civitas Virginis:

> Maria advocata,
> Mediatrix optima
> Inter Christum
> Et Senam suam.

CHAPTER IX

SIENA

THE CATHEDRAL GROUP

THE Piazza del Duomo of Siena differs both from that of Florence and from that of Pisa, for it is neither the centre of the life of the city like the former, nor a thing apart, a meadow spellbound like the latter; yet it has the silence of Pisa and the domination of Florence. Set on what may well be the highest point of the triune hill on which Siena stands, which is made one in the Piazza del Campo, the Cathedral of Santa Maria Assunta dominates the whole city, casting its shadow over it at sunrise and at sunset; yet it is withdrawn, surrounded by silence, and is separate altogether from those narrow streets, in which, nevertheless, everywhere its presence may be felt. It is, in fact, and in a more particular sense than in any other cathedral in the world, the votive shrine erected by the people of Siena to their guardian and liege lady, the Blessed Virgin Mary.

It is a citadel, too, in which long and long ago Siena placed all her hope, her pride, and her love. However one may come to it, whether by the Via di Città and the Via del Capitano, from the Campo, or by the Via del Fosso di Sant' Ansano from the Porta Laterina, or by the steps or by the Via del Poggiolo, from the Piazza di San Giovanni, one must go up, one must climb to that sunlit piazza which surrounds this shrine always with so mysteriously dazzling a space of silence. And this quietness is grateful to us of the modern world, who live perforce continually in a kind of hideous and useless noise.

As one comes into the Piazza, beside one stretches the whole length of the nave of the Cathedral; there rises the great palace of the Opera; beside it opens a long piazza, set here and there with numerous arches of white marble that look like ruins. Before the façade of the great church, closing the larger piazza, rises the golden Ospedale di Santa Maria della Scala, and everywhere around is a vast and beautiful space full of the sun.

All this has in it something of a miracle. It is only when one turns before the Ospedale to face the Cathedral that one is aware of a sudden disappointment.

In so many of the cathedrals of Italy the façade has little or no relation to the church which lies behind it; and here in Siena it might seem this is not so, though the three doors are of equal height. As a façade pure and simple, that of Orvieto, though it has little to do with the building behind it, is noble and lovely in design, in decoration, and in colour. This of Siena is fussy in design, it suffers from too much decoration, and this all in white marble. At Orvieto sculpture has, with very happy effect, been more sparingly used, but what there is, is of the best and noblest kind. When Lorenzo Maitano designed the façade of Orvieto, the Pisan influence was still living; and he worked mainly in relief. But when fifty years later the façade of Siena was decorated, not in relief, but with a host of figures, the effect, so splendid in the grey stone of Chartres, was almost grotesque in the dazzling marble of Carrara. Nor is this all. At Orvieto we find the façade glorified with mosaic, while at Siena only the gables have any colour. Thus structurally and in colour it is a failure, lacking in a sense of proportion, in order, and in repose, so that what effectiveness it has—and no one can deny it a certain element of surprise, and even wonder—soon wearies, till one comes to disregard it altogether as a mere ineffectual thing, set for pride before the church. One or two of the statues are possibly the work of Giovanni Pisano, but many are modern copies of the originals now in the Museo dell' Opera.

This hill on which the Cathedral stands, according to tradition has always been sacred to some deity; here it seems of Minerva. Pecci, the old Sienese historian, tells us that the first Christian building was erected here in the eighth or ninth century, when it became the centre of religion in Siena, for the earlier Cathedral had stood in Castelvecchio. In the twelfth century, too, we hear that the Sienese Pope, Alexander III, consecrated the second church upon this hill. But the building we now see belongs to the thirteenth century.

It was begun, according to Malavolti, in 1245, and in the following year there is documentary evidence that money was being spent on it. In 1257 a certain monk of San Galgano, a Cistercian, was Operaio here, and two years later was succeeded by another monk of the same monastery, a certain Melano. He repaired the work of his predecessors, and added to it, and in 1266 Nicola Pisano came to Siena to set up his great pulpit. The Cathedral, shorter than the building we see by two bays, was finished, with the exception of the façade and the present choir, in the following year. The church is really a Romanesque building transformed by Gothic decorators.

That the work was a failure seems to have been realized by the Sienese within fifty years of its achievement. The Cathedral of Florence promised to be not only larger, but more beautiful than theirs. They began by adding here and there to the church. The old baptistery which stood to the right of the façade was pulled down, and in 1315 the new baptistery to the east, and beneath the Duomo, was built. At the same time a choir above the baptistery, whose roof served as floor for it, was begun. But before they had gone far with the work, in 1322 it was pronounced to be unstable by Lorenzo Maitano, the great Sienese who was Operaio at Orvieto. It was then proposed to build a new church, "beautiful, large, and splendid, fine in its proportions of length, height, and breadth, and in all its parts". This scheme was strongly opposed by those who wished only to add to the old church. Their party was in power, and remained in power till 1339, when Maitano's scheme was at last adopted, and a vast church planned, of which the old building—the present church—was to form the transepts. Lando di Pietro, the Sienese architect, then in the employment of King Robert of Naples, was recalled, and the first stone of the great new nave was laid in February 1340.

But the work then begun was beyond the power or the wealth of Siena, for it soon proved to be impossible to use the old church at all. It was necessary to build this vast temple entirely new from the foundations. The work proceeded apace even in spite of the Plague of 1348, but it was that which killed it at last, for it half-depopulated Siena. The merchants were ruined, the city divided against itself, the energies which should have gone to the building of the Cathedral were absorbed by the struggle for existence or the petty and bitter politics of the factions. Then it was discovered that certain fatal defects in construction were already declaring themselves in what had been begun of the new building. Florentine architects were called in. They found the piers too light for the vast vaults, and advised a reconstruction. When this was known the Operaio, the Sienese Domenico d' Agostino, advised that the old Cathedral should be allowed to remain, and that the choir above San Giovanni should be finished; and though he by no means abandoned hope of finishing the new Cathedral, he asserted that it would take a hundred years to build.

In 1357 the unsafe parts of the new building were removed. The great days of Siena were over, and the new church was then tacitly abandoned.

Meanwhile work proceeded on the old Cathedral. In 1370 the choir was finished, and in the same year the piazza before the church was enlarged by the removal of the loggia of the Bishop's Palace. In 1374 it was decided to lengthen the nave by two bays, and these were finished in 1377, when Bartolommeo di Tommé and other sculptors began to work on the façade. By 1380 or 1381 the façade was finished. The beautiful eastern façade was then taken in hand, and built after a design by Giacomo di Mino di Neri del Pellicciaio.

A hundred years later Giovanni di Stefano built the small baptistery in the north transept. In 1495 the Piccolomini Library was added, and the only addition made to the Cathedral since then is the Cappella del Voto in the south transept, which was added by Alexander VII in 1661.

If one is always disappointed with the façade of the Cathedral, what is one's final impression of the interior? At first certainly one is bewildered and confused by those bands of black and white marble which so diminish the spaciousness of what is, after all, a very spacious building; they halve its height and breadth and rob it of its serenity. But when, if ever, one has become accustomed to this oddity, one recognizes that what charms one in a building full of contradictions, is that in it which carries out the idea of all Latin building, an effect, in spite of every sort of handicap, an effect of light and space, not so splendid certainly as in such masterpieces as the cathedrals of Pisa and Lucca or in the church of Santa Croce in Florence, but light and space nevertheless, here where the fundamental feeling is rather Romanesque than Gothic, the predominating lines horizontal rather than perpendicular; and the decorations of the church, mainly of the Renaissance as they are, confirm the impression one receives from the building itself.

The church possesses many treasures. The very pavement is a work of art, one of the most notable in the city, and, indeed, unique in Italy. It was the labour of centuries. Begun before the close of the fourteenth century, it was still incomplete when the sixteenth was half passed away. Among the masters who designed subjects for this extraordinary mosaic, or rather *opus sectile*, are Giovanni di Stefano, Federighi, Domenico di Bartolo, Benvenuto di Giovanni, Matteo di Giovanni, Neroccio, Cozzarelli, Pintoricchio, Beccafumi, and probably Francesco di Giorgio.[1] This wonderful pavement is spread like a rich carpet down the length of the church.

One comes upon the fine work of Federighi again at the very entrance to the nave, in the two holy-water basins, and on that of Neroccio, always so full of charm, in the tomb of Bishop Tommaso Piccolomini (1483), in the south aisle, close to the door of the Campanile. Beneath are bas-reliefs by Urbano da Cortona, another of the "pavement masters", representing scenes from the life of the Blessed Virgin.

Close by is the Cappella del Voto, added in 1661. The building of this chapel closed the ancient and famous Porta del Perdono. It was built as a shrine for the ancient Madonna del Voto, "she who hearkened unto the people of Siena what time the Florentines were routed at Montaperto", and who, according to the Sienese, is still full of miracles. She is invoked by the city or the peasants of the *contado* today chiefly in the matter of the weather. The late William Heywood[2] recounts from his own experience how the mere unveiling of Our Lady del Voto saved Siena from flood in 1902 when Rome was drowned. But a later story I have heard would seem to the profane, or at least to a Florentine, to throw some doubt on the present efficacy of this Advocata Senensium. For it was told me that not long since the whole Sanese was suffering from drought and this for so long a time that at last the peasants demanded that the Madonna del Voto should be unveiled. Their priests besought leave of the Archbishop, who shook his head. "*Pazienza,*" says he, "*pazienza, miei figliuoli!*" Doubtless it is easier to prate of patience in the Episcopal Palace of Siena than to ensue it as you watch your vines die in the *contado*. However that may be, the peasants sent again to the Archbishop, who, tapping his new aneroid barometer, gravely shook his head. "Unveil her if you must," says he, "but if you do you will make

[1] It is impossible here to enter into the details of this extraordinary and detailed work. The reader is referred to the excellent study of Mr. R. H. Hobart Cust, *The Pavement Masters of Siena* (1901).

[2] *A Pictorial Chronicle of Siena* (Torrini, Siena, 1902), p. 64.

a fool of your Madonna." It was only when at last the glass began to fall that with the greatest readiness he gave consent, saying, "Unveil her now if you will, for she will certainly hear the cries of her children."

The Madonna del Voto has played a great part in the story of Siena. It was to her on the eve of Montaperto, when Siena was in great fear of her life, not foreseeing her victory, that Buonaguida the syndic, "stripped to his shirt, barefooted and bareheaded, with a rope around his neck, came forth into the presence of all the citizens, and in his shirt betook himself to the Duomo". There, before the Madonna del Voto, in the presence of the Bishop and all the people of Siena, he dedicated the city to the Blessed Virgin.

Four times besides was the city rededicated—in 1483 when she was threatened by the exiles, in 1526 before the battle of Camollia, in 1550 when the Spaniards were at hand, and again in 1555 when Charles V and Cosimo I were about to put an end to her independence.

In 1260, at the time of the first dedication, the high altar still stood beneath the cupola, and over it was later set Duccio's Maestà, that, alas! is now imprisoned in the Opera del Duomo. It was not before this marvellous altarpiece, however, that Buonaguida knelt, but before the Madonna del Voto, now in the Cappella del Voto.

The present high altar was set up in the sixteenth century, and in a new place.[1] Upon it now stands Vecchietta's splendid bronze tabernacle, while on either side kneel Giovanni di Stefano's angels, and below them the lovelier statues of Francesco di Giorgio. No praise can be too fine for them. Around them, against the columns, is the work of Beccafumi in bronze.

In the right transept is the monument of him who built the Cappella del Voto—Alexander VII, Fabio Chigi—beside that of another and earlier Sienese Pope, Alexander III.

Turning now to the sacristy, there are two panels of S. Bernardino; in one, by Sano di Pietro, he is preaching before the Palazzo Pubblico. The picture of the Madonna is by Pacchiarotto.

But the finest and most interesting work of art in the Cathedral

---

[1] The Cathedral was transformed when in 1679 Francesco Mazzotti, a follower of Bernini, was commissioned to take down the old statues of the twelve apostles in the nave and supply new ones. These remained in the Cathedral for two hundred years, till in the nineteenth century these Baroque figures were removed. They now glorify the London Oratory. Cf. Borghesi e Banchi, *Nuovi Documenti* (Siena 1898).

SIENA: THE CAMPO AND THE CONTADO

ENTRY OF THE CORTEO, The Palio, Siena

is the pulpit by Nicola Pisano. He received the order for this splendid work on Michaelmas Day, 1265, and, thanks to the help of Arnolfo and his son Giovanni and others, he was able to begin it on 1 March, 1266, and to complete it in November 1268. The plan is the same as that for the pulpit in the baptistery of Pisa, but the work is richer and more clairvoyant. Octagonal in form, it possesses two more bas-reliefs than the pulpit of the Pisan baptistery, namely, the Massacre of the Innocents and a second scene of the Last Judgment. But in every relief we find a more dramatic life and an art more naturalistic than in the earlier work. It is a masterpiece a little uncertain of itself perhaps, but full of a new promise. The unfortunate addition of the steps was made by Riccio at the end of the sixteenth century.

Close to the pulpit is the Cappella di Sant' Ansano. Within is the magnificent bronze tomb of Bishop Pecci, made in 1426 by Donatello. It is a triumph of technique, exquisite in workmanship and colour, keeping about it too, in spite of the worn surface, a sense of calm and repose not always to be found in Donatello's monuments.

The north transept holds nothing of interest, but the Cappella di San Giovanni next to it was built by Giovanni di Stefano, and within there is a reliquary containing, as it is said, an arm of S. John Baptist, presented to Siena by Pius II. What, however, will no doubt detain one longer is the magnificent statue of the saint by Donatello. Very close to the statues of the Baptist, now in Venice and Berlin, and having much in common with the wonderful Magdalen of the baptistery at Florence, the S. John of Siena is an embodiment of that voice crying in the wilderness which seems to have haunted Donatello so persistently. On either side is a statue of S. Ansano and S. Catherine of Alexandria, the one a feeble work by Giovanni di Stefano, the other a wonderful but unfinished masterpiece by Neroccio. This chapel was the smaller baptistery, and the font is notable: its reliefs are the work of Federighi, and are concerned with Adam and Eve and the Garden of Eden—the garden of the Hesperides, it seems, for two labours of Hercules close the series. On the walls are frescoes by Pintoricchio and his pupils, representing Alberto Aringhieri as a young knight keeping vigil, and as a knight of Rhodes. Opposite is the Birth of the Baptist. The two frescoes over the door are the work of Peruzzi, but doubtfully.

8

The Piccolomini family, one of whose sons, Pius II, gave its relic to the chapel of San Giovanni, has its monument in the north aisle at the fourth altar, the framework of which was designed by Andrea Bregno (1485). Four of the statues which adorn it are said to be from the hand of Michelangelo, namely, S. Peter, S. Paul, S. Pius, and S. Gregory. Fine as they are, they but doubtfully come from the hand of the great Florentine.

Cardinal Francesco Piccolomini, who commissioned this altar, built also the famous Libreria, close by, to hold the manuscripts left him by his uncle, Pius II. The Library is, then, really a monument to the great humanist Pope who canonized S. Catherine of Siena. The bronze doors were made by Antonio Ormanni. Over them is a fine fresco by Pintoricchio of the Coronation of Cardinal Francesco as Pius III. Within are the ten splendid frescoes of the life of Pius II by Pintoricchio.

Pius II was born in 1405. He was an adventurer of fine character, but an adventurer. He had no great convictions, but, unlike so many who are without them, he was capable of learning from experience. And then, if he was without convictions, he was also without prejudices. He made the most of life in no vulgar way, but with a success that proves his superiority. He was not one to mould the world, but to use it and to enjoy it nobly. His early life is said to have been disorderly. He wrote much sensuous and even licentious verse and a *novella* that might have come from the hand of Boccaccio in a moment of ennui. At twenty-six he became secretary to the Bishop of Fermo at the Council of Basle. There he made his reputation, and in the years between 1432 and 1435 he was employed on missions in England, Scotland, and Germany. He then followed Frederic III, reformed his life, took Orders, reconciled himself to the Pope, and was created Bishop of Trieste, and, returning to Italy in 1456, he became Cardinal of Siena. On the death of Calixtus III, two years later, he was elected Pope, and, in reference to his name of Æneas, took the title of Pius II. His reign was disappointing; it revealed his want of conviction and his opportunism. Instead of forming that confederation of Europe against the Turks which was the most essential duty of Christendom at the time, he wasted himself, his eloquence— which was considerable—and his material power—which was small—in breaking the unruly barons of the Romagna and the Marche, and with a petty personal spite quite unworthy of him, and, indeed, unlike him, burnt Sigismondo Malatesta in effigy in Rome. The effort to regain Constantinople, worthy of all his energy, came to nothing, and, as though in remorse for his failure, we see him at last, feeble and suffering, borne to Ancona on a litter to bless and encourage the half-hearted and belated Crusade. There he died in August 1464. Looking back on his life now, it is as a scholar and a humanist he chiefly appeals to us. His Commentaries are full of human pages and a real love of nature that in the men of his day was only to be found again in Lorenzo de' Medici and Leon Alberti. He was a mixture more strange than rare, of weakness and strength, of an idealism and a vanity truly Sienese. He erred, but he did not deceive himself; he did not try to make himself out better than he was; and for his sincerity and his frankness we respect him, so that his very inconsistencies come at last to seem the most real things about him, and his thoughts about life, so plentifully recorded, really spontaneous impressions, are valuable to us on that account. And last, but not least, he had the courage of his opinions—he canonized S. Catherine.

The frescoes which Pintoricchio painted to illustrate Pius's life begin on the right with that in which one sees him starting for the Council of Basle with Cardinal Capranica. In the second he is at the Court of James I of Scotland. Later he is crowned poet-laureate by Frederic III; as envoy of the Emperor he meets Pope Eugenius IV; as Bishop he is present at the meeting of the Emperor and of Eleonora of Portugal, his betrothed, outside the Porta Camollia; he is made Cardinal by Calixtus III; he is elected Pope; he presides at the Congress he had summoned at Mantua to promote a Crusade against the Turks; he canonizes S. Catherine; he is borne to Ancona to bless the Crusade.

Full as these works are of the pretty detail that Pintoricchio loved, they are redeemed even from their faults of composition, even from their feebleness of structure, even from their lack of life by the spaciousness of their landscape and the charm of their thousand incidents. They are a complete decoration to the room, though not perhaps a really splendid one, and they remain the masterpiece of the artist and one of the brightest and most harmonious works of the Renaissance.

Leaving the Duomo at last for the spaciousness and light of the Piazza on the way to the Opera del Duomo, one passes under the beautiful Romanesque Campanile that is so splendid and so lofty a feature in any view of the city. It is a work of the first half of the thirteenth century.

Among the many fragments that go to make up the museum of the Opera, fragments from the façade of the Duomo, fragments from the Duomo pavement, it is the magnificent reliquary of S. Galgano by Lando di Pietro which calls for most attention. It dates from 1298 and its architectural treatment reminds one that the artist was not only a goldsmith but an architect of repute. He was in the service of the Emperor Henry VII, for whom he made the Imperial Crown used at the coronation in Sant' Ambrogio in Milan, and he worked too for King Robert of Naples.

But it is to that room on the third floor which holds Duccio's broken Maestà that one returns again and again. Before this marvellous altarpiece one often wonders whether this was not the greatest thing Siena ever accomplished in the world of action, in the world of art, in the world of the intellect. It, at any rate, endures.

Duccio was born about 1255, and already in 1278 he was employed as a painter by the State, and in 1280 was for some reason or other heavily fined. These are the two earliest notices we have of him. He was the true founder of the Sienese school, which was in its own way as lovely in its results as, and more decorative in its aim than, the other schools of painting in Italy. Duccio certainly seems to have got his training from some Byzantine master, perhaps in Constantinople itself, perhaps in Siena. Like many great artists, he seems to have remained poor his whole life long; at any rate, he was continually summoned for debt. Whatever vicissitudes Fortune may have thrust upon him, this at least he was allowed to do—to follow his art; and the Maestà, which is housed none too well in the Opera, is his masterpiece.

"It was the most beautiful picture that was ever seen or made," says Andrea Dei, his contemporary. "It cost more than three thousand gold florins, and Duccio, the painter, laboured many years at it." As a fact, he took three years to complete it; the work was commissioned on 9 October, 1308, and was borne to the high altar of the Duomo in triumph on 9 June, 1311. It seems possible that the rumour of its triumph was stolen by Vasari, probably unconsciously, and told again of the Rucellai Madonna in Santa Maria Novella. However that may be, an anonymous chronicler of the time, whose work is now in the Archivio of Siena, gives us a very circumstantial account of Duccio's triumph. "On the day that it was carried to the Duomo," he writes, "the shops were shut; and the Bishop bade that a goodly and devout company of priests and friars should go in solemn procession, accompanied by the *Signori Nove* and all the officers of the Commune and all the people; all the most worthy followed close upon the picture, according to their degree, with lights burning in their hands; and then behind them came the women and children with great devotion. And they accompanied the said picture so far as the Duomo, making procession round the Campo as is the custom, all the bells sounding joyously for the devotion of so noble a picture as this. And all that day they offered up prayers, with great alms to the poor, praying God and His Mother, who is our advocate, that He may defend us in His infinite mercy from all adversity and all evil, and that He may keep us from the hands of traitors and the enemies of Siena."

The picture thus honoured is one of the great works of the Middle Age. In the midst, on a vast throne, is seated the Madonna Advocata Senensium, with her Divine Child in her arms. Four angels on either side gaze at this wonder, leaning dreamily on the back and sides of the throne, while to the right and left on either side six others stand on guard. In front of these stand SS. John Evangelist, Paul, Catherine, John Baptist, Peter, and Agnes; and before all in adoration kneel the four bishops, the patrons of the city, SS. Savinus, Ansanus, Crescentius, and Victorius. On the footstool of the six-sided throne is written—

MATER SANCTA DEI SIS CAUSSA SENIS REQUIEI
SIS DUCCIO VITA TE QUIA DEPINXIT ITA.

This, being interpreted, prays, "Holy Mother of God, be thou the cause of rest to Siena, and to Duccio life, because he has painted thee thus."

But this was not all. This altarpiece was set up over the high altar of the Duomo, and in those days the high altar stood under the cupola. It had therefore to be seen from both sides: from the nave where the people worshipped and from the choir where the Chapter was gathered. The Madonna enthroned with the Divine Child and angels and saints, as I have described it, faced the people, and beneath this was a *gradino* of nine panels. On the other side Duccio painted twenty-six small panels illustrating the life of our Lord and the Blessed Virgin, above a *gradino* of nine panels. In all, with the *gradini*, the altarpiece consisted of forty-four small panels beside the Maestà, only thirty-five of which remain in Siena. The rest are scattered. Three of the western *predella* panels are in Berlin, three of the eastern *predella* panels are in the National Gallery, while three other panels are in America.

It is a pity that the Sienese authorities cannot find a better room in which to place this, perhaps the greatest work in their possession. As it appears at present it is impossible to appreciate its true effect. What it must once have been in the Duomo we shall never know.

It is difficult to look at the other pictures here in the light of this splendour. Yet they are worth looking at, especially a still lovely Pietro Lorenzetti, the Birth of the Virgin, and four spoiled but beautiful panels, early works by Ambrogio Lorenzetti.

The Pietro Lorenzetti is a triptych. In the midst S. Anne in bed has just given birth to the Blessed Virgin. She is sitting up leaning on her elbow while her servants wash the baby Mary. A friend has just come in to see her. On the left S. Joachim sits without; a messenger has just brought him the news. On the right are two majestic figures of waiting maids who have brought, one a flagon of water which she holds with quiet elegance in her left hand, having towels on her right arm; the other holds a dish with both hands covered with a towel. This picture is one of the finest of the Sienese school of the fourteenth century. It undoubtedly, too, suggested the Asciano altarpiece of the same subject.

I did not forget to enjoy the view over the city from the window at the end of the room.

Turning now to the Baptistery, one descends the steps into the Piazza di San Giovanni, and passing the Palazzo del Magnifico on the right, built for Pandolfo Petrucci by Cozzarelli, one is face to face with the unfinished façade of San Giovanni built by Mino del Pelicciaio which, though unfinished, is really a success. The interior is beautiful. In the midst is the great font, designed by Jacopo della Quercia, the greatest of Sienese sculptors; while the bronze reliefs, six in number, which adorn it are the work of some of the greatest masters of the fifteenth century, namely, Jacopo himself, Giovanni di Turino the Sienese, Lorenzo Ghiberti and Donatello the Florentines. Della Quercia's relief is that facing the apse, the Vision of Zacharias. It is flanked by two figures of Justice and Prudence by Giovanni di Turino. Beside it is the Birth of John Baptist by the Turini, the figure of Fortitude being from the hand of Goro di Neroccio. The Turini are also responsible for the next relief, the Preaching of the Baptist, the figure of Charity beside it being by Giovanni. Lorenzo Ghiberti made the two following reliefs—the Baptism of our Lord and the Baptist before Herod; while Donatello made the Feast of Herod, which comes next, as well as the two figures of Faith and Hope which flank it, and three of the delightful bronze *putti*. The extraordinarily vigorous and dramatic work of the Florentines, especially that of Donatello with its realism, strikes one strangely beside the more ideal and decorative work of the Sienese masters. The statue of S. John Baptist and the five marble reliefs of the Prophets, which complete the work, are by della Quercia. On the walls is the work, utterly spoiled now by repainting, of Vecchietta and his pupils.

Returning now to the Piazza del Duomo, one enters the Ospedale di Santa Maria della Scala, which fills the side of the Piazza facing the Duomo. Built first as a sort of poor-house in the eleventh century by the canons of the Duomo, it later became a lodging for pilgrims as well as a hospital. Here S. Catherine ministered to "the least of these My brethren", and S. Bernardino served the plague-stricken in the pestilence of 1400.

Passing a marble tomb by Cozzarelli and, in a room on the right, a fresco of the Visitation by Beccafumi, one enters the great hall or Pellegrinaio, where are the frescoes which tell the story of the hospital. They are chiefly the work of Domenico di Bartolo. One sees the Marriage of Foundlings, Almsgiving, the Care of the Sick. Opposite, Pope Celestine III takes the Ospedale from the care of the canons and gives it to the laity. Beside this last, one sees the reception of a Sister, a work by Primo della Quercia. Then, again, the enlargement of the hospital by Domenico di Bartolo, and close to it, full of little children, the Dream of a devout woman, a charming and lovely work by Vecchietta.

Leaving the Pellegrinaio one passes into the Deposito delle Donne, full of the spoiled work of Vecchietta in 1448; and so into the Infermeria di San Pio, where is a fresco in monochrome by Domenico di Bartolo of the Beato Sorore, to whom legend attributes the foundation of the hospital. Close by is the chapel, a building mainly of the fifteenth century. On the altar is a bronze of our Lord by Vecchietta—a magnificent work.

Leaving this church, one descends to the chapels of the Confraternities beneath the Ospedale. In that belonging to the Compagnia di Santa Caterina, where S. Catherine often came to pray, is a triptych of the Virgin and Child by Taddeo di Bartolo, his best work in Siena. Below is the chapel of the Compagnia della Madonna, now a small picture gallery. Among the many damaged works are a triptych by Duccio of the Crucifixion, and by the same master the wings of another representing the Entombment and the Flagellation. A Virgin with S. Catherine of Alexandria, S. Catherine of Siena, and other saints is by Fungai. On the next wall is a Madonna and Child by Sano di Pietro. Perhaps the finest piece here, however, is Benvenuto di Giovanni's S. Catherine leading Pope Gregory back to Rome. Not far off is another of Benvenuto's works, a Pietà, and beside it a Holy Family by Sodoma, and a Madonna and Child surrounded by angels by Paolo di Giovanni Fei.

CHAPTER X

SIENA

TERZO DI CITTÀ

THE city of Siena from very ancient times was divided into three divisions, or municipal districts, known as the Terzo di Città, the Terzo di San Martino, and the Terzo di Camollia. The districts seem to have sprung up about the three fortresses of which it seems Siena originally consisted—the Castel Vecchio to the south-west, the Castel di Val di Montone to the south-east, and the Castel di Camollia to the north. Thus there were three Sienas, not one Siena, and in Latin Siena was, in fact, often spoken of as Senae. The three *terzi* remained for ages separate communities, organized independently in civil, military, and economic affairs. And for long after Siena became one, the Magistracy of the Republic was in normal times composed of a multiple of three, the famous Nove—Nine—being perhaps the best-known example. And seeing that Siena lies on a hill which breaks starwise into three summits, it is not surprising that the division into *terzi* has, in fact, lasted to our own day.

As we have seen, the central government of the city—of the three divisions which had become one—was situated in the cup, or hollow plain, between the three summits, and thus in the very centre of the city. The Castel Vecchio, on the south-western height, when unity had been achieved, became the Terzo di Città, for there the Duomo was situated, and within this division was included the site of the central government—the Palazzo Pubblico. The Castel di Val di Montone, the south-eastern height, became the Terzo di San Martino, taking the name of its parish church; while the northern height or ridge, by far the longest of the three, retained its name, being called the Terzo di Camollia. It is proper to the history of Siena, then, as well as convenient, to fall in with this ancient division of the city into three parts when making an examination of it. As one stands in the Piazza del Campo, one is at the point of junction of these divisions. If one passes into the Via di Città, one penetrates that *terzo*; if one enters Via

Ricasoli, one enters Terzo di San Martino; if one turns into Via Cavour, one comes into Terzo di Camollia.

I have already examined the chief monuments of the Terzo di Città in the Palazzo Pubblico and the Duomo and its dependencies, and I now proceed by the Via di Città to find what remains to be seen in this *terzo*. Well, to begin with, there is the view of the Piazza and the Palazzo through the Costarella on the left as one follows on the way, and more than one fine palace on the right; and then just as one comes where the Via di Città bends away to the right, on the left stands the great Palazzo Saracini, which, though it is a building now for the most part of the fourteenth century, was standing in the day of Montaperto, for it was from one of its towers that Ceccolini, the drummer, watched the progress of the great battle miles away, and gave the news to those who remained in the city.

What once brought one, however, to Palazzo Saracini was its famous picture gallery. Its chief glory was, of course, the works it possessed of the Sienese school. Taking these in chronological order, here was a genuine work by Duccio—a mere fragment, however—a half-figure of an angel (1236). The trecento was further represented by two pinnacles (1266), comprising the Annunciation, by Andrea Vanni (1332–1414), and by one of Paolo di Giovanni Fei's (1372–1410) strange pictures, a Madonna and Child with saints and angels where Eve lies before the Virgin's throne (1269). It was, however, in works of the quattrocento, as one might expect, that the gallery was rich. Sassetta (1392–1450) is represented by two works—a charming small triptych (1278) and a most exquisite panel representing the Adoration of the Magi (933). The work of Sassetta's disciple, Giovanni di Paolo (1403–82) was to be seen here in one of his best works—a large panel, dated 1472, of the Madonna and Child in the midst of cherubim (1263), as well as in four little panels of the life of our Lord (1257–60). Andrea Vanni's Annunciation formed the pinnacles of Giovanni's large picture. There are also several pictures here by Sano di Pietro (1406–81), Sassetta's pupil: four fragments of saints (1237, 1238, 1277, 1278), our Lord in the hands of His Enemies (1265), and in one of the private rooms of the palace a fine Madonna and Child with angels and SS. Jerome and Bernardino on either side. Another pupil of Sassetta, Lorenzo Vecchietta (1412–80), was well represented by a fine small panel of S. Martin giving half his cloak to a beggar (1273); while one whom he influenced very strongly, Neroccio di Landi (1447–1500), that charming artist, was well represented by a Madonna and Child with SS. John Baptist and Mary Magdalen (8) and a Madonna and Child with SS. Catherine and Bernardino (14), both fine examples of that master's work.

With the work of Pacchia (1477–1535) we are on the eve of the cinquecento: he is to be seen in an excellent picture here, a Madonna and Child with SS. John, Bernardino, and Catherine (752). Beccafumi (1485–1551), altogether of the decline, has here a large but unpleasing Marriage of S. Catherine (15), a picture of the Rape of the Sabines (1422), and an earlier picture of the Madonna and Child (1029). And Balducci is seen in a rather charming and simple panel representing the Dream of Hercules.

As for the other Italian schools, that of Lombardy is best represented in the numerous works here of Brescianino; while the Florentine school is best seen in a portrait (205), the work of Mainardi, the pupil of Ghirlandaio.

Leaving the Palazzo Saracini, one follows the Via di Città noting the fine old palaces on the way, till one comes to the Piazza di Postierla, where on the right rises the tower of the Forteguerri de' Grandi. In this piazza the Via di Città ends, but one turns to the left into the Via di San Pietro, beside three fine Gothic palaces, of which the finest is the Palazzo Buonsignori, now the Picture Gallery. Where the street opens and turns, on the left is the church of San Pietro alla Scala. Here are some charming works by Sano di Pietro: in the sacristy two *tondi*—the Angel of Annunciation and S. Lucy; and over the second altar, on the north side, a fragment, usually covered. In the priest's house, adjoining the church, is a half-figure of Our Lord, by Giovanni di Paolo and a Virgin and Child by Ambrogio Lorenzetti.

Continuing on the way, one turns almost at once to the right into Via Tommaso Pendola, on the left of which is the old convent of Santa Margherita, in whose refectory are some frescoes by Fungai, while in the church is a spoiled statue of S. Margherita by a pupil of Quercia. Where Via Tommaso Pendola opens into a piazza, bearing to the left, passing through a narrow way under the Palazzo Celsi on the right, one comes into the broad Via Baldassare Peruzzi. The Palazzo Celsi is one of the finest buildings of

Peruzzi, and perhaps the finest specimen in Siena of the domestic architecture of the end of the fifteenth century.

Opposite the palace is the great sixteenth-century church of the Carmine, whose convent has been turned into a barracks. There is nothing of any great account to see; but the Well of the Diana, in the inner cloister, is curious as witnessing to the belief of the Sienese in a hidden river Diana beneath the city . The great need of Siena was water, and this well was sunk in the hope of discovering that fictitious stream. Perhaps the best picture in the church is Beccafumi's S. Michael, which is in its own way a masterly and dramatic piece of work. Vasari loved it. Beside the Cappella del Voto is a thirteenth-century Sienese Madonna.

On leaving the church one returns past the Palazzo Celsi and continues into Via Baldassare Peruzzi till one comes to the piazza in which stands the church of Santa Lucia. Here there is an old copy of Simone Martini's fresco over the outer gate of Camollia. It is certainly worth attention.

From Santa Lucia one can make one's way down Via di San Marco to the gate—there is a fine view all the way, and the gate is splendid; or returning to Palazzo Celsi and through the narrow passage under it into Via Tommaso Pendola, turn into the Via San Quirico over the height, and so into Via Castelvecchio on the right, through one of the oldest parts of the city. At the beginning of Via San Quirico, on the left, stands the church of Sant' Ansano, beside it a tower, where, as they say, S. Ansano was imprisoned. Within the church is a charming picture of the Epiphany, a fifteenth-century work with a figure of S. Ansano.

But perhaps the best way, certainly the least fatiguing, is, instead of following Via San Quirico and Via di Castelvecchio into Via di San Pietro, to return through Via Tommaso Pendola, or, from Santa Lucia, through Via della Cerchia past the Renaissance Palazzo Finetti to the Piazza di Sant' Agostino.

The church of Sant' Agostino is now a building of the eighteenth century, and uninteresting. But it possesses two treasures of a high importance; the one a Crucifixion, a late but lovely work by Perugino; the other, in the chapel of the Blessed Sacrament, a Massacre of the Innocents of an extraordinary vigour, realism, and horror, but of wonderful colour and fine effect, by Matteo di Giovanni. Beside this work Sodoma's Adoration of the Magi here seems even more insipid than in fact it is. One turns from it with relief to the beautiful triptych in the choir, the legend of the Blessed Agostino Novello, by Simone Martini, unique among his pictures.

Opposite Sant' Agostino is the little church of Santa Mustiola, whose delightful bell-tower is the most charming thing about her. On leaving her, one will do well to wander down to Porta San Marco to watch the sunset, or to return once more to the heart of the city, the Piazza del Campo, by Via di San Pietro and that winding, picturesque way, Via del Casato.

CHAPTER XI

SIENA

TERZO DI SAN MARTINO

THE smallest of the three *terzi*, the Terzo di San Martino, is best approached from the Piazza del Campo by the Via di San Martino, which leaves it in the extreme south-eastern corner on the left as one faces the Palazzo Pubblico. Passing thence, under the shadow of the Palazzo Piccolomini, one comes in a few yards to the parish church of San Martino, the sixteenth-century successor of a very ancient building. Just within, on the right, is a picture painted by Lorenzo Cini to commemorate the glorious victory of Camollia. That victory remains the most heroic in the later annals of the Republic, and in all respects coincides with that of Montaperto, though nearly three hundred years lie between them. Just as before the earlier battle Buona-guida had placed the city under the dominion of the Blessed Virgin, and led the people to her throne in the Duomo, so again, before the battle of Camollia, Margherita Bichi, widow of Francesco Buonsignori, a woman of prophetic soul, declared that the Blessed Virgin would protect Siena, and that it was her will that the city should especially honour the feast of her Immaculate Conception, not then proclaimed an article of Faith. On the following Sunday, as the Madonna had desired, all the magistrates went to the Duomo in procession, confessed and communicated and knelt before the Madonna del Voto, "to which at other times they had presented themselves"; and there, after the Mass of the Conception was over, they confirmed and renewed the donation of the city "to its true Patroness".[1]

The trouble in which Siena found herself was caused by the ambition of the Medici Pope Clement VII, who, taking advantage of the internal dissensions of the Republic, and the Sienese exiles, thought with help of the Florentines—those blind papal Florentines, *quei Papal Fiorentini ciechi*, as the people said—to bring Siena

[1] See the deliberations of the Balia and the Concistoro for 21 and 22 July in Pecci, *Memorie*, etc., ii, pp. 211-13. Cf. also W. Heywood, *A Pictorial Chronicle of Siena* (Torrini, Siena), pp. 82-6.

under the heel of the Holy See. But there is a God who disap-
proves of the inordinate greed of His ministers, who try to strangle
civil liberty and so put their own permitted existence in peril.
Moreover, the Blessed Virgin was the last person to refuse help
to those who earnestly call upon her, and least of all to her own
city of Siena. Is it any wonder, then, that in these circumstances
they placed their guns badly outside the Porta Camollia? Is it
any wonder that these guns did next to no harm? Is it any wonder
that when the Sienese issued out of the city, shouting for joy and of
great courage, they seemed to see S. Michael and his host of
archangels, so that for every mile the Sienese pursued, the Florentines ran ten? Truly that day the keys of Peter jingled unseemly
about the quaking knees of one who sought hiding in haste: the
triple crown was struck away, the blind papal Florentines, led by
the blind, fell, as the Gospel foretold, into the ditch; while the
victorious Sienese, returning with songs and thanksgivings to the
city of their Patroness, dragged within their walls the deserted
guns and banners they had won from the Church or from Florence.
"You know," wrote Francesco Vettori to Machiavelli, "you know
how unwillingly I allow myself to believe anything supernatural,
but this defeat seems to me to have been as extraordinary—I will
not say miraculous—as anything that has happened in the war
from 1494 till now; it seems to me like those stories I have read in
the Bible when a sudden terror fell upon a host, so that it fled it
knew not from what."

Here in San Martino we should remember those days, for it
might seem they are scarce to be found any more upon earth.

There is but one other thing of real interest in the church save
the very Querciesque statues of the Virgin, the Baptist and three
apostles—I mean the fine Nativity of Our Lord by Beccafumi.

Close by San Martino is the Misericordia, once an *ospedale* for
pilgrims. But one follows the Via di San Martino between the
ancient palaces, past the church of San Giusto, where is a spoiled
picture by Sano di Pietro, till at the end one comes to the church of
San Girolamo, where in the cloister is a notable panel by
Fungai of the Assumption, while in the church is a fresco of
S. Jerome by Pacchia, and in the sacristy a Coronation of the
Virgin by Sano.

San Girolamo, however, cannot keep one long from the best of
all, the great church of the Servi di Maria, at the top of the Via

dei Servi, whence one may see the desert that lies between Siena and her mountain—Mont' Amiata, a vision at evening. Here, on the ramparts of the city of the Virgin, towers the church her especial Servants have erected in her honour under the invocation of her Holy and Immaculate Conception. As one looks at that beautiful pierced Campanile, how can one but remind oneself of her beautiful names—

> Rosa mystica,
> Turris Davidica,
> Turris eburnea,
> Domus aurea;
> Foederis arca,
> Janua coeli.

Within at the base is a fresco of Madonna Refugium Peccatorum rescuing souls from the lively flames of Purgatory; and who that has spent a summer day in the fires of the *contado*, far away where there is neither shelter nor shade, but has understood this thing, and the refreshment to be found within the city of the Virgin after the purgatorial heat of July.

Within, the church, which is spacious and lovely, and full of such treasures as once abounded everywhere, but that now are only left in such rare shrines as this, has been all reburnished, a thing I regret.

Above the first altar on the right is the great Madonna del Bordone by Coppo di Marcovaldo (1261), truly miraculous and worshipful. Further, over the last altar on this side of the church, is another Massacre of the Innocents by Matteo di Giovanni, painted in 1491, and later than the more splendid composition of Sant' Agostino. Then in the right transept is a marvel, the Madonna del Popolo by Lippo Memmi, the most touching and lovely of his works, while over the sacristy door is a Madonna of the school of Cimabue.

Nor is this all, for in the next chapel one finds a great fresco by Pietro Lorenzetti, again the Massacre of the Innocents, but lately uncovered from the whitewash. Opposite to it is a Nativity by Taddeo di Bartolo. In the chapel, on the other side of the choir, are two more frescoes, by Pietro Lorenzetti, of the Dance of Salome, and S. John in Patmos.

Besides these pictures, over the high altar Fungai placed his

LA MADONNA DEL POPOLO, Lippo Memmi.
S. Maria dei Servi, Siena

PORTA STENDARDO IN FERRO. Palazzo Grisoli, Siena

Coronation of the Virgin, and though it has been spoiled by restoration, it still retains a shadow of its loveliness. While to the Madonna del Popolo, and the Madonna del Manto, and the Madonna del Bordone must be added the lovely Madonna del Belvedere by Mino del Pellicciaio over the second altar in the north aisle. Close by is a noble Crucifix by Ugolino.

In the chapel of the Holy Trinity close by, is a picture of the Madonna and Child with saints, by Sano di Pietro, and in the sacristy a Madonna and Child with the Baptist and S. Michael, a late work by Neroccio.

From the Santa Trinità one descends the steps in the Via di Val Montone, and turning to the right, when one comes to the Via Romana—which is the Via Francigena that enters Siena at the Porta Camollia—and so to the Porta Romana where it leaves it. Originally called Porta Nuova, it is the surprising and lovely work of Angelo di Ventura in the fourteenth century, and is the best example in the city of a double gate fortified. Over it is the still wonderful fresco by Sano di Pietro, quite spoiled by restoration. Returning on the way up the Via Romana, one comes, at the first turn of the great road, to the little church of San Galgano with its magnificent silver reliquary of the patron saint. The two fine statues to be found there of the Madonna and Angel of Annunciation are by a disciple of Jacopo della Quercia.

Where the Via Romana becomes Via Ricasoli one turns to the right, and gains admittance, if one can, to the Rifugio, where in the adjoining church of San Raimondo is an exquisite picture of the Madonna praying, which has been attributed to Domenico di Bartolo. In the schools are several fine Sienese pictures, a Madonna and Child by Fungai, and two spoiled works by Sano.

Close by is the Palazzo di San Galgano, where there is another Sano.

From here one follows the Via dei Pispini to the church of Santo Spirito, whose chiefest possessions are a Virgin in Glory by Matteo Balducci, perhaps his best picture, and a Crucifix by Sano di Pietro. In the Cappella degli Spagnuoli, in the south aisle, are frescoes by Sodoma: they are certainly nothing to boast of. The terra-cotta Nativity is by one of the later Robbia.

From this church one may follow the Via dei Pispini to the great Porta, taking on the way the church of Santa Chiara, a charming piece of architecture. In any case one will return along

9

Via Ricasoli, passing, just before, to the Palazzo Piccolomini on the left, the Loggia del Papa, a building of Federighi's in 1462 for Pius II. It has not its equal in all high Siena for charm and delight.

As for the Palazzo Piccolomini, let us hope it will stand for ever, as it was evidently meant to do. The finest architectural work of the Renaissance in Siena, it is now the Archivio of the city. Its chief treasures, perhaps, are those Tavolette, or covers of the books of the customs which form in themselves a history of the Republic.

This unique collection of delightful little paintings deserves a detailed description for it contains a sequence of little works many of which are by celebrated Sienese artists. The admirable little book by William Heywood, *A Pictorial History of Siena*, published by Torrini in Siena should be consulted.

CHAPTER XII

SIENA

TERZO DI CAMOLLIA

To explore the last *terzo* of Siena, the Terzo di Camollia, one leaves the Piazza del Campo on the north and follows Via Cavour, which, like Via Ricasoli and Via Romana which continue it, is a part of the great medieval highway from the north—the Via Francigena by which all the medieval Emperors marched to Rome.

Almost at once one comes on the right to the Piazza Tolomei, in midst of which is set the church of San Cristoforo, and which is closed by the great Palazzo Tolomei, the last remnant in Siena of all that once belonged to that tremendous family. This square was once one of their strongholds, almost surrounded by their houses. The church of San Cristoforo, which has played a great part in the history of Siena—for there the magistrates were used to assemble before the Palazzo Pubblico was built, while the Commune assembled in the Piazza itself—has been altogether rebuilt, and is now of little interest, save that it holds Pacchia's Madonna and Child enthroned between S. Luke and the Beato Raimondo, and a delightful S. George by Sano.

Hence, passing round the north side of the church, one crosses the top of the Via Sallustio Bandini and enters the piazza before the too late Renaissance church of Santa Maria di Provenzano. Begun in 1595 and finished sixteen year later, the church is the great shrine of that image of the Madonna which, owing chiefly to a quarrel between the Archbishop of Siena and an historian that prevented the usual adoration of the Madonna del Voto in the Duomo, was the object of almost universal devotion in the sixteenth century in Siena.[1]

In 1594 the people of Siena were afflicted by a very grievous famine, and decided to turn themselves to their advocate and to implore once more the pity of their suzerain Lady the Blessed

---

[1] See F. Bandini-Piccolomini, *La Madonna di Provenzano e le origini della sua chiesa* (Siena, 1895).

Mother of our Lord, Mary most holy. But as it happened at this
very time a furious contest was raging between Ascanio Piccolomini, Archbishop of Siena, and Giugurta Tommasi, historian and
rector of the Opera del Duomo, so that it was not possible for them
to go, as of old, to the Madonna del Voto in the Cathedral. Now
for some time it had been whispered that an image of our Lady,
which stood between two windows of a humble dwelling in the
Via di Provenzano di Sotto, was working miracles. On 1 July, the
Vigil of the Visitation, this suspicion was made certain by a very
remarkable occurrence, which happened while her shrine was
being decorated against the *festa*.

There lived in the same street a certain Giulia di Orazio, a
woman of notoriously evil life, who was tormented by an incurable
malady. She, beholding these preparations, began to scoff at those
who made them and at the Blessed Virgin. That same evening
at dusk she felt herself compelled by some mysterious force to go
and kneel before the sacred image, beseeching pardon and health.
On the following day she returned once more to offer up the same
petitions, and a few hours later was made perfectly whole; and
when her doctor arrived, as was his wont, to treat the sore produced by her illness, on removing the bandages which covered it
he found, to his amazement, that every trace of disease had disappeared. The woman hastened forth to offer praise and thanks-
giving for the mercy vouchsafed, narrating with emotion, to all
those who stood by, the great salvation which had been wrought
on her behalf. The tale passed from mouth to mouth, and ere
night fell the whole population thronged to the Contrada di
Provenzano to pray to the miraculous Madonna.

Thus began the great *festa*, one of the greatest in Siena, which
is held on the day of the Visitation in July: and thus was fulfilled
the prophecy of Brandano, Christ's madman, *Siena vedrai tutte
le tue donne andare a Provenzano*—"Siena, thou wilt see all thy
women go to Provenzano." The church of Santa Maria di
Provenzano, which was built as shrine for the miraculous image,
was begun in the following year, 1595.

Passing round to the north of the church, one follows the street,
which, after crossing the Via di Giglio, enters the Via de' Rossi,
to the Piazza di San Francesco.

This spot has been a Franciscan settlement since 1236, but the
church we now see is mainly of the fourteenth century. It is,

however, but a shell, for all the splendid monuments which once
made San Francesco to Siena what Santa Croce is to Florence
were destroyed in the great fire of 1655. Today the church contains little of interest, some frescoes by the Lorenzetti and the
fifteenth-century tomb of Cristoforo Felici by Urbano of Cortona.
The Lorenzetti frescoes are in the chapels north and south of
the high altar. In the first is a Crucifixion in fairly good condition, a work of great tenderness and dramatic beauty, by Pietro
Lorenzetti; in the second are two frescoes by Ambrogio, the
Martyrdom of the Franciscan friars in Morocco and S. Francis
before Pope Honorius III. In the first chapel to the right of the
high altar is an altarpiece of the Virgin and Child by Andrea
Vanni, an impressive thing.

Close by in the chapel of the Seminario is a panel by Ambrogio
Lorenzetti of the Madonna and our little Lord, one of his best
works, while in the refectory are some spoiled frescoes by both
artists. And in the museum of the seminary is a Madonna and
Child by Segna di Bonaventura. There is a wonderful view
of Mont' Amiata, Monte Cetona, and Radicofani from the
window at the end of the corridor.

On the south side of the Piazza stands the Oratorio di San
Bernardino, which contains some frescoes by the later Sienese
painters. In a room at the top of a flight of stairs over an altar is
a Madonna by Sano di Pietro.

After returning to the Via de' Rossi one takes the first street to
the right, and following it comes to the Porta Ovile. Above the
gate hangs an ancient Crucifix, and to the left is a fine but spoiled
fresco by Sano di Pietro of the Madonna between SS. Bernardino
and Ansano. Without the gate is the charming Fonte Ovile.

Returning to the Via de' Rossi, and following it into the
second street on the left, the Via di San Pietro Ovile, one comes
at once to the church of that name. Within, over the door, is a
Crucifix by Giovanni di Paolo. To the right is a very fine and
exquisite copy of Simone Martini's great altarpiece of the Annunciation, now in the Uffizi. The authorship of this work has been
the subject of much controversy. Mr. Bernard Berenson, I believe,
ascribes it to an unknown master of the later trecento. Was it he
who painted the Birth of the Virgin at Asciano till lately thought
to be the work of Sassetta's? The pinnacles above are by
Matteo di Giovanni. The Madonna enthroned opposite is perhaps

the work of Pietro Lorenzetti, the two saints, Bernardino and John Baptist, at the sides being the work of Matteo di Giovanni.

One returns to the Via de' Rossi and follows it to the left. Almost at once a street leaves it on the right. Following it one comes to the Piazza di San Donato, before the church of that name, where there is a painting of Pacchia's, and in the chapel a Madonna and Child by Andrea Vanni.

Following once more Via de' Rossi, one soon reaches the Via Trieste. Out of it one turns to the right and proceeds past the Palazzo Spannocchi, the Palazzo Salimbeni, and the Palazzo Tantucci, which holds a fine fresco of the Madonna and Child by Benvenuto di Giovanni. A little farther beside two towers, once the Roman gate of ancient Siena, one turns to the left and comes to the church of Santa Maria delle Nevi, with a façade by Federighi. Within is a fine altarpiece by Matteo di Giovanni over the high altar, from which the church takes its title—the Madonna of the Snows. The *predella* tells the story of the foundation of Santa Maria Maggiore in Rome.

Returning to Via Cavour, one presently passes on the right the Palazzo Costantini, a work, it is thought, of Francesco di Giorgio. Farther and still on the right is the church of Sant' Andrea, with its broken altarpiece by Giovanni di Paolo. Just there the Via Cavour changes its name and becomes Via di Camollia. Half-way to the Porta Camollia on the left stands the church of San Barto-lommeo, with a spoilt fresco of our Lord, without. Within is the tomb of Pintoricchio and some few pictures, a repainted altarpiece by Sano di Pietro over a side altar, a triptych by some pupil of Bartolo di Fredi, a Madonna and Child with angels by an unknown painter, and in the sacristy a banner with figures of SS. Vincenzo and Anastasio, the ancient patrons of the church, by Fungai.

Little is to be gained by continuing along Via di Camollia to the gate, which is for the most part a building of the seventeenth century. On the way one passes at the head of a street on the left the fifteenth-century church of Fontegiusta, where are several late pictures and an exquisite Coronation of the Virgin by Fungai.

Returning down Via di Camollia from the church of San Bartolommeo, if one takes the first street on the right, the Via Gazzani, one comes to the little church of Santo Stefano, where there is a fine polyptych by Andrea Vanni. The *predella* is the work of Giovanni di Paolo.

From the church door there is a view across the Passaggio della Lizza, which is the Sienese Cascine, or Park. Beyond it stands the Fortezza of Grand Duke Cosimo. Striking across the base of the Lizza from the church of Santo Stefano, one enters the Viale Curtatone, which presently leads to the great church of the Dominicans, San Domenico, which occupies the same position on the west flank of Siena as San Francesco does on the east. A vast and sober building of the late fifteenth century, San Domenico, like San Francesco, occupies the site of a much earlier building, for the Dominicans settled in Siena in 1225.

Within, the church has lost much of the simplicity which San Francesco now has. Its great attraction among its numerous possessions is the frescoes by Sodoma in the chapel of S. Catherine, where in a marble reliquary the head of the saint is venerated. I have never been able to love these works. They seem to me to sensualize what was wholly spiritual, wholly lovely and simple in the life of the great saint. Even the most famous scene of all those represented here, the Swoon of S. Catherine, seems to me meretricious, admirable though it may be as a composition. How much I prefer those humbler pictures: the spoiled Sano on the second altar on the south, Giovanni di Paolo's panel of the Beata Caterina de' Lenzi close by, Francesco di Giorgio's picture of the Nativity, the Pietà by Matteo di Giovanni, and his S. Barbara between S. Mary Magdalen and S. Catherine of Alexandria in the second chapel north of the high altar, his broken altarpiece in the next chapel, and that of the Madonna enthroned by Benvenuto di Giovanni. But best of all that San Domenico holds is the surprising view of the Duomo and the world to be had from a little window at the back of the choir. It is a vision, and beside it the pretentious works of Sodoma pass into nothingness.

But with San Domenico one has entered upon that district of Siena which may be said to be S. Catherine's own. The greatest of all Tuscan saints and one of the greatest women of all time, after the Blessed Virgin she seems to me to be the liege lady of Siena. Like the city she dreamed, but unlike the city she realized her vision. She lost herself in God, she tended the sick and weary, she dominated the Church and led the exiled Pope by the hand back from Avignon. And close by the church of San Domenico—for she was a Dominican Tertiary—she has her chapel, the Cappella delle Volte, which in her day was actually a part of the church. Here she loved best to pray, and here she was granted many of her visions. Today over the high altar stands her portrait by Andrea Vanni—an authentic and contemporary portrait.

From San Domenico, from the apse of San Domenico one descends steeply by a rough way to Fontebranda, probably the most ancient of Siena's fountains—those fountains which first among so many other things still remind us of her ancient connection with Rome.

Before the fountain passes the Via Benincasa, the street of the dyers, and here S. Catherine had her home. The house, the oratories which have taken its place, stands half-way up the steep street on the left. The first chapel one enters, the Oratorio della Contrada dell' Oca contains many reminders of her, best of all Neroccio's wonderful statue, which beside Pacchia's realistic frescoes seems always more delightful. Above, by a flight of steps, one enters another chapel, covered with modern frescoes. Here was her cell, where she gave alms; today it holds many of her relics —her pillow, her lantern, her veil, her hair-shirt, a piece of her staff, and such. The third chapel, entered from a loggia, is the chapel of her Confraternity. Over the altar Fungai has painted her receiving the Stigmata, with how much finer an understanding than Sodoma has been able to show. Higher still, and on the other side of the court, is the fourth chapel of the Most Holy Crucifix, where there is a wonderful Crucifix by some disciple of Giunta Pisano.[1] It was before this Crucifix that S. Catherine is said to have received the Stigmata.

---

[1] This impressive Crucifix was once in the church of Santa Cristina in Pisa.

CHAPTER XIII

SAINT CATHERINE OF SIENA

"AT HER VOICE, NAY, ONLY LOOKING UPON HER, HEARTS WERE
CHANGED"

CATHERINE BENINCASA, Saint Catherine of Siena, was born
on 25 March—the Feast of the Annunciation—1347,
here in Fontebranda in her father's house in the Contrada
dell' Oca. She was the daughter of Giacomo di Benincasa, a dyer
of the middle class, well-to-do and pious, and of Lapa di Puccio di
Piagente, "a woman, utterly alien from the corruption of our
times" as Raimondo, the Saint's confessor and biographer, tells
us, "albeit she was exceedingly careful and busy over the affairs
of her household and family, as all those who know her are aware,
for she is still alive". Catherine was one of the younger children
in a very numerous family, and Lapa seems to have loved her
above the rest. Indeed, as a child she was the darling of her little
circle of friends and neighbours, who named her Euphrosyne, as
who should say Joy. We know little of her childhood, but we see
her a baby of five years kneeling to salute the Blessed Virgin "on
every step as she passed up and down the staircase of her father's
house".[1] It was at this age, too, that we are told, as she passed
down the precipitous Vallepiatta towards Fontebranda, hand in
hand with her elder brother, "she looked up and saw, over the
summit of San Domenico, Christ seated on an imperial throne clad
in purple robes and wearing the tiara, attended by S. Peter, S.
Paul, and the beloved disciple S. John. He smiled upon her and
blessed her, and the girl, absorbed in ecstasy, knew not where she
was or what she did."

This seems to have been the beginning and the cause of her
withdrawal from the ways of the world. She would fast and
discipline herself and dream of entering the Dominican Order
disguised as a boy. All this and more. She determined when she
was seven, she told her confessor later, to dedicate her maidenhood
to Christ.

[1] See E. G. Gardner, *S. Catherine of Siena* (Dent, 1907), p. 6. This is the best study
of the Saint. We have more than 400 of her letters and her wonderful "Dialogue"
that has often been translated. Gardner's book is fully documented.

Now above all her other sisters Catherine loved Buonaventura best; and it was she who, when the child was twelve years old and marriageable, at their mother's suggestion persuaded Catherine to give herself to life, to dye her hair, and to conform to the fashions of the world. But in 1362 Buonaventura died, and Catherine, perhaps taking this for a sign and certainly in bitter repentance, dedicated herself once more to God. Her family was angered and invoked the aid of a Dominican friar, Fra Tommaso della Fonte, a man of sincere piety and her confessor. He failed to move her, however, and since she was resolute, counselled her to pursue her way, to cut off her beautiful hair, and to wait upon the Will of God. Her family, however, was obdurate. Her room was taken from her, she was compelled to do all the hard work of the house, and no time was left her for prayer or devotion. But she found a silence of which none might deprive her, and where Time is not there is time for everything. "She made herself in her mind, by inspiration of the Holy Spirit, a secret cell that could not be taken from her, and this she never left." Moreover, "she firmly pictured to herself that her father represented our Lord and Saviour Jesus Christ, her mother the most Glorious Mother of God, and that her brothers and the rest figured the holy apostles and disciples, and because of this imagination she served them all with such great gladness and diligence that every one marvelled". She had dreams and visions too. S. Dominic appeared to her and offered her the habit of the Sisters of Penance and promised it to her.

Her father by now was convinced of her vocation, for one day as he passed through the house he came upon her praying in her brother's room, and over her head he saw a snow-white dove hovering. And presently he gave her leave to follow the Will of God.

Shortly afterwards she took the habit of the Sisters of Penance, the Mantellate, an Order really of widows. At first they refused it to her, but when she lay ill and asserted that God and S. Dominic would take her from the world unless she were received, they gave way and accepted her as a sister. She received the habit from a Dominican friar in the Cappella della Volta in San Domenico, probably in 1363.

From this time her life became of a terrible austerity. For three years, we are told, she spoke to none but God and her confessor. Her whole time was spent in religious exercises, in mortification, in discipline, and in contemplation. A demonic possession followed. The devil, in whom we are much too clever to believe, but who nevertheless in his quiet way is always getting the better of us, assailed her imagination with every sort of abomination and her heart with the basest temptations. There followed what I think is known to mystical theology as "the Night Obscure". An immense and frightful darkness and dryness descended upon her soul. She seemed to be on the brink of an unspeakable precipice and to be about to be cast down. Her arms were tireless in prayer, but no God answered. Her lips ceaselessly pronounced the invincible name of Jesus, but she seemed lost in the darkness and loneliness. Yet was she in perfect safety in the shadow of His wings.

> Scapulis suis obumbrabit tibi:
> et sub pennis ejus sperabis.

Then in this desert of the soul, in the emptiness that broke her heart, she cried out, "Where wert Thou, my divine Spouse, whilst I lay in such loneliness and fear?" And out of that vast silence a still small voice made answer, "I was with thee." "What!" she cried in horror, "amid those filthy abominations with which my soul was infested?" And again that voice answered, "Even so." And she fell down in anguish but cried out no more.

Then God, because He loved her, gave her His supreme last gift of patience, and when the devil, neglecting neither violence nor stratagem, solicited her pride, He covered her with the invincible buckler of His Love so that she escaped those fiery arrows and remained in quietness.

> Scuto circumdabit te veritas ejus;
> non timebis a timore nocturno.

She sought humility and ensued it. Coming out of herself, she ministered to the poor; they were His brethren. She served old Cecca, the leprous woman who was sent out of the city, who did nothing but curse her; and one afflicted with cancer she tended lovingly in ways unspeakable, though all she had in return was calumny. Most of all she strove with the turbulence, inconstancy, and hatred of her fellow-citizens, with too little effect, yet Pio II says there was not one who ever spake with her who went not away a better man.

It was probably in 1366 that Catherine began to go forth from her retreat. At this time, while she devoted herself to the poor and the sick, she was the victim of the jealousy and detraction of the sisters. A certain Suor Palmeria hated her, but she was converted; others succeeded in alienating some of the friars, and for a time she was deprived of the Blessed Sacrament.

The years which followed were full of evil for Tuscany, and indeed all Italy. In April 1367, Pope Urban V left Avignon for Rome, where he arrived in October, only to leave the Eternal City again for Avignon in September 1370. Siena was in a state bordering on anarchy. It was in the midst of this disquiet that Catherine's public life began. It opened with a number of conversions, and when, in 1374, pestilence laid waste the Sanese, Catherine served the sick, and thousands came only to hear her. The Pope himself commissioned two Dominicans to hear the confessions of those whose hearts she had changed.

In 1375 she went to Pisa. Florence was ready to rise with Perugia against the absent Pope. On their banners they emblazoned the terrible and impossible word "Libertas". And Catherine marked it, and, throwing off her dreams, descended to deliver her people from their own folly. By her words she prevented Siena and Arezzo from joining the Florentines. Her acts were of an incredible swiftness and wisdom. In a kind of despair the Florentines appealed to her. She agreed to come to them, and when she arrived the chief magistrates met her at the gates. In their behalf, in behalf of Italy she set out for Avignon, which she reached on 28 June, 1376. She, aged twenty-nine, a woman and yet the ambassador of Italy to the Pope, compelled him to arrange terms of peace and faced his Cardinals alone. But she was in no way daunted, she was incapable of fear.

> Quoniam angelis suis mandavit de te:
> ut custodiant te in omnibus viis tuis.

Moreover, she was successful, more than successful; she gained the mastery, and bent the Papacy to her will. "I put the affair entirely in your hands," the Pope told her; "only I recommend to you the honour of the Church." But she was to find that it was not peace that Florence desired, but surrender.

Her greatest triumph, the true miracle of her life, was achieved, however, on this mission. She persuaded the Pope to return to

Rome. Thus in her genius was found the highest fulfilment of the Dominican idea—a union of the mystical and practical life. "Be a brave man and not a coward," she dared to say to Gregory, but she had said it first to herself.

From Gregory in Rome she went to Florence to bring him peace, and after a terrible struggle she won it for him. Amid scenes of daily violence and murder, in which again and again she risked her life undaunted, even when swords were drawn against her, she conquered in 1378, and immediately returned to Siena to her cell. Against her will she had left that silence, and at the first opportunity she returned to it to lose herself in God.

And there our Lord discovered to her mysteries, let us admit it, far beyond our understanding. Her whole life became a continual miracle absorbed in a Divine contemplation. We hear of almost incredible fasts, of humiliations and calumnies unthinkable. She rejoiced. One day Christ offered her two crowns, of gold and of thorns, and bade her choose. And she answered, "I desire, O Lord, to live always conformed to Thy Passion, and to find pain and suffering my repose, my delight." Then, taking the crown of thorns, she pressed it down upon her white forehead.

To torture her last years there befell the Great Schism, when Urban VI was chosen in Rome and Clement VII at Anagni. Then she wrote those wonderful letters that none can read without tears. She wrote to the republics of her fatherland, to the princes of this world, to the great men of the Church, and to the Queen of Naples she dared to say "I will".

I pass over the ecstasies, the visions, the innumerable miracles God vouchsafed her. I pass by the reception of the Stigmata; these cannot well be spoken of in such a book as this. Of her writings, too, I say nothing. It remains but to record her death, which befell in 1380, on 29 April, when she was thirty-three years old.

> Clamabit ad me, et ego exaudiam eum:
> eripiam eum, et glorificabo eum:
> et ostendam illi salutare meum.

CHAPTER XIV

THE SIENESE SCHOOL OF PAINTING AND THE PICTURE GALLERY OF SIENA

THE fourteenth and fifteenth centuries in Siena, which witnessed the political decadence of the city, are chiefly remarkable in her story for her achievement in the fine arts; indeed, the only really great figure of those years is S. Catherine, perhaps the greatest personality she was ever able to produce.

Almost devoid of interest, then, as those two centuries prove to be from a political point of view, they are of very great importance by reason of the fine artistic achievement of which they were witnesses.

The end of the thirteenth century produced the Palazzo Pubblico and the Mangia Tower, and with the opening of the fourteenth we come upon the magnificent work of Lorenzo Maitani, to whom we owe the façade of the cathedral of Orvieto. The same century saw the building of the Baptistery of Siena and the choir of the Duomo, while the fifteenth century gave us the beautiful church of Santa Maria delle Nevi and the Palazzo dei Diavoli, the convent of the Osservanza, and many of Siena's most splendid palaces.

In sculpture, too, Siena produced during those years some masterly works, her achievement culminating in the work of Jacopo della Quercia, who is now but poorly represented in Siena by the beautiful debris of the Fonte Gaia in the Palazzo Pubblico and by the relief of the Expulsion of Zacharias from the Temple and certain figures on the great font in San Giovanni.

During the fifteenth century we have the work of Antonio Federighi, of Vecchietta, of Neroccio, of Giovanni di Stefano, of Francesco di Giorgio, and of Cozzarelli, all of whom combined the art of sculpture with that of painting or architecture. Vecchietta is a most remarkable sculptor, especially in bronze. His statue of the Risen Christ in Santa Maria della Scala is among the finest work of the sort of the Renaissance. His pupils Neroccio and Francesco di Giorgio, too, deserve more attention as sculptors than they have received. Federighi would seem to be less gifted.

But it is in painting that Siena's greatest achievement lies. This was the true art of Siena.

It is idle to discuss whether Florence or Siena were earlier in the production of painters. Cimabue, great as were his position and achievement, had very little to do with Florentine painting as we know it, and Guido of Siena, whose famous signed Madonna of 1221, or more probably 1281, is the earliest signed Sienese work we possess, has as little significance in the school of Siena.

The two great men who founded respectively the schools of Florence and Siena are Giotto and Duccio di Buoninsegna, and of them Duccio is the earlier, but they can in no sense be called rivals. Giotto's aim in his art was to endow painting with all the solidity and actuality of life, and this, through his genius, became the aim of the school of Florence. Duccio, on the other hand, was concerned with a subtler, a more spiritual, and a more purely aesthetic ideal. He found in painting an exquisite decorative splendour, which he set himself to develop, and by his genius compelled every Sienese artist who followed him, during some two hundred years, to pursue the same road. Florentine painting, with a few exquisite exceptions, is a representation of life; Sienese painting, with a few negligible exceptions, is an expression of it. It is thus we may, perhaps, define the difference between the two schools.

In every history of Sienese painting we hear much of the conservatism of the Sienese, and we are told that such conservatism is natural and proper to a mountain people. But the Sienese are not a people of the mountains, but of the lower hills on the verge of a desert; their political history shows almost every weakness but that of a confirmed conservatism. They are unstable, hasty, easily roused, quickly appeased, without persistence in anything. And, indeed, it is on the morrow of their forsaking the Ghibelline cause that their painters begin to be famous. It is true that Siena seems to us to have been more isolated than Florence, and in part we impute her fall to this. But it is doubtful whether, in fact, she were so isolated in the Middle Age. The Via Francigena, the great medieval highway of Italy, passed through the city. No such great artery of traffic and international movement passed through or even near Florence; the Vie Aretine, old and new, were of an infinitely less importance, and it is not till late that we find them in any sense international. The truth is that the development of

these two schools of painting had very little to do with conservatism or its opposite. The Sienese advanced and developed their
art as deliberately as the Florentines, but on different lines. What
we see, what we are far too ready to explain by such vague terms
as conservatism, is really a fundamental difference in the apprehension of life, an aesthetic difference too, in its representation as
in its expression. The Florentine expressed himself once for all in
Giotto. What we have here, then, is a difference in fundamentals,
not in development, and with fundamentals conservatism can have
nothing to do.

Duccio saw life and wished to express it in a different way from
Giotto. His intention was different; not necessarily less fine or
splendid or less beautiful. To the nineteenth-century critic Florentine painting seemed not only to be the direct ancestor of the art of
his own time, but, in fact, to profess the same principles he himself
thought he saw practised. Moreover, Sienese art was very im-
perfectly known. It had no Vasari, and the historians and men
of letters of Siena were out of all comparison feeble beside their
Florentine brethren. It is thus we have been led to consider
Florentine art as "true art", fruitful and "progressive", while in
the art of Siena we have been told there is nothing but reaction
and conservatism. Nor was this verdict wholly unreasonable. The
Florentine school founded on the Roman—on the study of nature,
that is, and first through the antique—was the true heir, if any
heir there was, of Roman antiquity; it was essentially western in
its derivation and in its ideals. Hence its success. But the Sienese
school, it may be more original than the Florentine, derived not
from that great western school which has always insisted upon the
importance of realism and of the nude, but from the Byzantines
whose ideal was very different, who denied realism any vast
importance, and expressed themselves in a wonderful symbolism,
an exquisite decoration. The laws which govern, the ideals which
inspire, Sienese art, are essentially different from those which
govern and inspire Florentine art. Let this be understood, and we
shall soon be reasonably convinced of what our eyes have assured
us from the first, that what the Florentine was trying to do was
very different from what the Sienese was attempting.

It might seem obvious to the most casual observer of Simone
Martini's Annunciation in the Uffizi that the man who painted
that masterpiece—and the hand of man can do no more—might

SAINT CATHERINE, Andrea Vanni.
San Domenico, Siena

THE ANNUNCIATION, Francesco di Giorgio. Pinacoteca, Siena

very easily, had he wished, have given us a realistic representation of it. Simone could see, at least as well as ourselves, that the sky is blue, and not gold, and that there are three dimensions in the world and not two alone. He disregarded such mere facts as unessential, and without concern for him. Why? Because, like every art that has ever existed in the world, his art, too, was a convention, and such facts as those were to a large extent outside his convention. He used gold where blue would have been in reality; he used two dimensions where three are found in life, in the same way as a poet uses metre and rhyme, neither of which has any place in actual human speech or the language of the world. He used them not for the sake of ornament or for anything less than that they were part of the essential language of his art and for the sake of beauty.

A vast and representative number of pictures of the Sienese school has been brought together in the Reale Pinacoteca in the beautiful Palazzo Buonsignori. It is the best collection anywhere to be found of the Sienese school of painting. To begin with, there is a number of altarpieces of the thirteenth century and in the Italo-Byzantine style, which are often of great beauty and illustrate the roots, as it were, of Sienese art; but the true founder of the Sienese school, which only in our own day has found any wide or general appreciation, is Duccio di Buoninsegna, who painted between the years 1278 and 1319. We know very little of him, but such of his work as remains to us might seem to prove that he must have had his training from some great Byzantine master, possibly but improbably in Constantinople itself.

The greatest work from his hand that is left to us is the wonderful Maestà in the Opera del Duomo, which was carried in triumph to its place over the high altar of the Duomo on 9 June, 1311. It was then that the Madonna delle Grazie, which had, as the Sienese believed, procured them the victory of Montaperto, was deposed and removed to a place of less honour, Duccio's splendid double altarpiece being enthroned in its stead, only to be itself deposed in the sixteenth century when the present high altar was built.

Other works by the master are to be found in Siena: in the Gallery an early work, an exquisite small panel of the Madonna enthroned with three Franciscan friars kneeling at her feet (20); a panel of SS. Peter and John Baptist (22); fragments from some altarpiece; a Madonna with four saints (28), of which the Madonna and Child alone are from Duccio's own hand, the rest being the work of an assistant; a polyptych of Saints, Patriarchs, Prophets and Angels (47).

The closest and most devout of Duccio's followers, so far as we know them by name, were Segna and Ugolino. By the first there remain in Siena a Madonna with SS. Paul, John Evangelist, and Bernard (40), a signed work in the Gallery; while in the reception-room of the Seminario of San Francesco is a Virgin and Child. The Gallery possesses a small Crucifixion (34) and a polyptych of the Madonna, Child and saints (39) by Ugolino.

The greatest of Duccio's pupils, the most exquisite, too, and the most in love with life, was Simone Martini (1285 (?)-1344). Nothing by him is to be seen in the Gallery, but his splendid though damaged frescoes of the Madonna and Child with saints and the equestrian portrait of Guidoriccio da Fogliano in the Palazzo Pubblico, painted respectively in 1315-21 and in 1328, with the fine triptych, the Legend of Beato Agostino Novello, a later work, in Sant' Agostino, happily survive.

Duccio's pupil, Pietro Lorenzetti (1305-48), and his younger brother, Ambrogio Lorenzetti (1319-48), are the first Sienese painters who were touched by outside influences, those of Giovanni Pisano and Giotto. By the elder, Pietro, much remains in Siena. In the Gallery are a reconstructed tryptych of the Baptist, S. Cecilia and S. Bartholomew (79, 81, 82), four scenes of a Carmelite *predella* (83, 84), an Allegory (92), and two beautiful panels—S. Agnes and S. Catherine (578, 579). In the Opera del Duomo is an important alterpiece of the Birth of the Virgin (63), painted in 1342. In San Francesco, in the first chapel on the left of the choir, is a fine fresco of the Crucifixion. In the Servi is a fresco of the Massacre of the Innocents. Other frescoes in a chapel on the left of the choir—Salome dancing, the Ascension of S. John, and certain saints, are perhaps from his *bottega*.

Nor has Ambrogio left us less. In the Gallery are eight works or fragments from his hand: a small Madonna and saints (65), a triptych of the Madonna and saints (77), and an Annunciation (88), painted in 1344; a Deposition (77a), a reconstructed triptych (77e), a Madonna and Child (605), and two landscapes (70, 71). In the Opera del Duomo we find four fragments: panels of S. Francis (69), S. Mary Magdalen (71), S. Catherine (72), and S.

Benedict (73). In the Palazzo Pubblico, in the Sala della Pace, we find his famous but obscure frescoes of Good and Bad Government, painted in 1338–40, and in the Loggia a damaged fresco of the Madonna. In San Francesco, in a chapel in the convent, is a fine panel of the Madonna and Child, painted in 1340. In Sant' Agostino there are the heads of some saints in fresco to the right of the great doors, and in the Piccolomini Chapel a recently re-discovered and very beautiful fresco of the Madonna, Child and saints. A fine Madonna was formerly in the Monistero di Sant' Eugenio, but it has gone to America.

The Lorenzetti may be said to mark the highest achievement of the school of Siena. Barna has apparently left nothing in Siena, but Lippo Memmi (c. 1375), the brother-in-law of Simone, and a very charming artist, has left three works in that city—a panel of the Madonna in the right transept of the Servi, over the altar of the Madonna del Popolo; a fresco in the cloister of San Domenico of the Madonna and Child with S. Paul and an angel; and a Madonna and Child (595) in the Sienese Gallery.

There follow Bartolo di Fredi (1330–1410) and Andrea Vanni (1332–1414). Bartolo di Fredi, a follower of Lippo Memmi and the Lorenzetti, was considerably influenced by Barna. His works in Siena are very numerous, there being more than twelve in the Gallery alone, beside works in the Spedale and elsewhere. In the Gallery we find various saints on two *pilastri* (97, 102), two *predelle* (98, 99), four Scenes from the Life of the Blessed Virgin (100), the Assumption of the Virgin (101)—these six being various parts of a work completed in 1388—another *predella* with five panels (103), an Adoration of the Magi (104), and a panel of SS. Antonio and Onofrio (106).

Andrea Vanni, too, was perhaps the pupil of Lippo Memmi; at any rate he was the partner of Bartolo di Fredi, and he came under the same influences. His work, unlike his friend's, is not very plentiful in Siena. The Gallery possesses only one piece from his hand—a tabernacle with the Crucifixion and various saints (114).

He is followed by Taddeo di Bartoli (1362–1422), who developed under the influence of Bartolo di Fredi. The Gallery possesses some eleven of his pieces, and his work is plentiful elsewhere in Siena. His works in the Gallery include a Crucifix (55), the Adoration of the Magi (127), a small triptych of the Madonna and Child with saints (128), panels of S. Peter Martyr (129) and

S. Agnes (130), an Annunciation (131), painted in 1409, a Nativity (132), a triptych with the Nativity in the midst, between S. James and S. Domenico on the one side and S. Caterina delle Ruote and S. Maria Maddalena on the other, while above is the Resurrection of Our Lord, with the Annunciation in the pinnacles. The remaining three pieces seem to be fragments. They consist of the Martyrdom of SS. Cosma and Damian (134), a S. Matthew (135), and S. Francis receiving the Stigmata (162).

One of the most poetic and charming painters of the fifteenth century in Siena was Stefano di Giovanni, called Sassetta (1392–1450), who was probably the pupil of Paolo di Giovanni Fei (1372–1410). Very little of Sassetta's work remains in Siena, but a few small pictures and fragments have been gathered into the Gallery—a S. Antony Abbot (166), a Last Supper (167), two panels each with four saints (168, 169), a small triptych of Madonna, saints, and angels (177), and a Madonna (325); they give but a small idea of his loveliness. His master, Paolo di Giovanni Fei, however, is fairly well represented, not less than six of his works being found in the Gallery, namely, a Birth of the Virgin (116), a panel with S. Jacopo, S. Giovanni Battista, and a warrior saint (126), a triptych of the Madonna enthroned with our Lord, whom S. Catherine weds, two angels, S. Lucy, S. James, and S. Bartholomew; on the right panel S. Francis and S. John Baptist, on the left S. Anthony and S. John Evangelist (137). Besides these works there remain a diptych of the Madonna and saints (146), and a polyptych of the Madonna and saints (300). Fei was unrivalled in his day as a painter of small panels. Almost all of his smaller works are, in fact, wonderfully delicate in workmanship and of surprising decorative effect. In his large paintings he was not always so successful.

His contemporary, Luca di Tommè, is represented in the Gallery by a large and beautifully preserved polyptych of the Virgin, Child, angels and saints—an early work in collaboration with Niccolò di Ser Sozzo Tagliacci, and an altarpiece of S. Anne with the Blessed Virgin and Child, S. Catherine and the Baptist, S. Anthony and S. Agnes (109), which comes from San Quirico d' Orcia, a polyptych of the Madonna, Child and saints, a triptych (594), a triptych (580) of the Marriage of S. Catherine, and four pinnacle-pieces with half-figures of saints (123, 124, 138, 139).

The fifteenth century, in which the most charming figure in

Sienese art is Sassetta, opens really with Domenico di Bartolo, who was made free of the Guild of Siena in 1428, between which date and 1444 we find him active. He is of the school of Taddeo di Bartolo, but has tried to assimilate some influence from Florence: in this he was not very successful, and his rare work is often disappointing. One picture from his hand, signed and dated 1433, hangs in the Gallery of Siena—a Madonna and Child surrounded by angels (164). Another—a truly beautiful work—is in the church of San Raimondo.

As for Giovanni di Paolo (1403–82), a pupil of Fei, but strongly influenced by Sassetta, he is one of the most markedly original and individualistic of all Siena's painters. More than twenty of his works are here. His contemporary, Sano di Pietro (1406–81), the pupil of Sassetta, is one of the most prolific painters of the school, a delicate and sumptuous master, whose works fill the fourth and fifth rooms of the Gallery and run over into the sixth, fifty pictures in all finding a place there.

His fellow-pupil, Vecchietta (1412–80), is represented by four pieces in the Siena Gallery—the doors of a shrine (204), painted in 1445, a panel of S. Bernardino (205), a Madonna and four saints (210), painted in 1465, and a S. Laurence (577). Gifted painter though he be, he does not charm us as his master can do; nor has he, I think, the brilliance and versatility of his pupil, Francesco di Giorgio (1439–1502), who, like himself, was architect, sculptor, painter, and engineer, and who was influenced by the Pollaiuoli of Florence. His works, rare elsewhere, are plentiful in Siena, ten pieces from his hand hanging in the Gallery, namely, Joseph and Potiphar's Wife (274), Susanna and the Elders (275), Joseph sold by his Brethren (276), an Annunciation (277), a Madonna and Child with an angel (288), a Madonna and Child with S. Peter and S. Paul (291), a Madonna and Child with two saints (292), a fragment of an Annunciation (306), a Nativity (437), painted in 1475, and a Coronation of the Virgin (440), painted four years earlier.

Another and even more subtle and charming pupil of Vecchietta was Neroccio di Landi (1447–1500), the most gracious product of the Sienese school of the fifteenth century. The five master works which hang in the Gallery are, perhaps, the loveliest things there. In his masterpiece, the Madonna and Child with S. Jerome and S. Bernardino (281), the S. Bernardino is like a fifteenth-century bust in terra-cotta. His other works here are only less lovely—the Madonna with S. Catherine and S. Bernardino (285), the triptych of 1476 (282), the Madonna with six saints of 1492 (278), and the Madonna with four saints (287).

One of the best and most widely-gifted of Sienese painters, Matteo di Giovanni (1435–95), frequently seems on the point of emerging into the more living art of Florence. Seven of his pictures are preserved in the Sienese Gallery, but not one of them can compare with his masterpiece, the Assumption of the National Gallery. His follower and imitator, Cozzarelli (1450–1516), is not to be named with his master, though his work is by no means without delight. Seven works from his hand hang in the Gallery.

Another less-known painter, but often a very charming one, though his later work is apt to become unduly austere, Benvenuto di Giovanni (1436–1518), is represented in the Gallery by two works—the Ascension of 1491 and an earlier painting, a triptych with *predella* (435, 436) of 1475. One of Benvenuto's most beautiful works—a large polyptych of the Madonna, Child and saints—used to be one of the chief ornaments of the Gallery, but it has recently been returned to the town of Montepertuso, its original home.

His son and pupil, Girolamo di Benvenuto (1470–1524), one of the last painters of the true Sienese school, is a lesser master well represented in the Gallery by nine works—the Nativity (342), the Deposition (369), a panel of four saints (370), the Birth of the Virgin (372), the Dead Christ with two angels (373), two pictures of the Madonna and Child (380, 395), an Assumption (383), and the Madonna with saints and angels (414) of 1508.

With Girolamo di Benvenuto and with Giacomo Pacchiarotto, by whom the Gallery possesses a very pleasing Visitation (426), we come into the sixteenth century, to the work of Pacchia, of Sodoma and of Beccafumi. But this is not Sienese work at all. It is a careful and too informed eclectic art, the imitation of what other men of other schools have been content to do with the realistic tradition.

CHAPTER XV

TO THE OSSERVANZA, IL MONISTERO, BELCARO, LECCETO AND THREE VILLAS

S EEING that the country, a perfect and delicious garden, begins at every gate, it is not long before even the most hurried traveller finds himself compelled to venture forth on foot or by car, if only for an afternoon, to explore those winding and lovely ways that lead him through the olive gardens and vineyards in and out of the valleys that gird Siena round about. And these valleys, these hills, hold treasures not less splendid, though much less numerous, than the great *contado* of Florence, which is so rich in little towns and villages and country churches full of the simple pictures and shrines of four hundred years ago. There are four expeditions that every one will undertake from Siena, if, indeed, he be anything more than the merest tourist, and even the tourist can scarce omit them. I mean a visit to the Osservanza, and that is the briefest; to the monastery of Sant' Eugenio, to the Abbey of Lecceto, and to the villa of Belcaro.

And first as to the Osservanza. This Franciscan church was destroyed in 1944. Direct hits by bombs caused the complete collapse of the roofs of nave and aisles, chapels and sacristy. The cupola, too, was almost entirely destroyed. All is now being rebuilt. Most of the works of art had been removed to safety before the attack, but the terra-cotta relief of the Coronation of the Virgin and the terra-cotta group of the Deposition by Cozzarelli were heavily damaged, if not in fragments. I will describe the church and its works of art as they were before the war, for all should be in order again very soon.

That is a good way to reach the Osservanza which takes one on foot out of Porta Ovile, turning left where the road reaches the railway, passing the line, and then following a steep and rough path to the convent. By this way one may go in half an hour; to drive by the carriage road is quicker, but many of the views of the city will be lost.

The convent stands on the hill called Capriola, across the deep valley through which the railway runs southward from Siena, and commands some marvellous vistas. S. Bernardino was the founder who here restored the strict Observance of the Rule of S. Francis, which during the centuries many papal dispensations had considerably relaxed.

S. Bernardino of Siena, the S. Francis, as we might almost call him, of the fifteenth century, was born at Massa Marittima in the Sanese in 1380, of the noble family of Albizzeschi. When he was but three years old he lost his mother, and before he was seven he was orphaned, for his father, the chief magistrate of Massa, was carried off by the plague. He was brought up then by his aunt Diana, who loved him, we are told, as her own son, and educated him piously, so that he was modest, humble, and devout, and even as a child took delight in visiting churches, serving at Mass, and, above all, in hearing sermons, in the art of preaching, of which he was to become so great a master.

Beside the love of eloquence which we find so early in him there was also a great compassion for the poor, which, not less than his preaching, was to mark him out from his fellows. One day, we read, when he was still but a child, seeing his aunt send away a poor person from their door without an alms, for, indeed, there was but one loaf in the house, he exclaimed, "For God's sake let us give something to this poor man; otherwise I will not dine nor sup this day." This, and other things, his aunt kept in her heart, encouraging him in pious customs, such as fasting every Saturday in honour of the Blessed Virgin. Then, at eleven years of age, he left Massa to join his uncles in Siena, who put him to school there, and so modest was he withal, so pure of heart and conversation, that the most impudent were kept in awe by his presence, and when the conversation grew too free, if he passed by, the very loosest would say, "Hush, hither comes Bernardino!" And this was no more an effeminacy in him than in Cato, who in ancient Rome by his mere presence restrained the lewdness of a festival. Yet Bernardino did not altogether escape the touch of the brutality of his day, though he shamed that man who would have injured him. For, indeed, he was comely and beautiful, but his virtue secured him from more assaults, and he grew up to scourge the vileness of his time.

Now when he had completed the course of philosophy, and had applied himself to the study of civil and canon law, at the age of seventeen he enrolled himself in the Confraternity of Our Lady in the Spedale della Scala, and there served the sick for four years till in 1400 the plague once more descended upon Italy, so that in Siena twenty persons died every day in the Spedale, and almost all the priests, apothecaries, and servants belonging to the place were carried off. In this predicament Bernardino gathered about him twelve young men to aid him in the service of the Spedale, and for four months he kept the place in order. Then, the pestilence being over, he returned home sick at last of a fever brought on by his fatigues, which kept him abed for some months. He was scarcely recovered when he returned to the same works of charity, nursing with incredible patience during more than a year an aunt of his called Bartolommea, who was blind and bedridden. When she died, he retired to a retreat he had found on the hill of Capraja, or Capriola, where lately stood his Convent of the Observance. Here he lived in solitude, till he took the habit of S. Francis, among the fathers of the strict Observance, who had a convent on the hill of Colombaja not far away. After a year of novitiate, he made his profession on the day of the Nativity of the Blessed Virgin, and his own birthday, it seems, in 1404. There he dwelt, always striving to make the Rule more strict, pleased with insults and humiliations. When he went abroad it was in a threadbare short habit, to be pelted with stones by the young rascals of Siena, and greeted everywhere with contempt. His relations (he was of noble family) naturally objected to his utter disregard of their position in the city; they abused and reproached him; but he heard Christ whisper, "If thou lovest Me, follow Me." And now, having prepared himself for preaching, he was ordered to practise it. For long he suffered an impediment in his speech, but the Madonna took it from him, and for fourteen years he laboured in Siena, and her *contado*, and became there a light and a beacon to the whole Church.

Of his labours throughout Italy this is not the place to speak. For him, at least, the truth was so clear and so full of all delight that his continual wonder was that men would not hold to it. "O ye sons of men, how long will ye be dull of heart?" It is the burden of all his sermons.

His day was an evil day, a day of indescribable vices which he combated lucidly and freely with all his strength. He would have had men love our Lord altogether. To this end he caused the

Perugian, whose business it was to make cards for gambling, to make instead little boards on which the sacred name of Jesus was curiously inscribed in gold letters for a remembrance of His love for man. Nor was he without offence. Pope Martin V imposed silence upon him, and he acquiesced, but when the Pope had heard the truth he dismissed him with his blessing, and pressed upon him the Bishopric of Siena in 1427. This he declined, no less resolutely than that of Ferrara, offered to him by Eugenius IV in 1431, and that of Urbino in 1435.

In Milan he rebuked the Visconti, and when the threat of death did not silence him, the Duke sought to bribe him, but he gave the money to those who for debt were in prison. This contempt for money appealed to Visconti. He could not imagine it. And ever after he venerated Bernardino as a saint. Bernardino's travels covered all Italy; he pacified Perugia and Ancona. In 1433 he went with the Emperor Sigismund to Rome, and then returned to Siena, where he founded this Convent of the Observance, and finished the other work he had begun, and in 1438 he was appointed Vicar-General of the Order of the Strict Observance in Italy. As General he laboured for five years, when in his age he began to preach through all Italy. In 1444 he was once more in Siena, and then, setting out for the Abruzzi, he was taken ill with fever on the road, and died at Aquila on 20 May, 1444, in the sixty-fourth year of his age.

It is to this true son of S. Francis that we owe the Osservanza of Siena. The buildings he left were but a small part of those lately destroyed, it is true. But the enlargements of Pandolfo Petrucci at the close of the fifteenth century were made in his honour, and the restorations at the end of the seventeenth century were in some sort a tribute to him, as was and will be the big new church of a single nave with a large choir, without aisles or transepts. On either side all up the nave were chapels, and over their altars pictures of great beauty. In the first chapel on the north was a picture of the Madonna and Child with angels by Sano di Pietro, partly repainted. Over the altar of the second chapel was an exquisite terra-cotta by Andrea della Robbia of the Coronation of the Virgin. Over the altar of the third chapel was another picture by Sano di Pietro—the Madonna and Child with S. James and S. Bernardino. Its *predella* was placed under a polyptych by Taddeo di Bartolo in the next chapel.

On either side the high altar were the Madonna and the Angel of Annunciation in glazed terra-cotta by Giovanni della Robbia. The altar itself contained relics of S. Bernardino in a fifteenth-century casket. In the choir on either side the window were a picture of S. Catherine with a donor, by Girolamo di Benvenuto, and a picture of S. Bernardino, signed and dated 1439, by Pietro di Giovanni.

The chapels on the south side of the nave were not less rich than those on the north. In that nearest the high altar was a splendid altarpiece of the Madonna and Child with S. Ambrose and S. Jerome, with above an Annunciation, by Sassetta. This was the great treasure of the church, and the finest work perhaps by Sassetta in Italy. In the next chapel was a Crucifixion ascribed to Sodoma, but certainly not from his hand. The last chapel contained a S. Anthony of Padua by Cozzarelli. A Pietà by the same artist was in the sacristy, where, too, was to be seen the tombstone of the magnificent Pandolfo Petrucci. In the crypt was the cell of S. Bernardino.

The beauty of the country in which the Osservanza stands, the splendour of the views thence, for one does not only look upon Siena, but on the perfect shape of Mont' Amiata southward and northward to Monte Morello, invite one to linger in the country, and so it was by many a byway and olive garden that I came to Il Monistero. The less haphazard traveller, however, will do well to return from the Osservanza to the city, and to leave it again by the Porta San Marco; the Monistero lies a little farther from that gate than the Osservanza from Porta Ovile. And, indeed, it is but few who will care to visit these two shrines in one day; they are best seen and enjoyed if an afternoon be devoted to each.

The way out of Porta San Marco lies as nearly south as may be, and the road winds down picturesquely from the city, giving you your first real idea, perhaps, of its remoteness and height. The views all the way are fine. At the gate Il Monistero comes in sight, and beyond and beyond, Mont' Amiata and Cetona, and between them the bizarre stronghold of Radicofani.

In the eighth century, when the first quarrel arose between Siena and Arezzo about the jurisdiction of a convent, Siena was administered by a certain Warnefred, and it was he who founded the Abbey of Sant' Eugenio, known today, when it is no longer in the hands of religious, but a country house, as Il Monistero. It is thus possibly the most ancient abbey in all the Granducato. One climbs from the valley to reach it on its hill over the road to Grosseto, which it dominates. The situation is very splendid, and one is not surprised to learn that it was here in 1270 the Count Guy de Montfort encamped with the army of the Guelf League only ten years after Montaperto. Guy was Vicar of King Charles of Anjou, and was intent on spoiling Siena and the *contado*. Nearly three hundred years later—in 1553—Pietro Strozzi erected fortifications here on the eve of Siena's fall. The abbey always belonged to the Benedictines, who in 1446 received here, by order of Pope Eugenius IV, the monks of Badia a Isola. The great abbey was suppressed in the eighteenth century, in much the same way as its sister house on Mont' Amiata.

Today all we see is a fine Baroque church, a few cloisters and buildings, and a magnificent villa. The church has still some treasures left, though they are fast slipping away. On either side of the nave, by the high altar, are frescoes of the Resurrection and the Crucifixion by Benvenuto di Giovanni. In the chapel, on the north side, was a picture of the Madonna and Child with angels by Francesco di Giorgio, but this is now in America as unfortunately is another picture which used to make a visit here so interesting. In the chapel on the left side there is nothing now, but till lately there hung here a fine Madonna by Ambrogio Lorenzetti. On either side the high altar was SS. Peter and Paul by Vanni; while by the west door is a dead Christ watched by two angels by Fungai.

In the church of San Bartolommeo near by there was a picture of the Madonna and Child by Giovanni di Paolo which somewhat made up for the missing pictures.

From the gardens of Il Monistero one may see many fine things —the city of Siena and Mont' Amiata—but among those near by none finer than the tufted and lofty villa of Belcaro, dark with ilex. But to reach Belcaro from Siena one must leave the city by the Porta Fontebranda, whence it is a walk or a drive of some three miles. It is certainly not farther from Il Monistero, and the way is not less beautiful.

Belcaro is one of the most splendid of those fortified villas of the fourteenth century which remain to us. The Salimbeni held it in

1384, then the Marescotti; in 1482 it was ordered to be dismantled. Since then it has passed through many hands: the Bellanti have held it, and the Turamini, who reduced it to a pleasure-house, building a chapel, which was painted in 1535 by Peruzzi. Fortified again in 1554 for the great siege, it was taken by the Spaniards in the same year, but not without exacting toll.

From the beautiful rampart over the age-old ilexes there is today one of the most splendid views of the country about Siena, with the city herself in the distance. In a small room at the end of this noble pacing is a picture of the Madonna with two saints by Cozzarelli, with two trecento panels by different hands. The frescoes of Peruzzi in the chapel, I fear, have been spoilt, but in a chamber on the ground floor of the fortification is a ceiling frescoed by his hand with the Judgment of Paris.

Away to the north of Belcaro, some three miles to walk or drive, stands the Abbey of Lecceto, occupied in summer by the students of the Seminario of Siena. The forest of ilex which surrounded it, and from which it had its name (*lecci*), has for the most part been cut down, and, save in summer, the place is almost deserted, a *contadino* and his family being its only inhabitants for three parts of the year.

But that forest was of very ancient planting and of great fame. There, it is said, the converts of S. Ansano took refuge, and in 388 S. Augustine, so it is said, visited it by reason of its quietness and the holy life of its hermits: while S. Monica, S. Jerome, S. Dominic, and S. Francis, we are told, enjoyed its hospitality.

The place was well known, too, for its miracles; in the beginning a holy hermit, by merely touching the ground with a reed, had caused miraculous waters to spring forth and transform a desert into a fair garden, whose flowers had wonderful medicinal qualities; while here, too, were found the precious stones of Calvary, like diamonds and rubies, glistening white and rosy red, the tears and the blood of our Redeemer. Indeed, the whole place was full of mystery. The woods which surrounded it, the legends, some of them gay and delicious stories almost worthy of the *Fioretti*, caused it to be considered everywhere as a reverend and holy place.

The most human, and perhaps the most characteristic, of its

sons has in his *Assempri* left us many records of the place. Fra Filippo, who is William Heywood's hero in his fascinating and too little known work, *The Ensamples of Fra Filippo*, tells of many of these miracles, and among them I choose, for its own sake, the following:[1]

"In that place," says Fra Filippo, "abode very holy and virtuous friars, who were exceeding strict and fervent in the observance of the rule [the place had long been in the hands of the Augustinian Friars] and of the ceremonies. Now the Prior of the said Convent was a very holy man and venerable friar, by name Bandino dei Balzetti of Siena. And it came to pass upon a certain day at noon, the same being the time of silence when the friars were in their cells, that the blessed Fra Bandino looked, and lo! a thief had stolen the ass of the place and was leading it away. But rather than break silence himself or cause the friars to break it, he suffered the thief to lead away that ass. Nevertheless he betook himself to the church and kneeled down before the picture of the Saviour which was above the altar, and he besought God for that thief that He would turn him to repentance and would save his soul. Now the thief had departed with the ass and had well-nigh gone forth from the wood. But when he came to the place where he should have gone out, the ass stood still, as it had been a rock embedded in the ground; neither for all that he could do would the ass pass out of the wood. Whereupon the thief, fearing to be overtaken, was minded to depart thence and to leave the ass. But in like manner, when he sought to go forth from the wood, the ass became, as it were, a wall before him, and on no wise could he go forth. Then, seeing himself in such straits, he was pricked to the heart, and he vowed a vow unto God and unto the Virgin Mary that if he were permitted to go thence he would return to that Convent and would restore the ass, and from thenceforth would amend and correct his life. And when he had so vowed, the ass turned back of its own accord, and anon he found himself free to move. And he returned with the ass and asked for the Prior of the place, to wit, the blessed Fra Bandino, who was prior. And to him he delivered the ass and confessed his fault with many tears and besought pardon, and he told him of the miracle which had happened. Then the blessed Fra Bandino forgave him and caused large alms to be given to him. And with much love and charity

[1] Cf. *The Ensamples of Fra Filippo*, by W. Heywood (Siena, 1901).

he entreated him to sin no more, but to amend his life. And when he had promised so to do he sent him away in peace."

That is but one of many such wonders; indeed, so vastly numerous became the miracles, that about 1336 the prior, in his robes, "betook himself to the place where their dead had been buried, and in the name of holy obedience charged the blessed dead to abstain from obtaining further miracles from God . . . for by reason of the vast concourse of people who besieged the convent the pious meditations of the friars were in no small degree disturbed".

By that time the place had become an embodiment of medieval legend. It was deserted in the fifteenth century for fear of the Companies of Adventure, and was at last suppressed in 1810, when it was given to the Seminario Vescovile of Siena as a summer residence.

What the life of the friars was may be seen in one of the cloisters, where a series of frescoes sets forth in contrast the life of the convent and the life of the world. They are traditionally ascribed to Paolo di Maestro Neri. In another cloister are restored frescoes of considerable merit of the fifteenth century, in which are depicted scenes of the life of S. Augustine and again of the friars. Over the church door is another fresco, a Christ, said to be by Paolo di Maestro Neri, and some remnants of work, possibly by him, remain in the church itself, which now contains scarcely anything of interest but a tomb of some knight of the Saracini family.

San Leonardo al Lago, a hermitage of the convent, suppressed in 1781, lies in the plain some few miles beyond. The church there alone remains as in old time; its splendid frescoes in the choir of the Life of the Virgin are by some follower of the Lorenzetti.

The real charm, however, of Lecceto does not lie in the works of art that by chance rather than by design remain to it. One finds it rather in the beauty and tranquillity of the place itself. I like to return to Siena by way of the Villa Santa Columba where in the neighbouring church are some interesting frescoes ascribed to Niccolò di Segna.

Some seven or eight miles south of Lecceto above the main road from Siena to Chiusdino there is Sovicille which has been fought over by Sienese and Florentines from the thirteenth to the sixteenth century. Close by at Ancariano there is a parish church, which dates from the seventh century, and there at Cetinale is one of the most delightful villas in all the Sanese. It was built by Carlo Fontana for Cardinal Fabio Chigi in 1680 and is worthy of the architect of San Marcello in Rome. The villa is not large but exquisite. A great clipped ilex stands before the statued gate and within is a long *tapis vert* which ascends between an avenue of clipped ilexes to a statue on the crest of the hill. It is on this the villa looks across its courtyard. A double flight of steps leads up to the *piano nobile* of the house. But the most splendid thing here is the park called La Tebaide, to which a long grass path, wide as the house, between high walls, leads to another statued gateway with ivy-clad niches and obelisks and balls. Thence one passes into great *boschi* of ilexes, and thence by a rude flight of steps to Fontana's Romitorio on the highest point hereabout, to be rewarded by a wide and magnificent panorama all over the Sienese *contado*.

The Chigi had another villa at Vicobello to be reached out of Porta Ovile which was perhaps built for them by Peruzzi and is certainly earlier and in its own way not less charming than Cetinale. It stands on a ridge, is approached by a noble gate in a semi-circular wall, which encloses a series of ilex-clothed terraces. The villa is an oblong Renaissance building with lemon house and *bosco*, a fine well in the courtyard and walled terrace gardens.

Not far from this exquisite villa of the Chigi is La Palazzina of the Gori family. This is a small house of the seventeenth century with chapel and outbuildings and well in the courtyard. The charming voluted garden façade of the house, approached by vast tunnels of clipped cypress, enchants one. Another such tunnel of clipped ilex leads to an open-air theatre, a unique feature of this lovely house.

CHARITY, Jacopo della Quercia. Palazzo Pubblico, Siena

THE RISEN CHRIST, Vecchietta. Ospedale, Siena

CHAPTER XVI

BUONCONVENTO AND MONTE OLIVETO

SOME twenty miles to the south of Siena on the Via Francigena, the highway to Rome, lies the little city of Buonconvento and the neighbouring monastery of Monte Oliveto, famous for its frescoes by Signorelli and by Sodoma. Today, by motor-car, I suppose it is easy to visit both these places in a day and return to Siena at evening. I am a more leisurely traveller and like to linger by the way.

I left Siena by Porta Romana (where Sano's ruined fresco still remains and where Sassetta caught his death from cold while painting what Sano finished), past the beautiful thirteenth-century façade of Santa Maria in Betlem where within—I said I was a leisurely traveller—is an altarpiece of the Virgin and Child somewhat repainted of the school of Guido da Siena.

But it is the wonderful view, where Mont' Amiata fills the horizon, that took all my attention, as far at any rate as Colle Malamerenda, where one enters that strange wilderness of barren clay hills which forms the landscape of so many of Giovanni di Paolo's pictures. There one twice crosses the Arbia and Montaperto fills the mind:

> Lo strazio, e 'l grande scempio
> che fece l'Arbia colorata in rosso.

Buonconvento is the capital of all this region and, in old days before the railway, was the first post out of Siena on the road to Rome.

This small but interesting walled town was the witness of the great tragedy that marked the end of the Middle Age, that brought Dante to his knees, and in reality finally disposed of the Imperial power in Italy—the death of Henry VII, Dante's Emperor.

That barbarian, of whose nobility we hear so much and see so little, descended into Italy in 1310, dreaming of the feudal union of Germany and Italy. Nor was he alone in his dream. Every disappointed ambition in Italy, noble and ignoble, greeted him with feverish enthusiasm. Bitter with loneliness, imprisoned in the adamant of his personality, Dante, amid the rocks of the Casentino, hurled his curses at Florence, who, with her allies, refused to receive him or, in fact, to call him anything but "Enemy" and "German King". Hailing Henry as "the Lamb of God who taketh away the sins of the world", Dante urged him to attack Florence, and in language at once blasphemous and runagate bade him destroy his native city. Henry, who seems to have been less intelligent than Dante had hoped, preferred to enter Rome, where he easily won the Capitol, but was fiercely opposed by King Robert of Naples, the head of the Guelf cause, when he tried to reach S. Peter's to win the Imperial crown. The Roman people, then certainly a mere rabble, took his part, however, and by threats and violence insisted on his coronation in the Lateran on 29 June, 1312.

Then the Emperor followed Dante's advice, and proceeded to lay siege to Florence. In this he was completely unsuccessful, and after six weeks, in which he never dared to make an attack, he raised the siege and set out for Poggibonsi, his health already ruined by anxiety and hardship, and his army, as was always the case both before and since, broken and spoiled by the Italian summer. He spent the winter and spring between Poggibonsi and Pisa, then, with some idea of retrieving all by invading Naples, he set off southward in August. On the 24th of the month, the day of S. Batholomew, he was in Buonconvento, and there on that day he died worn out, or poisoned, as some say, in the Communion.

What that invasion which Dante hailed with so much enthusiasm meant to Italy, we may gather from an old chronicle in the Communal Library of Siena.[1]

"The said Emperor Henry of Luxembourg moved his camp from Pancole with all his host Thursday, the sixteenth day of August, and came burning. And he pitched his camp at Stigliano and at Orgia Thursday, the sixteenth day of August.

"The Emperor Henry of Luxembourg moved his camp from Stigliano and from Orgia Wednesday, the twenty-second day of August, and went burning and pitched his camp the said day at the Badia Ardenga and at Buonconvento.

"Also during the said Signoria, the Emperor Henry of

---

[1] Published in 1893 by N. Mengozzi and A. Lisini (per le Nozze Patini-Sarrocchi.)

Luxembourg died in camp at Buonconvento, Friday, the twenty-fourth day of August, the day of Saint Bartholomew."

In these few and simple words we learn all we need know of the "noble" ways of Dante's idol. When he died, either from disease or poison, on 24 August, there can have been few in all Tuscany but sang *Te Deum*.

But it was not only in the Middle Age that Buonconvento had some fame. All through the Renaissance down to our own day almost, it was of international importance as being a post on the great highway to Rome. There all our fathers have slept and cursed the bed and the fare as heartily as some of us will do.

To go no further back than the early years of the nineteenth century, we find evidence of its importance to travellers. Even the inn was called *Il Cavallo Inglese*—the English Horse—a sure sign of its foreign fame.

A traveller, one of our own countrywomen, writing in 1817, just after the close of the Napoleonic War, has left us an account of the place and what it stood for in the journey to Rome.

". . . Night closed in upon us long before we reached our destined place of rest, the wretched *osteria* of the still more wretched village of Buonconvento. Thither, where a wearisome pilgrimage of four mortal hours had at last conducted us, its half-starved-looking denizens would not admit us into the humble pig-sty in which they wallowed themselves, but conducted us to a lone, uninhabited house on the other side of the way, in which there was not a human being. We were ushered up an old ghastly stair-case, along which the wind whistled mournfully, into an open hall, the raftered roof of which was overhung with cobwebs and the stone floor was deep in filth. Four doors entered into this forlorn-looking place, two of which led to the chill, dirty, miserable holes which were our destined places of repose, and the other two to rooms that the people said did not belong to them; neither did they give any very distinct or satisfactory account of who might be their tenants—one old woman assuring us they were inhabited by '*nessuno*', while the other maintained they were occupied by '*galant' uomini*'.

"It was miserably cold; the wind blew about us, and we could get no fire. But there was no remedy for these grievances, and we resigned ourselves to fate and to bed. The two hideous old beldames who had brought us our wretched supper had left us for the night, and no human being was near us, when we heard the sound of a heavy foot on the creaking staircase, and a man wrapped in a cloak and armed with a sword and a musket stalked into the hall.

"He informed us that he had the honour of lodging in the house, that he was the only person who had that honour, and that he should have the honour of sleeping in the next room to ours.

"Finding him so courteous, and being aware there was no means of getting quit of him, we treated him on our part with the utmost civility, perhaps upon the principle that the Indians worship the devil; and, exchanging the salutation of '*Felicissima notte*', our whiskered neighbour retreated into his apartment, the key of which he had in his pocket. We contented ourselves with barricading our doors with the only table and chair that our desolate chamber contained; then in uncurtained and uncoverleted wretchedness, upon flock beds, the prey of innumerable fleas, and shaking with cold, if not with fear, we lay the livelong night; not even having wherewithal to cover us, for the potent smell of the filthy rag which performed the double duties of blanket and quilt obliged us to discard it, and our carriage cloaks were but an inadequate defence against the blasts that whistled through the manifold chinks of the room."

Evelyn passed this way in 1644 and so did Smollett in 1765 and had a strange adventure here which he describes in Letter XXIX of his *Travels*.

Buonconvento today is by no means so poor or so rough a place as it seems to have been in the last century, and for its poverty there are many consolations in the way of pictures.

In the church of the Misericordia there is a fine picture of the Assumption of the Virgin by Pietro di Domenico and a *predella* of the Life of the Blessed Virgin. But it is the Opera di SS. Pietro and Paolo, the ancient *pieve* in the Borgo di Mezzo, where the Palazzo Pubblico and the Palazzo Taj stand, that the best pictures are to be found. Here are works by Taddeo di Bartolo, by Matteo di Giovanni, by Girolamo di Benvenuto, by Sano di Pietro, and by Pacchiarotto. The Taddeo di Bartolo is a panel of S. Antony Abbot and the Magdalen. One Matteo di Giovanni stands over the high altar, the other is of the Madonna and Child, lovely but much damaged. Girolamo di Benvenuto's best picture is on the right; it represents the Annunciation with S. Francis and S. Antony Abbot. By Sano di Pietro are two works—a triptych of the Madonna with S. Catherine and S. Bernardino and a panel of the Annunciation. On the left wall of the left transept is an Annunciation by Andrea di Bartolo. The altarpiece here is a fine Sano. On either side of this are two panels painted on both sides, perhaps by Beccafumi. On the left wall of the nave is a much damaged picture of the Virgin and Child of the school of Duccio. On the right wall of the nave is a fresco of the Coronation of the Virgin by some follower of Sano. As for Pacchiarotto, his picture is in the sacristy, and represents the Madonna and Child with S. John Baptist, S. Peter, S. Paul, and S. Sebastian. The Cozzarellis should not be missed.

There was not much else in Buonconvento nowadays to cause me to linger there, so I set out for that monastery of Monte Oliveto on the hill north-east of Buonconvento, hidden away among the worst precipices of the desert, which here the monks had made to blossom like the rose.

The great block of brick buildings which form the monastery, with its church, cloisters, and conventual house, are the centre of a veritable oasis in this bare country, of an oasis which little by little the desert is claiming again. For the place is no longer a monastery, the monks having been deprived by the jealous Italian government not only of the fruits of their labours, the houses they had built, the smiling garden they had contrived in the desert, but of the right to labour at all. The abbey of Monte Oliveto, a monastery no longer, is now a sort of pension for *forestieri*—the Italian *contadino* and labourer are deprived of their employers; the land carefully and laboriously redeemed and cultivated by the monks has been lost.

It was about the year 1320 that there began to rise among these barren clay hills and dreadful precipices this *Arcicenobio* in which the Congregation of Olivetani had its origin. The region in which it stands, so bitter and savage and sterile, was known as the desert of Accona, and, save where the splendid labour of the monks has redeemed it, it is still an unmitigated wilderness.

The man to whom in the first place we owe the foundation of this house is a certain Bernardo of the Tolomei of Siena, who fled into this solitude in the year in which Dante's Emperor, Henry VII, died at Buonconvento, close by, the year 1313. Bernardo was the son of Mino Tolomei, the head of the Ghibelline branch of this house, and of Fulvia Tancredi. He was born in 1272, and we are told was christened not Bernardo but Giovanni. As a boy he was studious and pious, and as a young man became the leader of the social life of Siena, and seems to have exercised no little influence in the politics of the Republic. It was, however, his learning which chiefly delighted his fellow-citizens, and it was indirectly his learning that was the cause of his conversion. One day, we read, as he was about to deliver a lecture on some philosophical subject to the Studio of Siena, he was struck blind. In his darkness visions came to him, and presently, after praying to the Blessed Virgin, he recovered his sight, and instead of a philosophical discourse he preached a sermon, *De Contemptu Mundi*, in which he deplored the condition of Italy, the exile of the Popes, and the general state of enmity in which the world then lay. At length, giving all he had to the poor, only retaining a few acres of barren land he possessed here in the desert of Accona, he left Siena for this bitter place with his two noble friends, Patrizio Patrizi and Ambrogio Piccolomini. The first thing they set about was the building of a tiny chapel, which they did with their own hands, and when it was finished they placed it under the protection of S. Scholastica. Changing his name, Blessed Bernardo began to redeem the land round about. All through that desert men heard of him and came to see him, thinking him mad. Certain Guelfs in Siena, smelling a Ghibelline plot, tried to poison him, but he was warned from heaven of his peril, and escaped. Then both Bernardo and Ambrogio Piccolomini were accused of heresy, and summoned to Avignon, but the Pope received them with kindness, and sent them back with a recommendation to the great Bishop of Arezzo, Guido Tarlati, who at the Pope's bidding gave them the Rule and the habit of S. Benedict, and sent for the Camaldolese, who inaugurated the new Order under the name of the "Congregation of the Blessed Virgin of Monte Oliveto", and all this was confirmed by the Pope in 1319.

When Blessed Bernardo had achieved so much, he began to build the church and the convent we see today, not without opposition, for we read that over the new buildings "the Archangel Michael and the devils renewed the war they had fought in heaven before God made the world". The Pope, who seems to have appreciated the Blessed Bernardo at his true worth, began now to send him on several missions for the reconciliation of the factions in many of the cities of central Italy; but the noblest work of Bernardo and of his fellow-monks was accomplished in the Black Death of 1348, when, under his direction, they left the convent two by two for the different towns of the Sienese *contado*, with instructions to nurse the sick and minister to the dying, and to assemble all together in Siena two days before the Feast of the Assumption in August in their last new convent outside Porta Tufi. All assembled, as he had said, safe and sound, and he spoke with them for the last time. For the city of Siena had suffered more severely than any other place from that appalling pestilence, some eighty thousand persons dying in the city and the suburbs (*ne' borghi dentro alla città*); indeed, Tommaso Fecini tells us that out of every ten Sienese nine died, and presently Blessed Bernardo sickened and died also. From him their father, or from the pestilential city itself, the rest of that company also took the infection, the greater number of them dying with those they would have succoured.

Those who returned to Monte Oliveto were a remnant. They built and tilled the soil till what had been the most desolate spot in a wilderness of desolation blossomed into smiling vineyards and olive gardens and fields of corn. So that not much more than a hundred years later, in 1459, Pius II, Piccolomini, coming there in summer-time, writes of it, describing it in detail, and adding, "Happy are the monks who dwell in such a place." He remained there three days, eagerly searching for the tombs of his ancestors. Again, about a hundred years later, in 1536, the Emperor Charles V was entertained here with two thousand men. It was about this time that the church we now see was built, being added to later in 1777.

It is difficult to understand the policy of a government which suppressed a community from which Italy has received nothing but benefits. Nevertheless so it is. The last Abbot of Monte Oliveto, the holy and courteous Abbate di Negro, of the family of S. Catherine of Genoa, died in 1897. He remembered the now empty cloister and choir filled by fifty white-robed monks. And then the peasants sang in the vineyards, and the corn was golden in July and reaped with joy, and the whole countryside was glad in those days. And now?—well, now there is only a horrid silence.[1]

The chance wayfarer today must expect but a pitiful welcome from the few monks who remain in the convent as servants of the government. If he wishes to sojourn there, it is not as a pilgrim he must go, to visit a noble and holy place, but as an enthusiastic student of the art of Sodoma, of the splendid art of Signorelli. And so he must provide himself with a ticket, which he must obtain at the Accademia delle Belle Arti in Siena. Armed with this permit, which he must send to the "Sopraintendente del già Arcicenobio di Monte Oliveto Maggiore" two days in advance of his advent, he is graciously permitted by the Italian government to remain two days to contemplate the wanton ruin it has contrived out of a smiling garden. The ordinary English traveller, however, seeing that his own land is strewn with ruins more terrible by far, will make little of this. The rape of Monte Oliveto will not move him any more than murdered Glastonbury has done these four hundred years. He will wander about the tangled garden and the dying woods, and pass half-indifferently through the beautiful quiet rooms, the half-empty library (the books have for the most part been taken away and are now in Siena), and the noble cloisters. The wanton stupidity that has drained away the life of such a place will probably not touch him. He has come to see the frescoes of Signorelli and Sodoma, which are a continual and unanswerable impeachment of all he now sees going on there around him; but he is intent, if at all, on the study of art; the life of the people, brutally sacrificed to make a Liberal holiday, scarcely interests him.

It is to be hoped that the art he will find there, all that is left now, a mere corpse of what was till lately pulsing with life, will please and amuse him. It might seem doubtful. Signorelli's work is but a fragment, and that is not of his best, and as for Sodoma's, though there be plenty of it, it is what he has taught us to expect. It quite fills three sides of the great cloister, and makes, of course, the fame of the place.

It would be an error to expect from Sodoma the art, or the faith that produced the art, of Duccio. He was of the sixteenth century, a painter of what seems to us the production of the study and

---

[1] The Olivetani have been turned out almost everywhere, like the rest of the Orders. Their General now lives at the little monastery of Settignano. There are ten monasteries and about 120 monks now in the Order.

imitation of many masters. Even here his work is not original, but in every sense a continuation of that of a much greater painter, Luca Signorelli. And, curiously enough, what is valuable in it seems to be due to the influence of that great and heroic man who in 1497 painted here eight frescoes of the life of S. Benedict as told by Pope Gregory the Great in his *Dialogues* and then departed for Orvieto to achieve his masterpiece in the Cappella di San Brizio in the Duomo there. Signorelli, no doubt acting under instructions from the monks, had begun in the middle of the legend. It was left for Sodoma, who began to paint in 1505, to begin and to finish the story.

Vasari, the inimitable story-teller of the Italian Painters, tells us that Sodoma "was a man of joyous life and cheerful manners, a lover of pleasure, and ever ready to contribute to the amusement of others, even though it were not always in the most creditable manner, for which cause he obtained more than one by-name, among others that of *Mattaccio*, or the arch-fool; whereat, instead of being displeased and resenting the same, he must laugh and glorify himself—nay, he would make sonnets and *canzonetti* upon these opprobrious epithets, which songs he would then sing to the lute, and that without reserve."

He had, too, a fancy, Vasari tells, for keeping all sorts of animals in his house: "Badgers, apes, cat-a-mountains, dwarf asses, horses and barbs to run races, magpies, dwarf chickens, tortoises, Indian doves, and other animals of similar kind—whatever he could get into his hands, in short; he was always surrounded by children and young men, in whose society he took much pleasure; and besides the animals above named he had a raven, which he had so effectually taught to speak, that this creature counterfeited his voice exactly in some things, more especially in replying to any one who knocked at the door—nay, this last he did so perfectly that he seemed the painter's very self, as all the Sienese well knew. The other animals also were so tame that they constantly assembled about his person while he was in the house, and came round all who approached him, playing the strangest tricks and performing the most extraordinary conceits ever seen or heard, insomuch that the dwelling of this man seemed like the very ark of Noah.

"This unusual manner of living, the strangeness of his proceedings, with his works and pictures, some of which were certainly

very good ones, caused him to have such a name among the Sienese
. . . that he was considered by many to be a very great man.
Wherefore Fra Domenico da Leccio, a Lombard, being made
General of the Monks of Monte Oliveto, and Sodoma going to
visit him there, the principal abode of that Order, some fifteen
miles distant from Siena, found so much to say and used so many
persuasions, that he received commission to finish the stories which
had been partly executed on a wall of that monastery by Luca
Signorelli. The subject which had been chosen was from the life
of S. Benedetto, and Sodoma undertook the work for a very low
price, with the addition of his expenses and that of certain boys,
colour-grinders, and other assistants by whom he was attended.
But the amusement which these fathers found in his proceedings
while he worked in that place is not to be told; nor could one easily
describe the pranks which he played there, insomuch that the
monks there bestowed on him the name of *Mattaccio*, before
alluded to, in requital of his follies.

"Returning to the work itself, however, Sodoma having finished
certain stories in a manner which showed more readiness of hand
than care and thought, the General complained of that circum-
stance, when *Il Mattaccio* replied that he worked according to his
humour and that his pencil only danced in harmony with the
sound of the coins, adding that if the General would pay more,
he was quite able to produce much better work. Thereupon Fra
Domenico promised to pay him better for the future, when Sodoma
painted three stories, which still remained to be executed in the
angles, with so much more of thought and care than he had given
to the others, that they proved to be much better works."

It is perhaps doubtful where Sodoma began to work on the
frescoes of the story of S. Benedict. As has been said, he followed
Signorelli, whose work is concerned with the latter scenes. The
narrative begins in that corner of the cloister nearest the church,
but the most important paintings in the series are those in the
corners of the cloisters, namely, S. Benedict leaving home, the
Broken Cribble, the Temptation of the Monks, the Reception of
the Novices Maurus and Placidus, and the Destruction of Monte
Cassino. Eugene Muntz thought that this last fresco was the first
to be painted. However that may be—and it might seem almost
impossible to decide the matter now—one takes the frescoes in their

narrative order, beginning with that in which S. Benedict leaves his father's house at Norcia in order to go to Rome to study.

S. Benedict, the Patriarch of Western monks, sprang from a family of note, and was born about the year 480. The history of the great Order he founded is for centuries the history of monasticism. With his advent monasticism proper may be said to have begun, for the Benedictines always have been, and are still, not only the greatest community in the Catholic Church, but its most civilizing force, its most cultured class, as it were its aristocracy. Of all the Orders of Western Christendom, then, the Benedictine stands first. Of all the Rules that of S. Benedict is the most profound, the most comprehensive. In something less than five hundred years this great Order began to produce branches of Black and White monks and nuns. It is natural, then, that its remotest descendants should look behind their mediatory founders, as here the Blessed Bernardo Tolomei, to their great parent, S. Benedict himself.

The first thing S. Gregory, one of the greatest of S. Benedict's sons, tells us of this great saint is that he early left his father's house at Norcia to go to the Roman schools (1)[1], and it is with this incident Sodoma opens his series of frescoes of the Saint's life. We see Benedict setting out with his nurse. In Rome he acquired learning, it is true, but, disgusted at the licentiousness of his companions, he decided presently to bid the world farewell (2); and in the second of Sodoma's frescoes we see him setting forth from the Eternal City. His nurse, Cyrella, who "tenderly loved him", went with him till they came to a place called Aeside, and there she borrowed a vessel to winnow some wheat; but for negligence the vessel fell to the earth and was broken in two pieces. And Cyrella fell to weeping, and when S. Benedict saw it he had great pity, and prayed to God, and after made the vessel as whole as it had been before (3). Then they of the country took it and hung it on the front of the church in witness of this fair miracle. "Then," S. Gregory tells us, "then left S. Benedict his nurse and fled secretly and came into a hermitage, where he was never known of no man but of a monk named Romanus, which ministered to him meat for to eat (4). And because that there was no way from the monastery of Romanus unto the pit where S. Benedict was, he knit the loaf in a cord and so let it down to him, and because he

[1] The numbers refer to the frescoes.

should hear when Romanus should let down the bread he bound a bell on the cord, and by the sound thereof he received his bread, but the devil having envy of the charity of that one and of the refection of that other, cast a stone and brake the bell, but nevertheless Romanus left not to minister to him (5). It happed that there was a priest on an Easter Day that had arrayed his dinner for himself, and our Lord appeared and said: 'Thou ordainest for thyself delicious meats, and My servant dieth for hunger in such a pit,' and named him the place. Then the priest arose and bare his meat with him, and sought so long that he found S. Benedict in great pain. When he had found him he said to him: 'Arise now and take thy meat and refection, for it is Easter Day' (6). . . . It happed after this that a black bird that is called a merle came on a time to S. Benedict and pecked with his bill at his visage, and grieved and noyed him so much that he could not put it from him, but as soon as he had made the sign of the cross anon the bird vanished away (7). After that came to him a great temptation of the flesh, by which the devil tempted him in showing him a woman, and he burnt sore and was inflamed in his courage, but anon he came again to himself (8). . . . It happed that the abbot of a monastery was dead, and for the good tendance of this holy man S. Benedict, all the monks of the abbey gave their voices and elected S. Benedict for their abbot (9), but he accorded not thereto nor agreed to them, for he said that his conditions and manners were not according to theirs. Notwithstanding, he was vanquished, and so instantly required that at the last he consented. But when he saw they lived not nor were ruled according to their religion and Rule, he reproved and corrected them vigorously. And when they saw that they might not do their wills under him, they gave him venom meddled with wine for to drink, but S. Benedict made the sign of the cross over it and blessed it, and anon the vessel brake in pieces, which was of glass (10). . . . Then went S. Benedict again into the desert, where God showed him many signs and miracles, and founded there twelve abbeys.

"Of the twelve abbeys that S. Benedict had founded three of them stood on high rocks, so that they might have no water but great labour (11). Then came the monks to him and prayed him that he would set these abbeys in some other place because they had great default of water.

"Now it happened that in one of the abbeys was a monk that

might not endure long in prayers, and when the other of his fellows
were in prayer he would go out of the church. Then the abbot of
that abbey showed this to S. Benedict, and anon he went to see if
it were true. And when he came he saw that the devil in likeness
of a little black child drew him out of the church by his cowl. Then
S. Benedict said to the abbot and to S. Maurus [the reception of
S. Maur and S. Placidus is not recounted by S. Gregory, but is
included by Sodoma (12)]: 'See you not him that draweth him
out?' They said: 'Nay.' Then he said: 'Let us pray to God that
we may see him.' When they had made their prayer, S. Maurus
saw him, but the abbot might not see him. The next day S.
Benedict took a rod and beat the monk, and then he abode in
prayer like as the devil had been beaten, and durst no more come
and draw him away, and from then further he abode in prayer
and continued therein (13).

Then went S. Benedict about the mountains, and made his
orisons and prayers much devoutly; and when he had long
prayed he saw three stones in a place for a sign, and on the
morn, when the monks came for to pray, he said to them: 'Go
ye to such a place where ye shall find three stones, and there
dig a little, and ye shall find water—our Lord can well provide
for you water.' And they went and found the mountain all
sweating, where as the three stones were, and there they digged,
and anon they found water so great in abundance that it sufficed
to them and ran down from the top of the hill unto beneath into
the valley (14).

"It happed on a time that a man hewed bushes and thorns
about the monastery, and his axe or instrument of iron that he
hewed with sprung out of the helve and fell into a deep water;
then the man cried and sorrowed for his tool, and S. Benedict saw
that he was sore anguished therefor, and took the helve and threw
it after into the pit, and anon the iron came up and began to swim
till that it entered into the helve (15).

"In the abbey was a child named Placidus, which went to the
river for to draw water, and his foot slid, so that he fell into the river
which was deep, and anon the river bare him forth more than a
bow-shot. And when S. Benedict, which was in his study, knew it,
he called S. Maurus, which was a monk, and said that there was
a child that was being drowned, and bade him go to help him.
And anon S. Maurus ran upon the water like as it had been on dry

ground, and his feet dry, and took up the child by the hair, and drew him to land, and after, when he came to S. Benedict, he said that it was not by his merit, but by virtue of his obedience" (16). The next fresco (17) tells of the drunken monk who saw the devil issue forth from a bottle. It is not recounted by S. Gregory.

"There was a priest named Florentius which had envy of S. Benedict, and he sent him a loaf of bread envenomed (18). After, when S. Benedict had this loaf, he knew by the inspiration that it was envenomed. He gave it to a raven that was wont to take his feeding of S. Benedict's hand, and commanded him to bear it unto such a place that no man should find it. Then the raven made semblant for to obey to the commandment of S. Benedict, but he durst not touch it for the venom, and fled about it howling and crying. . . . When this priest, Florentius, saw that he could not slay S. Benedict, he enforced him to slay spiritually the souls of his disciples. He took seven maidens, all naked, and sent them into the garden to dance and carol for to move the monks to temptation (19). When S. Benedict saw the malice of Florentius he had fear of his disciples and sent them out of that place."

The next fresco (20), perhaps by Riccio, recounts how S. Benedict sent S. Maurus to France and Placidus to Sicily. S. Gregory omits this incident. There follow the frescoes by Signorelli (21–28).

"Now, when Florentius saw that S. Benedict and his monks went out, he demened great joy and made great feast, and anon the *solar* [the upper chamber] fell upon him and slew him suddenly (21). When S. Maurus saw that Florentius was dead, he ran after S. Benedict, and called him, saying: 'Come, for Florentius is dead.' When S. Benedict heard this he was sorry for the perilous death of Florentius, and because S. Maurus was glad for the death of his enemy, as him seemed, he enjoined him penance therefor.

"After this he went to Monte Cassino (22). . . . It happed on a time that as the monks should lift a stone for a work of an edifice they might not move it, then there assembled a great multitude of people, and yet they all might not lift it, but anon as S. Benedict had blessed it, they lifted it anon. Then apperceived they that the devil was upon it, and caused it to be so heavy (23). And when they had a little made the wall high, the devil appeared to S. Benedict, and bade him go see them that edified. Then S. Benedict sent to his monks and commanded that they should keep them well,

for the devil went to destroy them. But ere the messenger came
to them the devil had thrown down a part of the wall, and had
therewith slain a young monk. Then they brought the monk all
tobruised in a sack to S. Benedict, and anon S. Benedict made
upon him the sign of the cross, and blessed him and raised him to
life, and sent him to the work again (24). A layman of honest life
had a custom once in the year to come to S. Benedict all fasting,
and on a time as he came there was one that bare meat accompanied with him, and desired that he would eat with him, but he
refused it. After, he prayed him the second time, and yet he
refused it, and said he would eat no meat till he came to S.
Benedict. At the third time he found a fair fountain, and a much
delitable place, and began sore to desire him to eat with him, and
at the last he consented and ate. And when he came to S. Benedict,
he said to him: 'Where hast thou eaten?' Which answered, 'I have
eaten a little.' 'O, fair brother, the devil hath deceived thee, but he
could not deceive thee the first nor the second time, but the third
time he hath surmounted thee.' Then the good man knelt down
to the feet of S. Benedict, and confessed him of his trespass (26).

"Totila, the King of Goths, would once prove if S. Benedict had
the spirit of prophecy, and sent to him his servant, and did so array
him with precious robes, and delivered to him a great company
as he had been the king himself. When S. Benedict saw him come,
he said to him: 'Fair son, do off that thou wearest, it is not thine,'
and the man fell down anon to the ground because he mocked
the holy man, and died anon" (27).

The next fresco shows Benedict receiving the King himself (28),
an incident not recounted by S. Gregory. Through the next
fresco, the last of Signorelli's, a doorway has been cut. Sodoma
continues the series with S. Gregory's prophecy of the destruction
of Monte Cassino (29). There follow six frescoes, five of which
follow S. Gregory closely:

"It happed over all Campania, whereas he dwelt, that so great
a famine was in the country that much people died for hunger.
Then all the bread of the abbey failed, and there was within but
five loaves for all the convent; when S. Benedict saw that they
were abashed, he began debonairly to chastise and warn them
that they should have their hearts on high to God, and said to
them: 'Wherefore are ye in so great misease for bread? If ye have
none this day, ye shall have it tomorrow.' Now it happed that on

the morrow they found at their gate two hundred muddes of meal which were properly sent from God, for never man wist from whence they came. When the monks saw that they thanked God, and learned that they ought not doubt nor of abundance nor of poverty (30).

"It happed on a time that S. Benedict sent his monks for to edify an abbey, and said that at a certain day he would come see them and show them what they should do. Then the night before that he had said to come, he appeared to the master and to his monks, and showed to them all the places that they should build, but they believed not this vision, and supposed it had been but a dream. Then when they saw that he came not, they returned and said to him: 'Fair father, we have abided that thou shouldst have come to us like as thou promisedst us.' Then answered he: 'What is that ye say? Remember ye not that I appeared to you that night that I promised you, and enseigned and told how ye should do? Go your way, and do in such wise as I have devised to you in the vision'(31).

"There were two nuns nigh unto his monastery which were of much noble lineage, which were much talkative and restrained not well their tongues, but tormented overmuch him that governed them. And when he had showed this to S. Benedict, he sent them word that they should better keep silence and rule their tongues or he would curse them. But they for all that would not leave it, and so, anon after, they died and were buried in the church. And when the deacon cried in the end of the Mass that they that were accursed should go out of the church, the nurse that had nourished them, and that every day had offered for them, beheld and saw that, when the deacon sang so, they issued out of their sepulchres and went out of the church, and when S. Benedict knew hereof he offered for them himself and assoiled them. Then, after that, when the deacon said so as afore, they never issued out after as their nurse had seen them (32).

"There was a monk gone out for to see his father and mother without licence and blessing of his abbot, and the day after he came thither he died; and when he was buried in the earth, the earth cast him out again, and so it did twice. Then came the father and mother to S. Benedict, and told him how the earth threw him, and would not receive him, and prayed that he would bless him. Then took he the Blessed Sacrament, and made It to be

THE VIRGIN AND CHILD WITH SS. JEROME AND
BERNARDINO, Neroccio. Pinacoteca, Siena

CORONATION OF THE VIRGIN (detail), Sano di Pietro.
Pinacoteca, Siena

laid on the breast of the corpse, and when they had done so they
buried him, and the earth threw him no more out, but received
the body and held it (33).

"There was a monk that could not abide in the monastery, and
prayed so much to S. Benedict that he let him go, and was all
angry, and anon, as he was out of the abbey, he found a dragon
with open mouth; and when he saw him he had fear that he would
have devoured him, and cried loud: 'Come hither and help me!
Come hither, for this dragon will devour me!' Then the monks
ran, but they saw no dragon, and brought again the monk trembling and sighing. Then the monk promised that he would never
depart from the abbey" (34).

The last fresco (35) tells how S. Benedict, with a look, broke
the chains of a peasant that some knights had bound. It is not
related by S. Gregory.

Thus ends this great legend, as we have it now, without relating
the death of S. Benedict or his visit to S. Scholastica. But other
frescoes are still under the whitewash on the stairs leading to the
smaller cloister.

What Vasari has to tell us of Sodoma's work here, inaccurate
as it proves to be, seems to be authentic in so far as it suggests that
the master did not take himself very seriously. One cannot paint
the life of a saint with the unction of a Simone or a Sassetta, and
at the same time care so little for one's work that one does it well
or ill according to the price offered. "To do despite to the General
and the monks," Vasari tells us, "Sodoma depicted the story of the
priest Fiorenzo, the enemy of S. Benedetto, who brought a number
of public dancing-women to sing and frolic around the monastery
of that holy man, thereby to tempt and disturb the devotions of the
fathers. In this story *Il Mattaccio*, who was as eccentric in painting as in other actions of his life, exhibited a dance of nude figures
which was altogether offensive, and, as he knew that this would
not be permitted, he refused to let any of the monks see his work
while it was in progress. When this story was uncovered, the
General at once commanded that it should be instantly destroyed
and done away with, but *Mattaccio*, after much idle talk, and
seeing that the father was in great anger, added draperies to all
the figures in the picture, which is among the best of those to be
found in the Monte Oliveto."

What there is of splendour here we owe to Signorelli, even in the work of Sodoma.

The cloister, famous though it be, is by no means all there is to be seen at Monte Oliveto. The church is of the seventeenth century, and contains little of interest; only, indeed, the stalls by Fra Giovanni da Verona, brought hither in 1815 from San Benedetto of Siena to replace those taken in 1813 to the Duomo. But the Library is charming, with its few books bound in vellum, a noble room with an antechamber reached by a flight of steps, at the farther end, where are two ancient pictures: one a Madonna by some painter near to Segna, the other a S. Bernardino by Neroccio.

It is, in fact, in the convent itself, its cells and corridors and offices, that one takes most delight, in the conversation of the few monks who are left, not to serve God but us, and in the ruined gardens and *bosco* that still offer flowers and shade even in the autumn days. And wandering there, one still finds remnants of the ancient beauty that must once have filled the place. Over the entrance tower still the Madonna is enthroned with her little Son—a polychrome terra-cotta from the hand of Giovanni della Robbia. The companion figure of S. Benedict on the other side is only a work of the *atelier*, but it is charming nevertheless.

ON BEING WRONG FOR THE RIGHT REASON

One afternoon while at Monte Oliveto, I happened to be in the Chiostro Grande when to my dismay there arrived one of those motor-coaches now so common everywhere in Italy, full of a mixed company of tourists. It was the "Marian Year", the centenary of the definition of the dogma of the Immaculate Conception and these people, a sort of modern pilgrims I conjectured, had no doubt been in Rome for the occasion and were now returning through Italy on their way to their various homes.

Among them, rather conspicuous in his black and white habit, was a little Dominican friar, but the most outstanding person was a tall though stooping and rather cadaverous figure who looked like a professor of some sort. He was obviously the centre of the group as they went round the Cloister looking at the frescoes of the life of S. Benedict by Signorelli and Sodoma.

I had avoided them as well as I could, but presently the "professor" began to hold forth, and out of curiosity I strolled nearer to hear what he was saying. As I came within hearing, on the edge of the small crowd, this is what I caught.

". . . In matters theological the Benedictines are generally right and for the right reason; the Dominicans—*scusi*, Padre—wrong for the right reason, the Jesuits wrong for the wrong reason and the Franciscans right for no reason at all."

It seemed to me a witty, if malicious, summing up of the various Religious Orders, and I was not surprised when the Dominican padre protested.

"Why," said the professor, turning on him, "you Dominicans were wrong in this very matter of the Immaculate Conception defined a hundred years ago.[1] Your S. Thomas denounced the doctrine. It seems he could not understand how the Blessed Virgin could be redeemed if she had not sinned. Your Order supported his conclusion. As I have said, you were wrong for the right reason. You even refused the feast of the Conception, calling it the Sanctification of the Virgin, whatever that may mean."

"If S. Thomas," said the Dominican, "had known the doctrine in the sense of the definition of a hundred years ago, he would have been the first to defend it."

"You think so? On the other hand the Franciscans defended, if they did not invent, the doctrine; and though Duns Scotus supported it with irrefragable reasoning, the Franciscans before him were right by inspiration; as I have said for no reason at all."

The little Dominican, now thoroughly roused, protested again; but his opponent was irrepressible.

"Your Order," he said, "was so passionately obstinate in denouncing the doctrine and in support of your god S. Thomas, that the whole Church was torn with controversy; and though the Franciscan Pope Sixtus IV adopted the doctrine and the feast for the whole of western Christendom, you were so successful in opposition that he withdrew; and presently the Council of Trent also, shied at it. Still you stuck to your views until the scandal became so great that Pope Gregory XV in the seventeenth century had to impose absolute silence *in scriptis et sermonibus etiam privatis*, until the Holy See should see fit to decide the question."

[1] The doctrine of the Immaculate Conception is that our Lady alone of all mankind since Adam and Eve was conceived and born without the taint of original sin.

I felt sorry for the little Padre Domenicano who was quite unable to stem the torrent.

"Why," went on the professor ruthlessly, "it was to Gregory XV that one of your company ran one day crying—(but how to express his falsetto?): 'Santo Padre, Santo Padre, those miserable Frati Cappuccini have built a church by Piazza Barberini and are going to dedicate it in honour of the Beata Vergine Immacolata.' "[1]

"Hm-m-m," said Papa Ludovisi, "Are you certain of your information, *figlio mio?*"

"Perfectly certain, Santità."

"Ve-e-e-ery well," said Papa Ludovisi. "We shall look into this. Meanwhile, *figlio mio*, do you run away and—a-ah yes—build a church and dedicate it in honour of the Madonna born in sin."

There was an uneasy silence, till someone turned to the frescoes and the group broke up, though several gathered round the little Dominican and did their best, no doubt, to restore his equanimity.

An unpleasant episode. It spoilt, if it enlivened, the afternoon. And most out of place I thought, here in the Sanese where but for a certain Sienese, a Dominican Tertiary, they might all have been returning from Avignon instead of from Rome. I was doubly glad when they went off in their motor-coach and left the place in silence and to me.

[1] Santa Maria della Concezione (I Cappuccini) in Piazza Barberini.

CHAPTER XVII

TORRI AND SAN GALGANO, CHIUSDINO,
RADICÒNDOLI AND MASSA MARITTIMA

THERE is really nothing for it but to take a motor-car if one wants to see the great ruined abbey of San Galgano, visit Chiusdino, and get to Massa Marittima for the night. There is no railway line and the public motor-coach is not much use, for it passes San Galgano by, as it does Chiusdino, and if you stop it and alight you have to find your way thereafter on foot.

I left Siena by Porta San Marco on a day of late autumn and crossing pleasant country, just after passing the village of Rosia on the edge of the Merse Valley under Monte Acuto I turned off the high road to see the ancient abbey of SS. Trinità and S. Mustiola at Torri, which once belonged to the Vallombrosan Order. It is a magnificent Romanesque building with a triple cloister, little visited, but worth some trouble to see, indeed better worth a visit, as I found, than the more famous abbey of San Galgano. Founded in the eleventh century, the church itself is notable, but the lovely cloister of black and white marble in three stages, with its various columns and capitals is entrancing. The abbey was suppressed by Pius II, the last abbot being Dom Antonio da Firenze in 1464.

I went on to San Galgano in about an hour. The old abbey lies almost under Chiusdino, which is piled up on its hill a little to the west.

S. Galgano Guidotti, in whose honour the great ruined church was founded, is one of the patron saints of Siena; one sees him pictured, his great sword struck into the rock, in the Palazzo Pubblico and in the Opera del Duomo; and in the museum at Pisa, I remember, there is a *predella* in which are scenes from his legend.

He was born in Chiusdino of a noble house and quarrelled one day with a youthful knight, who, being jealous of his good looks, jeered at him because his sword hilt was in the form of a cross. "One day," he sneered, "he will turn into a rascally monk, for like a monk he wears a cross at his girdle." Galgano, who was quick-tempered, drew his sword and ran him through. One night soon after he dreamed that the Archangel Michael came to him and demanded that he should become a knight. Galgano was delighted to consent, but when S. Michael saw his sword stained with a brother's blood he had to refuse him, saying: "Thou canst not follow me."

When Galgano awoke he was in great distress and determined to change his way of life. He prayed and fasted. Two years later S. Michael appeared to him again and leading him through many perilous ways brought him into the presence of our Lord enthroned with the twelve apostles. Our Lord spoke to him and told him his repentance was accepted and he might henceforth become His servant.

Galgano now resolved to forsake the world. He left the city and built himself a hut on the top of a hill called Siepi; in fact, on the hill just above where the abbey stands today. Then he took his sword and thrust it up to the hilt in a mound there which suddenly turned into solid rock and held the sword fast so that only the cross of the hilt appeared. Before this cross Galgano was wont to pray for many years. But at one time when there was the plague in Siena, while he was absent there, tending the sick, evil men burnt his hut and broke his sword hilt. Finding the sword broken on his return, he held the pieces together which by miracle were made whole and friends built him another hut, where he lived till, being very old, kneeling before his sword, he died. He was canonized in 1185.

That is not a very interesting story as I have told it. S. Galgano lived in the twelfth century and presently Cistercians from Burgundy came down into Italy and founded their great abbeys at Fossanova in 1133 and Casamari in 1149, both in lonely places in the mountains south of Rome, and this abbey too they founded in 1201. The present building was begun in or about 1224, to be completed in 1288, also in a lonely place, lonely even today under the hill of Siepi with its woodlands and meadows and Chiusdino against the sky a few miles away.

The church, magnificent even in its ruin, is, if not the finest, among the finest Romanesque-Gothic buildings in Italy, and is of course of French Burgundian origin, if not actually built by French Cistercian monks. Its abbot came to hold very great powers, not only over other Cistercian houses in this part of Italy, but as arbitrator and judge in the quarrels internal and external in Siena and the cities of this part of Tuscany.

The abbey held vast possessions all through this country and was in every way a civilizing power, in engineering, in medicine, and in art. Its influence was powerful in the building of the Duomo in Siena, where its abbots had a great palace at the Porta Romana. The beginning of its end came when in the trecento it was twice sacked by Sir John Hawkwood and his White Company of Adventure, and before 1503 it was reduced *in commenda* and, of course, the *commendatori* took all the income of the abbey for themselves. The monastery and even the church began to fall into ruin and in 1653 it was secularized. In 1786 the tower collapsed and what was left of the ruined church was de-consecrated in the ominous year 1789.

Almost nothing remains of the monastery save the ruins of the chapter house, the refectory, and part of the cloister, but the abbey church is still a magnificent building, a most impressive piece of northern architecture, a typical Cistercian church. The façade, which was never completed, is modest, as becomes a Cistercian building. Of the three doors the middle one has a fine frieze in the architrave; the apse has two orders of windows surmounted by a single rose; the right transept also has a rose window; the left a large pointed window once trefoiled. Within, this great church of travertine and brick is about 200 feet long with three naves divided by sixteen pillars and a transept which is also divided, on one side into three aisles, on the other into chapels. At the end of the left transept is a door which gives access to a stairway, at the top of which I found I had the best view of the church.

I climbed up the hill, Monte Siepi, to visit the scene of S. Galgano's hermitage, where still today there is a Romanesque church, banded with marble stripes, where to my astonishment and delight there were frescoes in the lunette, perhaps by the Lorenzetti, one of the Madonna and Child enthroned with angels and Eve at her feet, by Ambrogio Lorenzetti (?), and another of S. Galgano before his sword in the rock, by the same master, who has also covered the vault with the figures of Prophets. Pietro Lorenzetti, his brother, has also a fresco here of the Resurrection.

I lingered at San Galgano through the afternoon and went on to Chiusdino for dinner. It is scarcely any longer worth while to leave the main road and climb up to this little town on its hill.

I used to come here to see the magnificent altarpiece by Sassetta, but that has been carried away to the Contini collection in Florence, and now, except the Casa di S. Galgano with its chapel where once the Sassetta altarpiece stood, there is little or nothing to see—a small Byzantine Crucifix in the church of San Martino, nothing more.

I had put up in Chiusdino in order on the morrow to go to Radicòndoli far away in the hills to the north, half a day's journey. Radicòndoli was an ancient Castello of the Aldobrandeschi, which commanded the road between Colle and Massa Marittima. It came into the hands of Siena in 1221.

I took this long journey for the sake of Pietro di Domenico, for the parish church at Radicòndoli possesses his masterpiece, a magnificent altarpiece of the Assumption, with a single long panel below of the Adoration of the Child with many saints. Above our Lady is borne to heaven to be received by God the Father and the celestial hierarchy.

The church itself, of the Assumption, is a Romanesque building of the twelfth century of considerable interest. Originally consisting of three naves, upheld by columns with apse and vaulted transept, it has white and black transversal arches.

Some three miles further on the road to Colle is the finely situated church of San Giovanni Battista at Mensano. This too is of the twelfth century with three naves upheld by columns and with a single apse. The columns have magnificent capitals carved with men's heads and fantastic animals, acanthus and other leaves. There is an epigraph or signature with the word AGLA, which I was told records the Pisan sculptor Bonamico (twelfth century).

All this was well worth the journey but it meant spending another night in Chiusdino. I went on to Massa the next afternoon.

The old Etruscan city of Massa Marittima stands on a hill about a thousand feet above the sea on the verge of the Maremma, by which it was destroyed in the fourteenth century—abandoned on account of malaria. It was subject to Siena and was actively loyal to her, when Cosimo I was making all subject to him as the master of Tuscany in 1554. In this affair it suffered a siege which ended in its capitulation to the imperial forces, but this defeat and the terrible scourge of the anopheles mosquito almost dis-peopled it, and it was only under the House of Lorraine that it recovered owing to their development of the mines of pyrite; and to some effect, for the city acted so vigorously in the war for the unity of Italy that Garibaldi called Massa "La Brescia Maremmana".

Its most famous son, however, was the great Franciscan saint, Bernardino da Siena, who was born in Massa, where his father was governor, in 1380, and it was in Massa after evangelizing all Italy, he preached his last Lenten sermons in 1444, on fifty consecutive days, before he set out for Aquila, where he died on the vigil of the Ascension. He was in his sixty-fourth year and had spent forty-two years as a religious.

I had not been five minutes in Massa when I hurried to the Palazzo Pubblico, for evening was drawing in, to see once again the stupendous altarpiece by Ambrogio Lorenzetti, unquestionably his masterpiece, of the Madonna and Child enthroned with angels and saints, painted in 1330. I do not know any great altarpiece which produces as a whole a more magnificent effect.

I returned to this majestic eikon many times during the next few days. Some have found the figures of the Virgin and Child clumsy, and many of the saints heavy and ungainly. For me, this great altarpiece is perhaps the most monumental in all Sienese art, only to be compared with his brother Pietro's very different and more spiritual masterpiece in Arezzo. Happy are they who have been persistent or fortunate enough to get as far as Massa Marittima to see this wonder.

I should like to quote here my friend Mason Perkins' description of this great, but, alas, mutilated picture, for I think it could not be bettered:

"On a richly embroidered cushion of scarlet and gold, upheld by two adoring angels, whose pinions, sweeping upward, form, as it were, the back to a unique throne, is seated the noble figure of the Virgin, sedate, majestic, hieratic, wrapped in a mantle of deepest blue. Softly nestled in her arms is her Son, against whose upturned face she gently lays her own. Behind her, her heavenly attendants scatter down about the holy pair a fragrant shower of red roses and white lilies. Below three high and divers-coloured steps, emblazoned with the words FIDES, SPES, and CARITAS, lead upward to the throne. Upon them sit three radiant beings, winged and crowned, though haloless and clad in shining raiment

—allegorical personifications of the three great theological virtues. Highest of the triad, directly at the Virgin's feet, sits Charity, a fair figure with a waving wealth of hair, arrayed in loose almost diaphanous garments of rose-red, fire-like hue. In one out-stretched hand she holds a flaming heart and in the other a keen-pointed shaft. To her right, below her, sits her sister Hope, in dark blue, gold-embroidered vestments, with the same flowing red-gold hair. On her knees she holds a tall four-storied tower and her eyes are cast intently upward towards the jewelled crown—Hope's guerdon—which floats above its battlemented top. Still lower yet, on the first step of all is seated Faith, attired in chaste and ample clothing of light emerald green, her hair bound tightly in a close-drawn head cloth. She seems lost in contem-plation of a mirror, in which shines reflected a double-visaged head—the Old Law and the New. To left and right kneel angels—rapt musicians, softly singing to lute and viol, while others gently swing their silver censers before the sacred presence. Behind, on either side, stand in close and serried ranks the great company of saints and martyrs of apostles, patriarchs, and prophets, in silent, ecstatic adoration about the heavenly throne."

I wonder if any altarpiece in Italian painting except Duccio's Maestà has surpassed this in combined spiritual beauty and monumental magnificence.

But Massa has many other, if lesser, treasures.

The Duomo, a Romanesque building of the thirteenth century, standing on a platform approached by a flight of steps, is in the Pisan style. It is said to have been designed by Enrico da Campione about 1228. The façade, with its seven lofty blind arches, has a single portal and in the architrave are bas-reliefs of scenes in the life of S. Cerbone in whose honour the church is dedicated. Four columns carry the symbols of the Evangelists and, above, one over the other in the Pisan style, are other blind arcades enclosing rose windows and a wall of rose and white stripes. The walls of the body of the church have white and green stripes. At the side is a heavy campanile recently rebuilt.

Within—one enters on the left side—the church is of three naves divided by columns of travertine. At the beginning of the right aisle is the magnificent baptistery with huge quadrangular font covered with bas-reliefs and figures of prophets, of the thir-teenth century. In the midst is a tabernacle of 1447, in the niches

in which are figures of patriarchs and, over all, a figure of the
Baptist. The holy water stoup close by is of the fourteenth century.

On the right is the chapel of the Blessed Sacrament. Here is
one of those great Crucifixes of painted wood. This is a beautiful
work by Segna di Bonaventura.

The high altar is of the seventeenth century and rather like a
Roman triumphal arch, but beneath it is the magnificent Arco
di S. Cerbone, the masterpiece of the sculptor Gori di Gregorio
of Siena, signed and dated 1324, with bas-reliefs and medallions.
S. Cerbone (Cerebonius) was Bishop of Populonium, near Piombino,
in the sixth century. Summoned to Rome he went to meet the
Pope, followed by a flock of geese, perhaps the first but not perhaps
the last bishop to do this. He died in Elba and was buried in
Populonium, whence his body was brought here. He worked
many miracles, among them the taming of a bear which set upon
him when Totila cast him into a den of these beasts. Hence his
symbol of a bear licking his feet. His legend is told by S. Gregory
in his *Dialogues*.

In the chapel at the end of the left transept is an "assimilation"
by Segna of Duccio's Maestà painted in 1316. The Virgin and
Child are very like Duccio's. The Passion scenes at the back are
some damgaed and some missing. In the chapel of the Relics,
entered here, are some fine reliquaries of Sienese goldsmiths' work.
In the left nave are frescoes of the fourteenth century of the school
of Bartolo di Fredi and several fine tombs.

In the crypt one finds a fourteenth-century fresco of the Sienese
school—a Crucifix with our Lady and S. John, S. Cerbone, and
S. Bernardino.

There are a few buildings of some interest still in Massa, such
as the remarkable Palazzo Comunale, the Palazzo Pretorio, the
cortile of the Fortezza dei Senesi, and the Romanesque church of
Sant' Agostino and the Cappella di Santa Lucia. Here is an early
painting by Pacchiarotto of the Adoration of the Child with SS.
Joseph, Bernardino and Anthony of Padua, and perhaps a donor
whose head is just seen behind S. Anthony. This picture is somewhat damaged, but not repainted, and has a charming landscape.
Above the shed under which the figures are grouped are two
angels in adoration.

But winter was now upon me and I made haste to return to
Siena.

OLIVE HARVEST IN THE SANESE

Yes, winter is come.

At the Villa of my hosts through all the three *poderi* they are picking the olives:

> Per San Simone
> Il ventaglio si ripone.
> Per Ognissanti
> Manicotto e guanti. . . .

The land has all been ploughed between the olives and the vines, with the almost Virgilian plough drawn by a pair of oxen, though in the more open fields modern iron ploughs are now used; I have seen them at work all along my way. Up and down the field the oxen go deliberately, delicately, between the vines drawing the plough which throws up as it goes to and fro two long waves. The *contadino* uses as his other implements the *vanga*, the long-handled triangular-bladed spade and the ancestral hoe and mattock.

Since San Simone (28 October) the *buzzurri* have been selling their boiled chestnuts in the piazzas of Siena and we have been eating them washed down with the new wine:

> Per San Simone
> Si mangian le ballotte. . .

And then Ognissanti (1 November) opened the season for sowing the wheat under the new moon, sown broadcast—a beautiful spectacle. And now winter is come and they have begun to gather the olive crop.

It is cold for all the genial sunshine. Here the women do much of the work except at the tree top. Each picks for herself, stripping the berries from one bough after another quite round each tree. The days are now short, on the mountains is a mantle of snow, but the work will go on till the winter is over. With a basket strapped to the waist, a sack for holding the fruit, a ladder to reach it, the picker stands on the rungs often for hours reaching with numbed fingers for the clusters of half frozen berries. Old Regina and the children glean between the furrows and beneath the trees for the windfalls. The baskets are filled again and again and emptied into sacks and carried to the mill-house at nightfall.

A chilly business. How comforting to get into the warm mill-house, the *frantojo*, dirty though it be, where a *monte*—about a hundred and twenty gallons—of olives is assembled to be divided in half for grinding in the mill.

> . . . teritur Sicyonia baca trapetis . . .[1]

The mill consists of a level bed-stone surrounded by a lip, in fact just like a saucer. In the midst arises a wooden spindle from a pair of stone millstones each a foot thick and between three and four feet in diameter. These revolve on their axis turning with the spindle. An ox is harnessed to the beam which is attached to the spindle and the patient beast plods round and round the mill in the track its many predecessors have made through the generations. After perhaps three hours the mill is stopped; the olives have been crushed to an unctuous mass, which is then scooped out and stuffed into rope sacks which, eight at a time, are stacked one above the other under a press which squeezes out the oil, as Otone and Pino, strong though they be, turn the beam with breast and shoulder. Then the mass is put back into the mill again; again ground up and again pressed. And a third time this is done, hot water being poured over the mass to extract the last of the oil, of course inferior in quality; *olio di sansa* they call it; and like the oil extracted from the windfalls, it is used for the lamps. What remains is sold for manufacturing soap.

The high quality oil from the first pressings is not at once ready for use, for it is still mixed with many impurities. So it is allowed to stand for some hours in the *chiaretojo* or clearing room, in a terra-cotta jar, when the impurities sink and the oil is skimmed off much as one skims off the cream from the dairy pan. Some weeks are then allowed to go by, during which the oil has again deposited a thick matter, from which it is drawn off, pure and clear and nutty in flavour, ready for use.

Yes, a chilly business. It is time I went into winter quarters, for I have long since learnt it is ill wandering about Italy between December and March.

---

[1] Sicyon's berry is bruised in the mill (Virgil: Georg. II. 519)

CHAPTER XVIII

SPRING IN ASCIANO

SPRING has come again at last and once more I find myself at evening in Siena, on that platform beside the Servi church. Before me across the narrow gardens that hem Siena in and fill all her valleys with plenteousness, lies a country of very different character, a strong and masculine country of vast and barren undulations, of low and wrinkled clay hills, tragic in aspect, forbidding, and yet full of mystery.

Almost invisible at midday in the glare of the summer sun, often hidden in early morning by the mists of the valleys, this strange wilderness reveals itself only at evening, when it seems to lie like a restless sea between the city and that far-away fair mountain, Mont' Amiata, whose beautiful and pure outline nothing can ever trouble or modify. Forbidding at first, little by little, as day by day, evening by evening, you gaze on that vast loneliness, it begins to attract you, to call you, to fascinate you; its little cities half-hidden here and there in the sombre billows of clay, or suddenly shining out in a glint of stormy sunshine, or delicately revealed in some virginal dawn, beckon you from Siena, till at last you set out to find them where they are, repeating their beautiful names—Asciano, Trequanda, Montepulciano, Pienza, San Quirico, Montalcino, Radicofani, Chiusi.

If one leaves the fruitful heights of Siena by train or motor-car to explore that strange desert, the first place one comes upon will be the walled town of Asciano, lying in a verdant hollow of that barren sea of clay. Always a place of some importance, since it held the Ombrone valley, Asciano is now the chief centre of this wild district between Siena and the southern hills; for though it is far from the great Via Francigena, it is the junction of the railway system which joins northern with southern Tuscany, which leads from Siena to Rome, to the mountains of Umbria and the marshes of the Maremma.

The ancient capital of this strange country which now looks to Asciano, was Buonconvento, on the Via Francigena, some twenty miles south of Siena. It was not through Asciano but through

Buonconvento that all our fathers passed to Rome, and before our fathers those medieval armies which so uselessly laid waste Italy. But, in fact, to the leisured traveller it will make but little difference whether he traverses the medieval highway to Buonconvento or goes by train to Asciano. In either case he must cross that region of solitude and desolation, for between Siena and Asciano road and railway cross a good part of that desert of clay hills which gives, as I think, so much of its character to the Sanese and, indeed, to the Sienese. There is, and indeed there can be, but little to see: only the desert has its own beauty and strength, and may be loved at last for its own great sake, as Giovanni di Paolo loved it, for it often appears in the background of his pictures.

On entering that sombre country, at some six miles from Siena the train draws up for a moment at the little wayside station of Arbia, without a village or even a house to account for it. It is there, however, one must stop if one would visit the battlefield of Montaperto with its great mound crowned with cypresses, a somewhat tiring, sentimental journey that might easily become a bore, but that on the way to the scene of the famous battle one finds the church of Sant' Ansano a Dofana, and, close by, the chapel which marks the supposed scene of the martyrdom of S. Ansano, the apostle of the Sienese.

At Sant' Ansano, in what was once a convent and is now a parish church, I found a fine Madonna by Baldassare Peruzzi; and it is to this sixteenth-century painter and pupil of Pacchiarotto and assistant of Pintoricchio that one owes the little chapel called Il Martirio, some quarter of a mile away to the west, which marks, as it is said, the scene of S. Ansano's martyrdom. Here I found a splendid picture, painted in 1328, by Pietro Lorenzetti, a Madonna and Child surrounded by four angels, with S. Nicholas and S. Antony Abbot, and *predella*, which is worth all the fatigue of the way.

Later I made my way through devious paths to Castelnuovo Berardenga on a hill over the Ombrone valley, amid a rich country of woods and olives and vines. The parish church possesses a picture of the Virgin and Child by Giovanni di Paolo signed OPUS JOHANNIS SENENSIS MCCCCXXVI from San Domenico in Siena. Castelnuovo Berardenga possesses a Palace of the Saracini with a fine park and far away in the woods an old Romanesque abbey

church and a group of monastic buildings with a four-square campanile: such was the reward of my journey.

I turned away at last from this to the lean and masculine
country which lay around, and through which, after a long tramp,
I made my way back to the station. It was evening. All around
me lay that vast and empty world whose ascetic outlines were
softened in the level light of the setting sun. On its desolation a
marvellous and delicate beauty seemed to have fallen from the sky,
which, trembling with light, seemed to bless it and to call forth all
that was best and most characteristic in its sombre strength which
that hour alone was able to reveal and to transfigure. Everywhere
around me lay a barren sea of clay, billow after billow rolling
away to the horizon, broken only by the far hills. Every line and
seam and channel in that desert of clay was visible in the evening
light, and seemed to disclose for the first time the incredible age of
the world. Then little by little it faded away, the merciful shadows
crept up from the valleys and wrapped everything in their
wonderful embrace. It was quite dark when I came to Asciano.

Asciano is a little town half-hidden in the fruitful clefts of this
desert of clay, that lies, it might seem so restless, between the
mountains. Half-hidden in its delicious valley, it lies some
distance from the railway, with which it seems to have but little
in common, so little, in fact, that, as any traveller may see as he
approaches by train, the line quite passes it by so close that you
might drop a stone on to its roofs, yet the station is set more than
a mile away from the town in a desolate place in the valley of the
Bestina.

With a good thousand years of life behind her, Asciano has left
us little history, and, in fact, there seems but little to know. Her
story is that of most of the towns in the *contado* of Siena. From the
ninth century we find the Conti Scialenghi dominating her till
they were divided into various branches, and were called Manenti,
Ardenghi, and Berardenghi. Of these last were the potent
Cacciaconti and Cacciaguerra, and that Caccia d' Asciano whom
Dante named among the luxurious fools of Siena in the twenty-
ninth *Inferno*. In 1169 Ildebrando of the Cacciaguerra renounced
his portion in Asciano to the Republic of Siena, and it was then
that Asciano first came under the influence of the city, which
ordered, as it is said, the destruction of the ancient fortress which
stood on the highest part of the old *castello*, where now stands the

MONTE OLIVETO MAGGIORE

ALTARPIECE (detail), Ambrogio Lorenzetti. Palazzo Comunale,
Massa Marittima

church of San Francesco. But Asciano did not cease altogether to be under the dominion of the Scialenghi till 1212. Then in 1234 the *castello* was besieged by the Florentines, who took it. A little later it came back into the power of Siena and was refortified, as it was again in 1351. Thereafter it remained Sienese, till in 1554 it fell, with all the rest of the *contado*, into the hands of Cosimo I.

But though her story can have but little interest, Asciano, as one soon finds, is to be loved for its own sake, and strictly for what it remains today, one of the most charming of those delightful towns that lie like flowers on the skirts of Siena. Its situation is delightful, cosily hidden among the vineyards in the billows of the desert; its people are honest and courteous and bid you welcome, the inn is clean and humble, and, knowing nothing of strange luxuries, is all for home, and has a quietude that many a place more famous might envy.

Asciano stands just so in a cleft of the desert. It seems, indeed, gradually to have slipped down a lowly hillside till it should be lost in the shade of the valley. Its oldest citadel, the *castello* proper, is set on the summit of a low hill. There of old stood the fortress, where San Francesco stands today. But this fortified place, called Il Prato, now in ruin, seems to have little to do with the town proper, which is some distance away, lower down the hillside, and utterly separate from it. On the other side of Asciano, and lower still—in fact, in the bottom of this narrow cleft in the hills where it opens into the valley of the Ombrone—stands the *borgo* called Camparboli, close by the Siena gate, but in truth not joined to the true town, but separated from it by the country.

But the true splendour of Asciano lies in its churches, which are to be found alike in its three divisions. There is Sant' Agata in the town proper, the Collegiata since 1542, a fine and interesting building of the Romanesque period. It is perhaps here that Asciano keeps its greatest treasure. For in the choir behind the high altar, on the left, is a magnificent altarpiece, till lately ascribed to Sassetta, but now to the Osservanza master, of the Birth of the Blessed Virgin, with scenes from her life. It is full of a sweet gravity, precision, and daintiness that still entrance us and lift up our hearts. In the midst, in a lofty room before a cheerful fire—Brother Fire, of whom S. Francis sang, comely and joyful, masterful and strong—sits some sister maybe, of S. Anne, with the baby Blessed Virgin in her arms. A servant warms some linen

13

before the crackling flames, while to and fro through the sunlit room angels softly pass and repass, intent on the service of their Queen. Nor are they forgetful of S. Anne, who, still abed, is served by one of them, while another waits on guard, fascinated by the little Virgin. To the left without sits S. Joachim, talking, it may be, with the doctor, while a little lad, perhaps S. Joseph, runs in from the garden, charmingly visible, with its well and cypress and border of flowers, through an open doorway. Above are three scenes: in the midst the Madonna and Child with four angels, to the left the death, and to the right the funeral of the Blessed Virgin. Nothing can exceed the intimate loveliness of this work which owes more than a little in its composition to the picture by Pietro Lorenzetti in the Opera del Duomo in Siena.

Around the choir on either side are panels with half-figures of saints perhaps by Fei, and guarding it, as it were, are set the four Evangelists of Fei. Then in the north transept one comes upon a fine picture by Taddeo di Bartolo of the Madonna and Child, and an Annunciation by Martino di Bartolommeo with an altarpiece by Giovanni di Paolo and two saints by Matteo di Giovanni. In the south transept of the church are a noble Assumption with side panels of full-length saints by Matteo di Giovanni and a large fresco by some painter near to Pacchia. To the left of the main entrance is a fresco of the Pietà by some pupil of Sodoma's; and lastly, over the high altar, a picture of the Virgin and Child by Segna di Bonaventura, or if not by Segna by some other close follower of Duccio. The long fingers of the Madonna are like those of the National Gallery Virgin by Duccio and like those of the Virgin in one of the altarpieces in the Siena Gallery ascribed to one of Duccio's closest disciples. This picture has been somewhat repainted.

The other church within the town proper is that of Sant' Agostino. Here in the nave, over the second altar on the right, is a part of an altarpiece by Matteo di Giovanni, consisting of four saints, an exquisite Annunciation, and the Blessed Trinity, with five *predella* scenes of great beauty. The centre panel of this altarpiece, which completes it, is the great and holy treasure of the church. It stands over the high altar, and represents the Madonna and Child, and can only be seen with some ceremony. This early work of Matteo's is one of the finest pictures of the later Sienese school anywhere to be found. There is always some delay in getting the picture uncovered. The *contadina* who eventually did this for me kneeled down beside me, on the altar steps, and gazing up at our Lady, suddenly whispered *"come è garbata"*, that is, "how courteous she is", a loving remark worthy of Tuscany, *madre di ogni cortesia*. Under the Madonna, over the high altar, is a beautiful gold Crucifix of the fourteenth century.

Over the second altar, on the left in the nave, is a picture of the Nativity between two saints, of much beauty, by Giovanni di Pietro d' Ambrogio, a pupil of Sassetta's. Here we see the Nativity as the dawn is breaking over the hills and the angels sing in the twilight.

From Sant' Agostino it is but a little way back past Sant' Agata and along a country road up to the old *castello*, where now, instead of a fortress, San Francesco stands. It is interesting, though mournful, to note how completely this church has been spoiled and its character changed. It was once a building in the Italian Gothic manner, such as we still find so lovely and spacious in Santa Croce of Florence. It had five pointed windows on either side the nave, and between and under them the walls were covered with frescoes by Giovanni d' Asciano, some fragments of whose work are still visible, especially in the chapel right of the high altar. All that, however, was changed in the seventeenth century, when the windows were blocked up or squared or destroyed, the whole church was whitewashed, and six Baroque altars, whitewashed, too, save where they were painted to represent marble, were set up to fill the place with their bastard splendour, the gaiety of a salon. And so today the church is no longer charming. Nevertheless some notable and lovely things remain to it amid the ruin. First, there are those two wooden statues of life-size, made in the fifteenth century, representing the Annunciation, that stand on either side of the main entrance, and the later Della Robbia altarpiece. Then there was, fairer far, the masterpiece of Barna, a Virgin and Child with donor, which hung at the entrance to the chapel, on the extreme south of the choir. It was one of the loveliest things of the fourteenth century even in the Sanese, rare and precious, and of an astonishing quality, but now imprisoned in some museum or gallery, it no longer gladdens the simple of heart in this ruined sanctuary. One used to linger long about San Francesco because of it.

Before I left the little town, however, I did not omit to visit the true *borgo* of Asciano, the little village called Camparboli, a few hundred yards outside the Siena gate. There in the midst I found a chapel of San Sebastiano with a fresco of the Assumption of the Blessed Virgin by Benvenuto di Giovanni, and a fresco of three saints—S. Lucy, S. Roch, and S. Jerome—by Girolamo del Pacchia. The granary close by has frescoes of the Seasons by Ambrogio Lorenzetti, but I was not permitted to see them.

The same great master will be found at the Badia a Rofena in the church at Pievina some three miles from Asciano. Over the altar is a polyptych from his hand of S. Michael between SS. Bartholomew and Bernard with our Lady and two saints in the pinnacles.

CHAPTER XIX

TREQUANDA, MONTISI, SAN GIOVANNI D' ASSO

I WAS very well placed in Asciano to explore those hills, scarcely a range of mountains, which divide the valley of the Ombrone, upon which Asciano stands, from the wide Chiana vale on the eastern frontier of Tuscany.

It was a fine spring morning when I set out for Trequanda, which lies on the high watershed, some four miles from the railway, at a height of over a thousand feet.

Trequanda is a fine little town dominated by its towered *castello* of the thirteenth century and the Romanesque church of San Pietro of the same period. Within the church I expected to come upon a lovely altarpiece by Giovanni di Paolo, but could not find it, only a fresco of the Transfiguration or Ascension, badly injured, by Sodoma, and in a niche another of the Virgin and Child enthroned with the Magdalen, the Baptist, and SS. Bernardino and Bonizella, signed by Bartolommeo da Miragna or Miranda, and painted about 1450. This fresco does not seem to be by a Sienese master, but who Bartolommeo da Miragna was I do not know. S. Bonizella, who stands beside the Virgin, is a local saint; the body is preserved in a carved urn under the altar. She was a Piccolomini-Cacciaconti of about 1300. The feast, I learned, was kept on 6 May.

But where was the picture by Giovanni di Paolo which I had come to Trequanda to see? I found it in the Pinacoteca and was disappointed. It seemed to me to be a work not from his hand but out of his *bottega*. It is an altarpiece of the Virgin and Child enthroned with angels and S. Bernardino kneeling at their feet. Above is God the Father in benediction and on either side a tall saint, on the left S. Sebastian, on the right S. Gregory the Great. On the pilasters which frame the picture are two small full-length saints on either side. Perhaps the central panel with the Virgin and Child may have been painted by Giovanni. I do not know. I was disappointed in the picture, and possibly prejudiced because it had been removed from the *pieve*.

However, a small boy, who now demanded *soldi*, led me to another church, where I examined a fresco of the Madonna and Child, perhaps by Guidoccio Cozzarelli, the follower and assistant of Matteo di Giovanni. And that was all I found in Trequanda. So on I went to the Eremo di Sant' Egidio, about a mile away, where S. Bernardino and S. Giovanni da Capistrano, who firmly re-established the Observant Franciscans in Italy, used to retire.

I went on past this hermitage in a beautiful countryside, up and down, to Montisi, again with a fine towered *castello* of the Cacciaconti, which came by legacy into the possession of the Ospedale of Siena. They made a grange of it according to Repetti, who says the town used to be called Monte Ghisi. It stands a thousand feet over the Valle dell' Asso. All about are more or less barren hills of clay, but there were olives and cypresses. Like Giovanni di Paolo, one comes to understand the charm of this landscape. Repetti speaks of a picture by Simone Martini in the *pieve*, which I immediately sought. He must have meant the small Crucifix of the school of Duccio, a fine thing much damaged, the ends, too, being cut off. He also speaks of the picture by Neroccio, which I was delighted to find still there. This is a large altarpiece in the choir signed and dated OPUS NEROCII BARTHOLOME DE LANDIS SENENSIS MCCCCLXXXXVI. The Virgin is seated on a throne adorned with cherubs, with her little Son, between the standing figures of SS. Peter, Sigismond, Ansano, and Paul. Above is God the Father in benediction, surrounded by four angels. This is a late and lovely work by Neroccio, very well preserved in colour, but falling to pieces.

Just beyond the little town stands, amid cypresses, to the left of the road, the small church of the Madonna delle Nevi. Within is a painting of the Madonna and Child of the school of Duccio. Farther, about a mile away, is Castelmúzio, where the Olivetan convent has been turned into a house of *villeggiatura* for the seminarists of Pienza. Within the church and in the refectory of the convent are many frescoes by Sodoma.

All the way as I went, the wonderful line of Mont' Amiata rose before me. It was up hill and down dale before I came to the Asso under San Giovanni d' Asso, another *castello*, this of the Conti di Scialenga, which like the others came into the possession of Siena. In the *pieve* of San Giovanni Battista, with its charming though incomplete Romanesque façade, I found in the sacristy three detached panels of an altarpiece, much restored, of the Virgin and Child with the two SS. John and God the Father, and the angels in the terminals. In spite of the restoration, these panels have much tender feeling. They are attributed to the school of Ugolino da Siena by Mr. Berenson, and by others to the Master of Montalcino. In any case they are of the school of Duccio and worth some trouble to see.

In the church of San Pietro in Villore near by, with a beautiful, though ruined, Romanesque façade and a remarkable crypt, I came upon a small Crucifix much damaged, a Sienese work of the twelfth century. I was unfortunately unable to see the Ducciesque triptych which used to be in San Giovanni Battista, but is now in the Pannilini collection in this village, and the Madonna enthroned, also of the school of Duccio, in the same collection. Here is the grange of the Ospedale of Santa Maria della Scala in Siena, now the property of the Pannilini family, an interesting fortified farmhouse probably of the fourteenth century.

I went on to Monterongriffoli, about a mile and a half away, another Sienese *castello*, where I found in the church of San Lorenzo a polyptych of the school of Ugolino, with the Madonna and Child, SS. Peter and Paul, two small saints and God the Father in benediction.

All this country is scattered with these early Sienese pictures. But evening was coming on, the long, early summer day was done, and it was already starlight when I got back to Asciano sure of a welcome.

CHAPTER XX

TO RAPOLANO, SERRE, AND LUCIGNANO

IT was on another perfect morning, after some welcome rain in the night, that I left Asciano for Rapolano, the key to the pass from the Valle dell' Ombrone into the wide Chiana valley. Rapolano is an ancient walled town still beautiful, with ruined fortifications and vast gates, possessing of old, and now, too, medicinal baths, which have a great reputation in this part of Tuscany. Its most ancient possession, however, is its *pieve* of San Vittorio—like all ancient *pievi*, not within the *paese*, but at the foot of the hill on which the little town stands. It existed in the eighth century, and appears in the first quarrel between Siena and Arezzo; but in 1776 the church was abandoned and the *pieve* translated to the church of Santa Maria Assunta, in the midst of the town, originally an abbey of Olivetan monks, which now bears the name of San Vittorio in Santa Maria Assunta.

Rapolano originally made part of the lordship of the Berardenga and of the Scialenga of Asciano. But as early as 1175 some of its Signori placed it under the protection of Siena. About thirty years later, in 1208, the Florentine chroniclers tell us that their compatriots took the place, as they certainly did in 1253. In 1260, however, the battle of Montaperto restored Rapolano to the Sienese, but in the meantime the town had acquired Guelf sympathies, and in 1266, acccording to Andrea Dei, the Sienese occupied it to suppress these rebels, who held the *castello*. In 1306 Ghibelline Arezzo attempted to seize it, no doubt on account of its strategical importance, and the Sienese, who were quite unable to defend it, destroyed its walls. It can have had no very considerable place in the confused history of the fourteenth and fifteenth centuries, when all Central Italy lay under the terror of the *condottieri*, and its fate, like that of every other city in the Sienese *contado*, was finally sealed in 1554, when it was sacked by the Austro-Spanish-Medicean army, and a little later included in the Granducato.

Its interest today lies in the treasures of art it may possess. I was not disappointed, for in the little church of the Fraternità, over the pulpit, hangs an old panel of the Madonna and Child in half length, by Pietro Lorenzetti (?). The Child, tenderly clasped by His Mother, is holding a small bird in His hand.

Then in the church of the Oratorio of San Bartolommeo there is a panel of S. Anthony of Padua by Cozzarelli, with four scenes from his legend.

Charming as Rapolano is, I did not linger there, for there is much to see in the country round about.

At Serre, for instance, a little town in a cleft of the hills some five miles south of Rapolano, in the *pieve*, there used to be a fine picture of the Madonna and Child on a gold ground by Ambrogio Lorenzetti, but they have taken it away to Siena, where it is now No. 605 in the Pinacoteca there. Few, indeed, visit this little place, so difficult of access and quite off the highways of travel; but it is in such places, and in such places only, that the Italy we used to know still lives.

I went on to Lucignano. The road passes quite round Rapolano and offered me a complete view of its walls, its gates, and terraced gardens. And after passing Poggio Santa Cecilia on the left, another of the Berardenga *castelli*, I found I had left the barren country of clay hills that lies about Asciano, and had entered a deliciously wooded valley full of peace. I lay down in the corner of a vineyard to enjoy all this and the wine and victuals my friends at Asciano had provided for me.

From an historical point of view Poggio Santa Cecilia is one of the most interesting places in the Sienese *contado*. When the Ghibellines were expelled from Siena in 1269 they took refuge where they could. No doubt their hopes were raised by the Sicilian Vespers at Easter 1282, but already Florence, Siena, Lucca, Prato, and Volterra were leagued against their cause, and they were afraid to move. In 1284 came the battle of Meloria, in which their last hope, Pisa, suffered the loss of her fleet. The exiles were then without a refuge. In October 1285, however, the Sienese *fuorusciti*, with the help of the Bishop of Arezzo, seized Poggio Santa Cecilia, a place then strongly fortified, and easily defended even today. "And," says the Chronicler, "they held the place against the Sienese and the Florentines and all Tuscany for fourteen months and eighteen days until they were compelled to eat rats and to gnaw the leather of their shields; and they collected the dew for the thirst which they had. . . . Finally on the night of Good Friday, being able to endure no longer, they abandoned the castle and issued forth and fled during a great rain; and so they saved themselves alive."

However, Andrea Dei tells a different tale. "Many of them were taken as they went forth and were led to Siena, and while they were in the Palace of the Podestà, whither they had been taken to be put to death, the people rose in tumult, crying, 'Peace! Peace!' and they began to attack the Palace. Wherefore the Nine who then governed the State were afraid, and they gave them the gonfalon and surrendered unto them the prisoners. Then the people took the prisoners to the Palace of the Bishop, who had come to their aid when the tumult commenced. And they were by themselves and the Guelfs with their followers set upon them in the Campo; and they brake them and discomfited them, the Monday after Easter; and they got them to the Palace of the Bishop and drew forth the prisoners and led them into the Campo; and there they cut off the heads of five of the chief among them and the rest they hanged between the Arbia and the Bozzone; and the number of them was sixty." Poggio Santa Cecilia was razed to the ground.

But the nightingales were singing:

> O fret not after knowledge—I have none,
> And yet my song comes native with the warmth.
> O fret not after knowledge—I have none,
> And yet the Evening listens. . . .

I went on. Presently in the golden light, the *castello* of San Gimignanello came into sight on the right. San Gimignanello, too, was part of the lordship of the Counts of the Scialenga, a picturesque place of towers. Then the valley opened as far as the eye could see; the wide plain of the Chiana, drained now, rich and healthy, stretched away between the tumbled hills, on one of which, at the very head of the valley, Lucignano was firmly set, a fine towered city aloft on her hill.

It is uphill all the way; but the place is worth some trouble to reach it, if only for the great view which greets one from the gate, whence one may see, across the wide valley, the vast and beautiful line of the Apennines, and the city of Cortona, like a white flower, on the skirts of those mighty hills. Here, too, for the first time something new comes into the landscape, a new spirit or atmosphere, something soft and mystical, a light that never was on any Tuscan hills—and, indeed, it is Umbria that lies there before you, secret and yet visible in every line, in the sweetness of the valleys, in the mystery of the mountains. Something severe has suddenly gone out of the landscape, and you look once more on Umbria, dark with ilex and sweet chestnut, through which run the valleys of the saints; where S. Francis and Blessed Angela pass and repass, lingering yet, and seem to stand for something in the world, for something, perhaps, we have lost and can spare so ill.

Lucignano, thus so nobly placed, was, as I have said, at one time a *castello* of very great importance to Siena, for it commanded the Val di Chiana, where the confines of the Republic marched with those of Arezzo. Its situation is, in fact, magnificent, for it stands on the highest point of a vast bastion of high land that is thrown out by the Chianti hills, dividing the great valley here into two parts. It thus enjoys to our delight one of the widest prospects of the wide valley of the Chiana, and from its gates one may see almost all the cities, towns, *castelli*, and villages with which that vast plain is peopled.

With all its splendour of situation, however, the *castello* of Lucignano does not appear to be of very ancient foundation, not older, indeed, than the thirteenth century, when, although it seems to have enjoyed a great measure of self-government, it was a civil and religious dependent of Arezzo, that city which is set under the hills at the head of the main Chiana valley where it meets the Val d' Arno. So securely does the power of Arezzo seem to have been established in the place, that a month after Montaperto (1260), we find the Bishop Guglielmo Uberti, then at the head of the government of that city, signing a decree in Lucignano in October 1260. After the victory of Campaldino (1289), however, in which the Florentines, with the Sienese and other allies, defeated the Aretines, Lucignano was handed over to the Sienese, and this was confirmed in the church of San Francesco, outside Lucignano, in June 1289. It proved to be the worst day's work that had yet been done for Lucignano. Even from the first the sympathies of the people of Lucignano seem to have been with Arezzo, and even so late as 1336 Giovanni Villani speaks of the place as Lucignano d' Arezzo, which seems to prove at least that the hold of Siena was disputed.

In 1337 Lucignano came into the power of Perugia, and in 1355 she was still Perugian, and in 1357 formed an important Perugian outpost in the war with Siena. Then in 1370, in Perugia's war with the Pope, she gave herself to Siena, but the hired *condottieri* in 1384 sold her to Florence. Indeed, the place, small as it was, a mere fortress in the eyes of the contending parties, was doomed to captivity. In desperation, to save themselves from slavery, in 1390 the people of Lucignano placed themselves, their town, and its territories under the protection of the Visconti, the most bitter enemies of Florence. This led to their coming again under the jurisdiction of Siena, and the conditions then imposed by the Republic are very interesting as an example of what Siena conceived to be the right way to govern a subject people.

In the first place Siena insisted that the *castello* and the territory of Lucignano should allow that they were for ever under the jurisdiction of her Commune; then that the subject town should receive as Podestà a citizen of Siena, whom she should pay every six months 400 florins of gold; that every year she would send to the Duomo of Siena for the Feast of the Assumption a *palio* of scarlet of the value of at least 60 florins, accompanied by eight guards, each of whom should be furnished with a candle of a pound weight; that every year she would buy from Siena 600 bushels of salt at the price of 30 *soldi* the bushel; that she would permit the Commune of Siena to build a fortress within her territory; that she would pay every year to the Republic 300 florins of gold as tribute; that she would not exact *pedagium* from the citizens of Siena; that she would permit all Sienese merchandise to pass freely between the two Communes; that all her landholders and citizens now and ever should become Sienese citizens; that all her notaries should now and ever matriculate in the University of Siena.

As for the *castello*, or fortress, mentioned in this convention, it was built by a certain Bartolo Bartoli within three years at a cost of 6,825 florins. And we find that the dominion of the Sienese was confirmed by a treaty with Florence in 1404.

I have given the convention which ensured the rule of Siena in Lucignano in some detail because it allows us to see exactly what the rule of Siena was like in her *contado*. That rule seems to have been as disastrous as it was short-sighted. Lucignano was to be ruled solely for the benefit of Siena. Siena ruled her *contado* not for its own good, but for hers. Lucignano had to pay yearly a large tribute, as well as vast taxes. Her trade was circumscribed and handicapped for the sake of Siena. The result might have been foreseen, but those who cannot rule themselves are not likely to succeed with others. Instead of strengthening the cities under her rule, and so raising a strong and even an impregnable bulwark of prosperity, contentment, and loyalty against the enemy, Siena quietly strangled, for purely selfish ends, every city that came within her grasp. Lucignano is but the figure of them all.

As the fifteenth century advanced the population of Lucignano decreased, and with its population went whatever wealth had once belonged to it. These evils had grown to such proportions in 1440, when the population had decreased by half, that the wretched town tried to obtain a diminution of the tribute and of the tax. However, Siena conceded the request—a fact which in itself speaks for the state of affairs—to this extent, that Lucignano was to pay 1,000 *lire* a year instead of 400 florins, and the 300 florins of tribute were reduced to 100 on condition that the other 300 were spent in repairing the walls and the gates; the 600 bushels of salt were also reduced to 300.

After considering this example of her government one is not surprised that the Austro-Spanish troops had so easy a victory. When the Imperial army took Lucignano in 1553 there can have been little to boast of in the exploit. However, when the Imperialists got in, in 1553, they nailed a woman to the gate like a hawk for refusing to cry "*Duca*" and continuing to cry "*Lupa*". This may have been a Lucignano woman; on the other hand, it may have been a Sienese.

No one, I think, who has once seen Lucignano would willingly pass her by again without paying her a visit. Her splendid situation, her quiet country aspect, her green hillside, her cypresses, her spring of water make the place a paradise quite apart from anything else she may possess. But it is impossible that so alluring a citadel should be quite devoid of pictures: and if there be such a place in all Tuscany it is certainly not Lucignano.

The old church of San Francesco, where the Bishop Guglielmo Uberti of Arezzo signed a decree in October 1260, is full of works of the Sienese school. On the south wall is a fresco by Bartolo di Fredi of the Triumph of Death. Over the high altar is a splendid polyptych of the Madonna and Child with saints by Luca di Tommè. Then in the north transept I found more of Bartolo di Fredi's work—frescoes of scenes from S. Francis's Life, the Madonna and angels, S. George and S. Christopher, and the

Adoration of the Magi. These are probably the work of a follower. Many of the pictures here have been restored, not to say repainted.

To my great disappointment I found most of the pictures I used to know in San Francesco now in the Gallery. Among the pictures gathered there are a signed triptych by Bartolo di Fredi of the Virgin and Child enthroned with the two SS. John; S. Francis receiving the Stigmata in the presence of Brother Leo, by Pietro di Domenico; S. Bernardino trampling on the mitres of the Sees he had been offered and had refused, by Pietro di Giovanni d' Ambrogio; and a Virgin and Child, a late work by Luca Signorelli or from his *bottega*. Here, too, is a Crucifix about two feet high, a Sienese work of the thirteenth century, traditionally coming from Sant' Antimo. The gallery has been established in the old convent next to an orphanage, where the good sisters were looking after and bringing up a number of small black-eyed children, full of mischief and noise.

Charming as all this was, it is Lucignano itself that every time I toil up to it seems to me more perfectly delightful because it is so completely itself. A little place scarcely worth a visit, the tourist may think: a little place scarcely worth improving, off the face of the earth. I feel sure my landlady was of that opinion. She was the *padrona* and cook and very efficient. Her husband— he seemed discouraged—was the waiter. He reminded me of Cecco d' Angiolieri's verses:

> Quando veggio Becchina corrucciata ...
>
> When I behold Becchina in a rage,
> Just like a little lad, I trembling stand ...

"Dio creò prima Adamo, e poi guardandolo, disse: Credo che potrei far meglio. E creò Eva." Yes, that was her view of things. Ah, well:

> Il mondo invecchia
> E invecchiando intristisce.

CHAPTER XXI

TO SINALUNGA, FOIANO, AND TORRITA

FROM Lucignano, from the station of Lucignano, to the station of Sinalunga is but ten miles, but from thence to the town is a good half-hour's walk. So I found fifty years ago when I first came this way, and I used to rejoice that this little hill town was not nearer the railway, for it had thus been able to keep something of its ancient character, its old-world air, and what beauty the centuries have left it. That saving isolation has been abolished by the motor-car and the motor-bus. The town itself is not among the more beautiful places of Tuscany, though the church of San Bernardino, with its campanile and lantern, towers up over its walls and lends it a charming dignity; but it is set in so fine a landscape, it is surrounded by so lovely a country-side, it is piled up so loftily on its strangely contorted hill and over-looks so noble and so splendid a world, that it can never be omitted in any journey through this delightful valley.

The birthplace of Ghino di Tacco, the famous brigand, of whom Boccaccio tells us in the Second Tale of the Tenth Day of the *Decamerone*, and who is to be met again at Radicofani, Sinalunga is a curious little nondescript and sunbaked *castello* set on a high hill in a charming world of vineyard and olive garden on the western bastion of the Val di Chiana. Reached by a long winding and delightful road, to which, according to Repetti— but who can believe this?—it owes its name, Sinalungo—*Sinus longus*, or as it became later Asinalunga—it is but rarely visited by travellers, and the one inn it possessed, and that a good one, had for the time being closed its doors when I last passed by.

Very few memories have come down to us concerning the place earlier than the twelfth century, when it formed a part of the dominion of the Conti della Scialenga, who presently brought it into the power of Siena, against which city it twice rebelled in 1313 and in 1322. But after the defeat of the Compagnia del Cappello near Torrita, its neighbour, in 1363, Sinalunga finally came into the dominion of the Republic, the counts in 1343 having sold to the town all their property and rights in it for some 2,250

gold florins. Then in 1399, when the Sienese for fear of Florence
handed over the government of their city and its *contado* to Visconti,
Sinalunga as part of that *contado* came into his power. In the year
1400 he built a great tower, called La Torre, which was destroyed
by lightning in 1563, but by then Sinalunga, like all its neighbours,
had for ten years been in the hands of Cosimo I, and presently
made part of the Granducato.

The ruins of La Torre, however, remained till 1590, when the
Grand Duke Ferdinando I pulled them down and used them to
build the new *pieve* of San Martino, giving the ground thus laid
bare for a public piazza, the great piazza we find today in the
loftiest part of the town before the *pieve* or Collegiata. The old
pieve, like all those of Tuscany, lies without the town at the foot
of the hill on which it stands, and may still be seen with its *borgo*
a little to the south of the railway station, beside the winding road
by which one reaches Sinalunga. It was dedicated to San Pietro,
and in 1591 by a Bull of Clement VIII all its rights passed to the
new Collegiata.

These dull facts will perhaps appeal but little to the traveller
who, on his way through this part of Tuscany, has had the courage
to visit Sinalunga for the sake of the pictures Mr. Berenson or
Mr. Perkins, that devoted student and lover of Sienese pictures,
has told him in some article he will surely find there. But let
him have patience. Pictures there are and to spare in this neglected town, but even today it would be unpardonable to take even
Sinalunga by assault without some sort of introduction. Indeed, if
it is thus one is to be compelled to visit the cities of our second
fatherland they will lose half their interest for us; and as for their
pictures, they might as well share the fate of their brethren and be
imprisoned in those vast emporiums called museums. In some way,
I know not rightly why, pictures fade and die in a museum as in an
intolerable captivity. Perhaps, like ourselves, these living and
lovely beings, which we are powerless to create, strike roots as we
do into their native earth, or into that place to which love has
brought them, which they have learned to regard as home.
Perhaps in the cold corridors of a museum they miss the prayers
of the poor, the tears of the sorrowful, the thanks of those they have
often assisted, the laughter of little children. Certainly there is
here some mystery we cannot wholly understand. Only we know
that, however carefully we bear it away from its altar, that

THE BATTLEFIELD OF MONTAPERTO (1260)

THE BIRTH OF THE VIRGIN, The Osservanza Master(?).
Collegiata, Asciano,

triptych, that panel, that picture of the Madonna will in its new place presently suffer some change, will seem to fade and die; will suddenly move us no more.

And since this is so, it is delightful, it is infinitely reassuring to know that pictures which have been here these hundreds of years remain here to be reverenced, to be loved, to receive the prayers of the poor, and to figure for them all that is left to them of divinity in their hearts.

Now certainly what I did first in Sinalunga after climbing into that lofty piazza before the church of San Martino was to wander through the narrow ways of the town, to visit the fine Palazzo Pubblico, to linger on the olive-clad bastions, and to wonder at the beauty that is surely to be found there in that church of San Martino which was built out of the ruins of La Torre, in Santa Lucia and Santa Croce in the Madonna delle Nevi, and San Bernardino.

In San Martino, besides the curious little shrine to the right of the western doors there is over the altar of the south transept a fine altarpiece of the Deposition, probably from the hand of Girolamo del Pacchia. Pacchia was the pupil of Fungai, and passed under the influence of many masters, Florentine as well as Sienese. His work has the usual composite quality of the sixteenth century, but here for once I think —or is it just my fancy?—he has brought something into a picture which but for that would be a little mannered, a little lacking in sincerity. In a wide and beautiful valley where afar off one seems to recognize the lovely lines of Monte Cetona and Mont' Amiata, the Cross itself hiding the height of Radicofani, Jesus has been lifted from the Tree and now lies in His Mother's lap supported by the holy women, while S. John carefully lifts away the crown of thorns from His brow, and S. Joseph of Arimathea and Simon of Cyrene wait in the background, the one with the precious ointment for His burial, the other with the holy relics—the instruments of the Passion— which he holds in his hands. And though yesterday it was almost summer, it is bleak winter now; the little trees stand forlorn, stripped of their leaves, and all the world is bare and still with the stillness of death, awaiting the Resurrection. Beneath the picture are seven *predella* panels, a Crucifixion at each end, and between them the Flagellation, the Bearing of the Cross, the Deposition, the Entombment, and the Resurrection.

14

To the right of the high altar is a *tondo* by the pseudo Pier Francesco Fiorentino, of the Virgin and Child with the infant S. John.

From San Martino I passed to Santa Croce, where on the right wall is a late or school picture by Luca Signorelli of the Sposalizio, an interesting and charming work.

From Santa Croce I went through the narrow streets to Santa Lucia, a curious and beautiful sanctuary, where over an altar on the left is an interesting work by Benvenuto di Giovanni—an altar-piece of the Madonna enthroned with her Divine Son on her lap between S. Sebastian and S. Fabiano, while two angels fly there on guard about her head, two play on strangely lovely instruments at her feet; above in heaven hovers the Dove. In the *predella* are three scenes divided by four panels of saints—the Martyr-dom of S. Sebastian, the Resurrection, and the Martyrdom of S. Fabian. In a recess in the eastern wall of the south transept is a fresco of the Madonna and Child between S. Roch and another saint, with S. Bernardino and S. John Baptist at the sides. This is perhaps a work by Neroccio.

I came upon Benvenuto's work not only in the Madonna delle Nevi, where over the high altar there is an archaic Madonna from his hand, but also in the delicious little Franciscan sanctuary of San Bernardino, to the west of Sinalunga.

Leaving the great piazza by a road on the right, and following it uphill, I came at last, at the end of an avenue of cypresses, at a turning of the way, to this little church and convent, with its cool loggia and country aspect.

Here in the summer quiet you may find—it maybe at evening, when Vespers are over and the antiphons of the *Magnificat* have reminded you of the morrow's feast, and the *Salve Regina* has died away in the cloisters—three pictures of exceptional beauty. The loveliest is in the choir, the Annunciation by Benvenuto di Giovanni. Under a loggia of marble beside the wonderful temple of Jerusalem, a poet's dream of a sanctuary, the Madonna rests at evening, drooping like a flower over her Little Office, her vase of lilies beside her; when suddenly like a star from heaven Gabriel falls before her on his knees, crowned with a garland from Paradise, a sceptre of olive in his hand, and whispers his *Ave*. And it is in truth from the very heaven of heavens he has come, as indeed Benvenuto has not forgotten, from the presence of the Father,

whom we may see bending down towards His angel, giving him
that branch of olive and the Message, too, which announced our
joy and that peace, also, which is surely ours, if anywhere in the
world, then here with these little friars this summer evening under
the cypresses among the corn and the flowers. This picture is
signed and dated 1470.

There are other works, too, in the church. In the choir is a
picture of the Salvator Mundi by Sano di Pietro. Over an altar
hard by is a fine triptych of the Madonna and Child enthroned
between SS. Francis and Bonaventura, while in heaven God the
Father rejoices with His angels and the Dove hovers over the head
of our Lady about to be crowned with no mortal diadem. This,
too, by Sano.

There are besides three pictures by Cozzarelli: two of the
Madonna and Child with saints and angels, one of which is signed
and dated 1486 and one of the Baptism of our Lord in a landscape
with three angels and S. Jerome, who is writing it all down, and
a haloed bishop in adoration. This is a fine picture, almost worthy
of Vecchietta.

It was with a sad heart I left San Bernardino of Sinalunga,
for who knows if I shall ever see it again?

Of the way to Foiano I cannot speak as I would. I can only
say that it is so fair that one should go afoot. I descended by the
winding road through the olive gardens to the Borgata di San
Pietro by the station, and crossing the line took the road east
across the valley, and climbing the hills by La Castellina descended
again into the valley of the Esse, a mere long tributary of the Val di
Chiana, and so climbing again came at last to Foiano towering
over the main Chiana valley looking straight to Cortona.

Foiano stands indeed on the highest of those hills, which from
the eastern bastions of that lofty promontory are thrust out
southward into the valley of the Chiana. It is a double town,
the older and loftier part forming the *castello*, the lower the *borgo*.
Surrounded once by two lines of walls, both of which had three
gates, the older included only the *castello* with its lofty tower and
two fine palaces.

In such a place, when the majesty and beauty of the landscape
have had their way with you, history, you might think, was bound
to have been glorious. But in fact we are ignorant of the origin of
Foiano, though some have conjectured that it got its name from

the Romans, who called it Fanum or Forum Jani. However that
may be, the *castello* and the *pieve* are spoken of in the earliest years
of the eleventh century as dependent on the Bishop of Arezzo,
though the Conti della Scialenga and Berardenga certainly had
some jurisdiction here, as in so many other places about Asciano.
To one's surprise, in the thirteenth century one hears almost
nothing of Foiano, but in the fourteenth one finds it an important *castello* in the immediate power of Arezzo, until in 1337 it came
into the hands of Florence, only to pass, if but for a moment, into
the dominion of Perugia. By 1353 it was once more in the hands
of Arezzo, but thirty years later it voluntarily submitted to
Florence on the eve of the final overthrow of its ancient mistress.
After that, till the whole of this part of Tuscany fell into the hands
of Cosimo I, its chief business was carefully to watch Lucignano,
the two strongholds, as it were, standing sentinel there for the rival
cities of Florence and Siena.

Fine though Foiano is and girdled with olives and golden with
corn and joyful with fruitful vineyards, it is rather by reason of its
wonderful views, for the ever delectable landscape that lies at its
feet, that one would come to it, but that in the Collegiata is
hidden away a signed and dated picture by Luca Signorelli of the
Coronation of the Blessed Virgin. This grand and noble picture
was painted in 1523, the year of Signorelli's death, and was, in
fact, the last he set his hand to. The Madonna, in a splendid robe
of rose with a mantle of blue, fairer than the angels who attend
her, kneels before our Lord, who crowns her *Regina Virginum*. On
either side two angels play, while S. Joseph, her guardian still,
stands beside her, and S. Gabriel, who was her messenger, waits
lest she should speak again and he not hear. Before her in the
foreground kneels S. Martino, whose altarpiece this is, dressed in
a golden cope, the which he won in exchange for the poor coat he
gave the beggar for Christ's sake. On his left hand stands S.
Jerome and three monks, and behind him S. Mary Magdalen;
and again on the other side some fine old saint introduces the
donor, Angelo Massarelli.

Signorelli was an old man when he conceived this majestic work,
and we may be sure that he received some assistance, for not only
are the figures of S. Gabriel and S. Mary Magdalen too feeble to
have come from his wise hand, even though it trembled then, but
in the *predella* only two of the four scenes are his. The four scenes

represent the story of S. Martin, and in the two Signorelli has given us with all his boldness and mastery of composition we see S. Martin in armour on his great white war-horse with his men-at-arms about him dividing his cloak with the beggar. In the other we see the Saint kneeling before a Bishop with his two acolytes— a beautiful picture.

I slept at Foiano and after Mass, when I had seen Signorelli's picture again, I made my way southward and across the valley to Torrita through Bettolle. It is a walk or drive of some ten, or, maybe, twelve miles. The way by Sinalunga, and so by train, is shorter, and the road is better, but so one misses Bettolle and a new vista of the great valley.

Bettolle, which may be counted half-way, is a garden—a garden of chestnuts and vineyards and olives. I do not know that Bettolle is famous at all for anything but its fairs; but for me it is a most charming village, with a fine wine and a courteous people, and I wish it every sort of good there is to be had, and that is the same thing as to repeat the old commandment to keep itself unspotted from the world. Some day, probably, Bettolle will be lost in a forest of tall chimneys, all the valleys will be hidden in a great pall of smoke, and a vast chemical works or what not will enslave the inhabitants from far and near. May this be far from thee, Bettolle!

Somewhere in this valley, between Foiano and Marciano, in August 1554, the battle was fought which made an end of the Sienese Republic and established, or rather made possible, the Grand Duchy of Tuscany, of which, later, Siena came to form a part.

It was in the January of that year that Cosimo de' Medici took the field with an army commanded by the Marquis of Marignano. On the 26th of that month Siena was invested. The Sienese general was Pietro Strozzi, a Florentine exile and a Marshal of France, whose father had died in a prison of the Medici. This fact doubtless embittered the campaign. With her usual bravery, Siena took the field, and after months of skirmishes and fights the two armies faced each other on the heights above the torrent of Scanagallo. It was the 2nd of August, about eleven in the morning, and the sun very hot, when the battle broke. "The Spanish horsemen advanced, and raising their visors as they passed the infantry, smiled upon them with joyful faces, to show their good

will to give them victory, knowing well [says the historian] that
in battle cavalry alone decide the day." The earth trembled
beneath their tread, and they seemed, as writes an eye-witness of
their charge, "a mountain of iron with plumes waving to heaven,
a spectacle as gallant as it was beautiful". About Strozzi were
gathered his fellow-citizens, exiles of Florence, while above them
floated a green banner bearing for motto the line of Dante:
"*Libertà vo cercando ch' è si cara.*" . . .

"Like two mighty waves, black below, foam-topped above, the
cavalry of either host hurled together. There was a thunder of
rushing hoofs, a crash of steel, and lo! with a shriek of treason and
fear the French standard-bearer turned and fled. In a moment
the splendid squadron divided, broke, and spurred hard out of
the fray, bought (it was said) with Spanish gold—*dodici fiaschi di
stagno pieni di scudi d' oro*—a treachery and a flight which lives
even today in the songs wherewith the *contadini* awake the echoes
of that solitary countryside—

> O Piero Strozzi in dù son i tuoi soldati?
> Al Poggio delle Donne in que' fossati;
> Meglio de' vili cavalli di Franza
> Le nostre donne fecero provanza.

"All was lost; but the Sienese were not minded to yield. . . .
High on the Poggio delle Donne, Strozzi, clad in black armour
inlaid with gold, mounted on an Arab charger and with his
truncheon in his hand, played the parts alike of general and
soldier, and played them well. He spoke words of comfort to his
infantry, declaring that the flight of the French was nothing but
a ruse; he bade the drummers and the pipers sound to battle;
all the banners waved as if for victory; and the Swiss charged down
the hill shouting *Francia! Francia!* while from the hostile ranks arose
the answering cry of *Spagna! Imperio!* . . . It became a butchery
pure and simple, and for two long miles, even to the gates of
Lucignano, the ground was strewn with the banners, arms, and
corpses of Strozzi's ruined army; while he himself, with bullet
wounds in the side and in the hand, and his head half crushed
by a blow from a mace, scarcely escaped to Montalcino."[1]

[1] A Sozzini: *Diario delle cose avvenute in Siena dai 21 Luglio 1550 ai 28 Giugno 1559* in
Arch. Stor. Ital. (Florence, 1842), pp. 270, et seq. O. Montalvo: *Historia de' fatti e guerre
de' Senesi* (Venice, 1599), pp. 98 et seq.

And so, considering of this on that fair summer morning, I crossed the great valley, mile after mile of it, and climbed into Torrita. Now Torrita is splendid, with seven towers on its *tufa* hill, and is probably of Etruscan origin—older then than Sinalunga, older than Foiano. Its history, so far as we may know its history, is that of every other little town between Siena and Montepulciano, and the best example of that is the story of Lucignano. It only comes really on to the stage even of Sienese history twice: it took part in the war with Perugia, and it witnessed the only honourable effort Siena was ever able to make to rid herself and her *contado* of the curse of the military companies. It happened thus. In the year 1363 Siena was ruled by that worst faction of all, the Dodici, who, not content with their own ineptitude, strove so far to obliterate even the memory of the Nove that they caused the very name to be erased from the public statutes. The times were perilous, and this gang of tradesmen was completely unfitted to deal with them. Many dependent towns had already revolted, and the Companies of Adventure which harassed the *contado* had again been bought off with great sums of money, when Messer Ceccolo degli Orsini, a Roman and no Sienese, in command of the Sienese levies, decided to save his honour in spite of the magistrates. Finding the Company of the Hat, a professional army of ruffians and pirates, ready to do any man's bidding who would pay them, lurking in the *contado* hereabout, against the order of the magistrates of Siena, he forced them to fight him in the valley between Sinalunga and Torrita and beat them, as you may see any day in the great Sala of the Palazzo Pubblico of Siena, for Luca di Tommè has painted the battle there, not without glory. "Messer Ceccolo was not confirmed in his office because he had been ordered not to join battle by reason of the peril which might come of it; and for this he was not re-elected." The Dodici, adding infamy to cowardice, however, were not ashamed to get what glory they could out of his victory, and that fresco of Luca di Tommè's is as much a monument to their dishonour as to his victory.

Torrita today shares with Sinalunga not only a glory of landscape, but a wealth of pictures little, if any, inferior to hers.

In Santa Fiora, over the altar is a magnificent signed altarpiece of the Madonna and Child with SS. John and Andrew and the Trinity in the *predella* by Benvenuto di Giovanni, painted in 1497.

That is perhaps the finest work in Torrita. In the Madonna delle Nevi I came upon some important frescoes about an altar by Girolamo di Benvenuto that in their exquisite country beauty are not less delightful. In the midst we see the Assumption of the Virgin among a crowd of musical angels, while S. Thomas, doubtful again, receives at once for his assurance and in token of her forgiveness her girdle, which now lies, they say, in Prato, where, in fact, I have seen it. Under the arch with His saints our Lord from amid the cherubim awaits His Mother and ours. On either side we see two saints, and above the Annunciation, in a quiet court looking on a garden plot.

Nor is this all, for hard by Cozzarelli has painted it all over again, though with less sweetness and sincerity.

Before I left Torrita I wandered by chance into the Prepositura, and found a beautiful triptych by Fei or some Sienese of the fifteenth century, where on a gold ground was set forth the Crucifixion of our Lord, with the Blessed Virgin and S. John, and weeping at the foot of the Cross, golden-haired Magdalen. In the side panels stood two saints as though at Mass, as indeed they were. Here, too, is a picture of the Nativity with saints by Bartolo di Fredi rather darkened.

Just before sunset I set out for the railway hoping to reach Montepulciano that night, though indeed I scarce knew how.

CHAPTER XXII

MONTEPULCIANO

However one comes to the lofty city of Montepulciano the way is beautiful. The whole valley of the Chiana and beyond is spread out like some gracious fairyland, in which lie three magic lakes, and one of them is not only lovely but famous—the lakes of Chiusi, of Montepulciano, and of Trasimeno; beyond lie the great mountains of Umbria, and over all is a supreme and luminous peace. Little by little, as one climbs to the city of the beautiful name, some great or delicate feature in the landscape impresses itself, only to be replaced again and again by others as fair as itself; the serene and graceful outline of Cetona, for instance, gives place to the tremendous and beautiful form of Mont' Amiata far away, or the eagle's nest of Monte Follonico, truly a city out of a fairy-tale, draws one's eyes from Chiusi, till at last Montepulciano itself suddenly appears over the lower hills at a turning of the way, the queen of all this country, a city of another world, a city aloof, piled up on its isolated hill-top.

It would be unprofitable to go into the almost inextricable details of the history of this hill city, which guarded of old so many ways and stood on so many confines. Called, as it is said, first Mons Politicus, then Mons Politianus, and finally Montepulciano, if we may believe tradition it is among the most noble of Italian towns, founded by Lars Porsena of Clusium, and already of account when there were kings in Rome. History, however, knows nothing of Montepulciano till the year 715 of our era, and though traces of Etruscan civilization have been found on its hillside, we know nothing of its life, if life there was, previous to the eighth century. Then it began to order itself as a free Commune, and its fate, like its story, is that of every other town in this region; in its comparative weakness it had to decide, not whether it would be free or enslaved, but which of two cities it would serve, Siena or Florence. Till 1202 it remained under the protection of Siena, but in that year it capitulated to Florence. This was but the first, if, indeed, it was the first, of innumerable surrenders, first to one party and then to another. For Montepulciano, commanding the Val di

Chiana at its narrowest part, before it divided into the two arms
which lead to Arezzo and Siena, dominating the only pass between
the Val di Chiana and the Val d' Asso, where the Via Francigena
entered the great defile between Mont' Amiata and Monte Cetona,
standing, as it did, on the verge of Umbria and Tuscany, was
continually the cause of war between Florence and Siena, both
of which claimed so valuable a fortress. Indeed, as you read the
story of those medieval Communes, you might think that their sole
cause of quarrel was this little hill city, so unfortunately placed for
herself in command of the great trade routes of Italy. Her fate
was decided by her geographical position; for though she was so
finely situated as a fortress, she was, even more than Siena, debarred
by that position from ever becoming a rich and populous city of
merchandise; and if these conditions be well grasped any detailed
account of her story will be superfluous. For we might prophesy
from them the very fate which overtook her. They destined her
to be a bone of contention for ever, and even as two dogs quarrel
over a bone, so Florence and Siena quarrelled over Montepulciano.
Sometimes the one seemed to be going to possess her, sometimes
the other, but till almost the end, in 1553, Montepulciano remained
a continual cause of quarrel.

To the agony forced upon Montepulciano from outside was
added in the fourteenth century internal troubles. The family of
Pecora, a family of ambitious merchants, seized the place, and
when they were betrayed by one of their own blood and the city
freed from their tyranny in 1352, it was only to fall into the hands
of Florence or of Siena or even of Perugia. Perugia, however, had
serious need of the city, and did something, at any rate, to restore
her freedom, till in 1359 Niccolò del Pecora returned, and there
followed riot, murder, and finally treason. Montepulciano herself
asked for the protection of Siena. By 1388, however, we are not
surprised to find she was tired of Siena, and appealed to Florence,
whereupon Siena placed herself and her *contado* under the lordship
of Visconti. Visconti took Montepulciano, but by 1404 Siena,
weary of his tyranny, got rid of him, and, making alliance with
Florence, exchanged Lucignano, which then belonged to the Lily,
for Montepulciano. There followed the futile wars of the *condottieri*,
which fill the fifteenth century with confusion. And, in fact, it was
not till Niccolò Machiavelli appeared, and, making treaty with
Siena, secured the lordship of that city to Petrucci and the lordship

of Montepulciano to Florence, that order rose out of chaos. But by then Cosimo I was at hand, and the Granducato something more than a prophecy. Thus peace came at last when the hegemony of Tuscany passed into the hands of Florence under the Medici.

There are but few signs left today of those centuries of struggle, of blood, treason, slavery, and destruction. Montepulciano is one of the most smiling, one of the most withdrawn of the smaller cities of Tuscany, and she sits there on her hill-top today above her vineyards and woods like a queen sure of her court and her own beauty.

It is true that the Marzocco inn is not so charming as I feel sure it must have been when Symonds made it famous, and if the wine be overrated, and today I think it is—I know many a better wine hereabout in Tuscany—it is difficult to praise too highly the interest of the city and the beauty of the country in which she reigns, or to tell of the works of art which still abide there—too many, alas! in a museum.

On entering Montepulciano one is struck at once by the splendour of her walls and gates, by the Porta del Prato especially, and once within the city, even as one comes to the inn, the palaces of Antonio da Sangallo astonish one by their splendour. From the Marzocco—that sign of Florentine domination opposite the Palazzo Avignonesi, just outside the inn, all one's way through the city is set with fine buildings—the Loggia del Mercato of Vignola, the Palazzo Tarugi, the Palazzo Cocconi, the Palazzo Contucci, perhaps the finest of Sangallo's buildings within the city, the magnificent Palazzo Pubblico (but with a tower that follows a long way off the Mangia of Siena), the whole of the Piazza Grande with its beautiful fountain, the Palazzo Cervini of Sangallo, the Palazzo Bombagli, so charmingly Sienese, the Palazzo Ricci-Paracciani— all the way is lined with fine buildings up to the modern *fortezza*, which stands on the ruins of the old Rocca of the Sienese.

All this without speaking of the churches, Sant' Agostino and Santa Maria, and the Cathedral, which is, as it should be, the best of all.

Climbing the narrow, steep street from the Marzocco, opposite which is the Palazzo Avignonesi, perhaps built by Vignola, one passes almost at once on the right the church of Sant' Agostino, with its good Renaissance façade, a delightful work of Michelozzo, and there, over the principal doorway, is the first of those art treasures in which Montepulciano is rich, Michelozzo's three fine figures in relief in half-length of the Madonna and Child with S. John the Baptist and S. Augustine. There are many older things in Montepulciano, but nothing, I think, that charms and delights one more than these fifteenth-century sculptures by a master not certainly the equal of Donatello, but a master, nevertheless, we may well envy the fifteenth century. Within, over the second altar on the right, is a panel by Giovanni di Paolo of S. Niccolò da Tolentino and, on the other side of the church, a Crucifixion by Lorenzo di Credi.

Climbing on, past the Palazzo Cervini, built by Pope Marcellus II when he was Cardinal, and designed by Antonio Sangallo the Younger, and so ever upwards through the town, one comes at last to the church of Santa Maria dei Servi, standing in an open space on the hillside, and commanding a wide and lovely view of that wonderful world of valley and mountain over which Montepulciano reigns. The beautiful tower and charming doorway and façade of Santa Maria take you at once, and within is a fragment of a polyptych, a Virgin and Child very like Duccio's Maestà, perhaps by Segna, altogether a remarkable work. In the apse is a copy of the famous Madonna of Correggio at Parma.

Just beyond Santa Maria one comes out on the hillside over the olives, and thence one may see Pienza, Montalcino, and Mont' Amiata, with Rocca d' Orcia and Campiglia d' Orcia on its skirts, and there lies Trequanda and nearer Monte Follonico, with, on a fair day, in the farthest distance to the north and west, the dim blue mountains of Elba over the midland sea.

Turning away at last from this vision of the kingdoms of the world, one makes one's way up past the *fortezza* to the Duomo, which, lovely in itself as it is, is the real treasure-house of Montepulciano.

A gaunt brick building, only partly cased with stone, flanked by a great square tower, it is the colour, perhaps, rather than the simple form of the Cathedral that wins one at first, but within is a noble church of a fine Renaissance type, spacious and full of light. And this somewhat worldly sanctuary possesses two treasures of great price, the one whole as ever it was, the other broken, yet even in ruin one of the finest things in the city—I mean the great altarpiece of Taddeo di Bartolo and the broken tomb of Aragazzi by Michelozzo.

Bartolommeo Aragazzi was secretary to Martin V, and Michelozzo's tomb, when it was still perfect, must have been one of the finest works of that master. Two fragments of it are now to be found just within the west doors of the Cathedral, but the main portion, the tomb itself, still stands over the high altar. There Aragazzi lies in friar's frock, his beautiful hands crossed carefully, seemingly sleeping, his wise and careworn face truly sympathetic, in the great peace which has smoothed away the restlessness that in his troublous time must often have tortured it. Beside him, one on either side the high altar, are two statues—S. Gabriel and S. Mary at Annunciation. The dead man lies sleeping between them, hearing in his dream the marvellous salutation.

Scattered all over the church are fragments of the once perfect monument, friezes of cherubs, and reliefs. No city, I think, in all southern Tuscany can boast of so much Florentine work as Montepulciano; but she is under no obligation, since she gave to the city of the Lily the greatest ornament of Lorenzo's court, Angelo Poliziano, who was born here, and called by her name. The greatest treasure of the church, however, is not this broken work of a Florentine sculptor, but a true masterpiece of Siena, Taddeo di Bartolo's vast altarpiece that towers over the high altar. It is a polyptych, towered and pinnacled, with a splendid double *predella*, perfect in every detail, of the Death and Assumption of the Blessed Virgin. In the midst we see the Madonna ravished into heaven, surrounded by angels, while below on earth the apostles weep for her, since she is gone from them. There are here many figures, and the character of the heads, the wonderfully living and lovely angels, the perfect completeness of the whole work, give to it a beauty, a nobility, and an importance beyond anything else we have from Taddeo's hand. One head among all those which bend over the frail body of the Virgin is especially vivid and full of life: it is, as the raised gold letters of the halo tell us, that of S. Thaddaeus, and there, I think, we see a portrait of the painter.

In the four pilasters are twelve figures of saints, and in the two side panels again other saints, each with his name or hers written in the gold of their haloes. Above, in the midst, is the Coronation of the Virgin, and on either side the mystery of the Annunciation. The *predelle* consist of twenty-three scenes, nine of which are concerned with the life of Christ, while fourteen are devoted to the saints.

The Duomo possesses other works of considerable interest; for instance, in the third chapel on the south side of the church is a panel of S. Vincent Ferrer by some pupil of Bonfigli; and a figure of our Lord by some later master. The font, too, is a work of much beauty.

One other church at least, within the city, that of Santa Lucia, is worth a visit. Here, in the chapel on the right, is a Madonna and Child, a very much damaged work by Luca Signorelli.

But most of the pictures which used to adorn the churches of Montepulciano have unhappily been gathered into the Museo Civico, where, it is true, they are well cared for, but where much of their beauty and all their meaning are lost. Here are some pictures of no great importance: a Coronation of the Blessed Virgin, with seven angels above and four below, by Bartolo di Fredi (?), but the heads of the Virgin and Christ are spoiled. The next picture is, though a late work, more interesting by reason of its subject. It is an Immaculate Conception by Lappoli of Arezzo, and was painted in 1547. In a garden Madonna treads the devil, half Cupid, half serpent, under her feet, bruising his head with her heel. God the Father blesses her, rod in hand. Beneath and around are S. Rosa of Viterbo, S. Francis, and S. Nicholas of Bari. The picture bears the following inscription: "Ioannes Ant. Lappolus Aret. Exprimebat Quod Alius ex Voto et Animo Concepisset Anno MDXLVII."

One then comes to a Madonna and Child with S. John the Baptist, a charming work with a lovely landscape, by some pupil of Filippino Lippi. The masterpiece of the collection, a delicate and lovely Nativity, is by Girolamo di Benvenuto, where our Lord lies on the ground just outside the shed where the ox feeds with the ass, and Madonna, like a tower of rosy ivory, kneels with S. Joseph to worship Him, while a shepherd in the background peers down in wonder and the Holy Dove hovers over "the place where the young child lay". In a cleft of dark rock an owl rests, and in heaven God blesses the world in a cloud of cherubim, and a tiny bright angel, like a gorgeous bird, flies earthward, with those glad tidings to the shepherds, which shall be to all people. Nothing more delicately fair than this Nativity is to be found in Montepulciano.

A few other works in the collection have some interest: a spoiled Crucifixion by some pupil of Filippino Lippi; a reliquary, the

Madonna and Child above, and under S. John Baptist, S. Biagio, and S. Sigismundo by some pupil of Fei; a Madonna and Child with S. Françis and a Bishop by some pupil of Bicci di Lorenzo; a *tondo* of the Madonna and Child in a landscape by Carli, and a charming picture by Bicci di Lorenzo of the Madonna and Child with S. Francis, S. Catherine, S. John the Baptist, and an Olivetan monk.

Seven pieces, reliefs in enamelled terra-cotta by the Robbia school, are gathered here; among them a lunette of the Madonna and Child with S. John the Baptist and S. Lucy; an altarpiece with a tabernacle about which stand four saints and over which hover two angels, while above, in a lunette, Madonna is at Annunciation, and below, in the *predella*, two angels wait; another altarpiece of the Madonna and Child between two saints, while above two angels crown her as Queen. Here, too, is an exquisite relief in marble of the Madonna and Child between four angels by some unknown master of the fifteenth century.

But it is on leaving Montepulciano for Pienza, perhaps, that one sees what is surely the most striking monument to her splendour at its greatest in the later Renaissance—I mean the beautiful church built for love by Antonio da Sangallo beneath the western height of the town. Coming upon Santa Maria della Consolazione, outside Todi in Umbria, I called it the most beautiful church in the world. Well, here you may see something very like it, without going to the trouble of marching to Todi. San Biagio of Montepulciano is, on a small scale of course, what San Pietro in Vaticano should have been, what it would have been, but for the barbarian Reformation—a Greek cross under a dome. As one stands on the threshold it is upward that one's gaze is drawn, irresistibly, by the great light and space of the design, the height and beauty of all the proportions. Here is a church full of light— a church not for repentance but for praise; the whole place seems to utter the great verses of the *Te Deum Laudamus*, and in itself to give visible form to words in which alone we hear some faint echo of those the great archangels sing:

Tibi omnes Angeli, Tibi coeli et universae potestates:
Tibi Cherubim et Seraphim incessabili voce proclamant:
Sanctus, Sanctus, Sanctus, Dominus Deus Sabaoth,
Pleni sunt coeli et terra majestatis gloriae tuae. . . .

CHAPTER XXIII

PIENZA

THE road from Montepulciano to Pienza, a distance of some eight miles, is picturesque enough. View after view, vista after vista, north and south, east and west, open before one, the glory of the world seems indeed to be spread out there for our joy. To the south rise the indescribably impressive forms of Mont' Amiata, Monte Cetona, and the huge bizarre rock Radicofani; to the north lie the low and tawny hills of the desert, closed at last by the distant range upon which Siena lies; to the west Pienza stands like a sentinel, and after Pienza, Montalcino, and behind Montalcino the blue mysterious mountains of the Maremma; while to the east Montepulciano rises high up above one into the sky. One may well sing *Te Deum*. In few other places do the strength and nobility of the Italian landscape so impress themselves upon one, nowhere else do the mountains seem so proud or the valleys so rare. Nor is the character of this landscape less splendid than its composition. It has before everything a beauty and strength of outline, of construction: it has colour, too, and spaciousness, but chiefly it has outline, decisive and affirmative. It has not the quietness, the repose, the softness and sweetness that one finds in Umbria; just these qualities it is content to lack; but it has always what is rarest in England, a beauty of outline without which there is no real or profound satisfaction, I think, no finality. So I thought as on that summer afternoon I rested in the shadow of a cypress on the road, far from the noisy cities.

Presently I came to a great castle at a turning of the way over the bare hills, and then at last and suddenly Pienza came into full view, still some miles away, so I went on with renewed heart and won the gate at sunset.

And as it happened my angel went with me, for as I came up the one long street of the place into the piazza where the Duomo of Rossellino stands and the Palazzo del Municipio and the Palazzo Piccolomini, and indeed all the great buildings of Pienza, he led me, and I swear I knew nothing about it, out behind the church on to a narrow terrace, and there I watched the sunset.

SAN BIAGIO, Montepulciano

BADIA DI SANT' ANTIMO

I could not have had greater good fortune. For it was not only
the sunset I saw, but the sunset over a great bare world of mountain and valley—Mont' Amiata, now quite close, and Val d' Orcia
—a world actually as strong as Castile, as barren,too, and as stony,
as tremendous in its significance. Desolate beyond expression,
that wide and desert valley, full of twilight, lay before me, and out
of it rose the vast bastions of Mont' Amiata, the greatest mountain
in Tuscany; and its foundations were as the foundations of the
world. Huge and sloping cliffs of tawny rock supported the enormous weight of the mountain, rising higher and higher till they
formed at last the platform from which rose the cone of this great
extinct volcano we call Mont' Amiata. Not a tree was to be seen,
not a house, not a sign of human habitation or toil, only this
primeval world of boulder and cliff and desert, out of which
the great mountain rose—the monument of some bygone and
departed age of stone. When the sun had set and the last faint
ghost of light had vanished from the earth, still, under a heaven
of stars, the mountain loomed out before me, blotting out the
whole western sky. And as I returned down the street of Pienza
to the inn it was that beautiful grave shape which I saw still
before me, that I could not put out of my mind or forget, that
haunts me still as I write; for I seemed to have seen something,
beyond the measure of man, that in its tremendous force and
silence was beyond my understanding. Something it held in
common with the constellations, those blazons of the sky, which
surely portend some message or express the meaning of some
godlike order, some universal ceremony in which the sun is served
at a heavenly altar by all the planets in order, and the stars in
their courses chant the winding antiphons in some universal
liturgy.

The story of Pienza is like the fairy-tale of Cinderella, which
after all has Christian authority, for is it not written that the last
shall be first? Before Pienza changed her name, before her
wonderful, her incredible fortune befell her, she was but a little
good-for-nothing village of a few hundred inhabitants, and her
name was Corsignano. Then in the first years of the fifteenth
century a certain poor nobleman, exiled from Siena, came to this
village to live by cultivating the few wretched acres which alone
remained to him, for he was ruined. With him came his young

15

wife, as noble as himself, and presently in their little homestead she gave birth to a son, whom they called Enea Silvio. This child of the race of the Piccolomini, after a life of adventure, managing his affairs with great astuteness, and meeting with much good fortune, was presently elected Pope, and taking, in memory of Aeneas, after whom he was named, the title of Pius, out of his vanity, in the twinkling of an eye, as only a pope can, he turned the obscure and dirty little village of Corsignano into the city of Pienza, building there a cathedral and certain palaces, and setting over it, to govern it, a bishop, that his name might be remembered for ever and his birthplace be held in honour *in saecula saeculorum*. Now the infallibility of a pope no one of good education will be found to question; but this infallibility, as is well known, is only to be found in matters pertaining to the Faith, and in them only when he speaks *ex cathedra* as S. Peter's successor, as the vice-regent of God here on earth—PP. Pont. Max. Serv. Servorm. Dei. Therefore it is not surprising that, do what he would, though Decree followed Decree and Bull followed Bull, Pienza remained Corsignano—that is to say, a little village—and nothing that the Pope and the Bishop could do with their cathedral and their palaces ever was able to make it otherwise. Let me hasten to add that as a village Pienza is one of the most charming and delightful places, exceptional, too, as villages go, in the possession of a fine cathedral and several palaces, to say nothing of pictures and a museum; and yet with all these, which Pius gave her, the finest thing and incomparably the loveliest and the best which she possesses is the great view she has of the mountains and the Val d' Orcia from her hillside. For this she should give thanks daily, and we with her; for the rest, we can accept it with a certain complacence, seeing that she is there, not for our sakes at all, but to satisfy the vanity of Enea Silvio, the most human of the popes, who, in the name of Pius II, filled S. Peter's Chair not unworthily from 1458 to 1464.

The most considerable buildings in Pienza, the buildings which she owes to Pius II, are set about the Piazza del Duomo, in which the Palazzo Pubblico faces the Cathedral, and the Arcivescovado the Piccolomini Palace. These are the sights of Pienza, but I always prefer first to visit the old *pieve*, the little parish church of Corsignano, which was here or ever Pius came and thrust upon the village an honour too intolerable—the honour of his name.

To reach this humble little sanctuary it is necessary to descend behind the apse of the Duomo for a few hundred yards southward, when it will be seen beside the way, a somewhat neglected flower of poverty and littleness. The church is dedicated to S. Vito and S. Modesta, and is very ancient, the Bishops of Arezzo and Siena having disputed its jurisdiction even in the eighth century. The present building, however, dates from the eleventh or twelfth century, and consists of three naves, divided by unequal round arches of stone. Beneath is a crypt. Two splendid Romanesque doorways, ornamented with sculpture, lead into the church; in the façade is a curious and half-ruined round tower. Here both Pius II and his father were christened.

Another relic of the village of Corsignano is the Franciscan convent church of San Francesco, that once had a little hospice of friars attached to it which in the eighteenth century was transformed into an episcopal seminary. Once covered with frescoes, now ruinous, the church was restored in 1892–1903. It still holds a few Sienese pictures—almost all that is left to it of its sweet country beauty.[1] The two churches of Corsignano are, however, but shrines for the sentimental traveller; for the rest of us there remain the Cathedral, the Piccolomini Palace, and the Museo, which after all are what has brought us to so out-of-the-way a place as Pienza.

Evil days befell the beautiful masterpiece of Bernardo Rossellino, which he began in 1457 and, with the Piccolomini Palace, finished in less than three years. In the series of earthquakes that fifty years or more ago proved so disastrous, the whole of the foundations of the beautiful apse of the Duomo of Pienza were destroyed; a vast winding chasm opened under the choir, and it was difficult to see how that part of the building could be saved. The devoted and loyal enthusiasm of Count Silvio Piccolomini was engaged in its preservation, and it is consoling to see that the church has been preserved.

The church which Count Silvio has saved is a fine Renaissance building, with a beautiful façade, with the arms of Pio II in the architrave; divided into three naves of equal height by eight travertine columns. The most charming feature is the apse, which was in such grave danger, and from outside, the tower, the most prominent feature in Pienza, as seen from a distance.

[1] In the apse are frescoes of the life of S. Francis by some follower of Bartolo di Fredi; a fine Ducciesque Crucifix, a Madonna of Mercy are here too, by some follower of Signorelli; and a repainted Sienese picture of the Madonna and Child.

One's delight in the church itself, however, is vastly increased when one finds that its ancient treasures of art—the best of them at least in the way of pictures—have been preserved to it and not hidden away in the Museo. Four masterpieces of Sienese painting greet one here each in its own chapel.

In the first chapel on the right is a splendid altarpiece by Matteo di Giovanni. The Virgin sits enthroned with her little Son; around her stand S. Bartolommeo, S. Lucia, S. Matthew, and S. Catherine, with two little angels. Above is a remarkable Flagellation.

In the first chapel on the left is a fine work by Sano di Pietro. The Virgin enthroned with our Lord—an apple in His left hand— is surrounded by S. James, S. Anne, S. Philip, and S. Mary Magdalen.

In the second chapel in this aisle there is a magnificent triptych by Vecchietta of the Assumption. In the midst our Lady, borne on a silver cloud by a crowd of angels, is caught into heaven, into Christ's arms, while beneath, beside her empty tomb, S. Thomas looks upward. On either side stand two saints, on the left S. Pio— first Pope of that name—and S. Agatha, and on the other S. Calisto and S. Catherine of Siena, whom the second Pio canonized. This work is, in fact, one of the masterpieces of the Sienese school of the fifteenth century; it gives us to understand to how great a place in religious art the painters of that school had been called.

Close by is a charming work by Giovanni di Paolo of the Madonna and Child with SS. Bernardino, Jerome, Francis, and Chiara; above in the lunette is a marvellously lovely Pietà hesitating to be realistic; while in the *predella* are three *tondi* of saints, and at each end the Piccolomini arms. The colour and quality of this work are remarkable.

The high altar is probably by Bernardo Rossellino and it holds reliquaries and relics given by Pius II. The stalls, too, are of course of his time.

On coming out from the Duomo one has on one's right the Arcivescovado, and it is there that the museum has found a home. This small collection, with its various treasures of tapestry, of Opus Anglicanum, of sculptures and paintings, is delightful. It is true I would rather see the marvellous Pienza cope, made in England and presented by Tommaso Paleologus to Pio II, worn by the Bishop in the Duomo for the Vespers of Christmas: it is true I should rejoice to hear Vespers sung from the wonderful

choir-books splendid with miniatures on some winter afternoon as
I sat under the great altarpiece of Matteo da Siena, but since that
is impossible, I will take care not to deprive my eyes of their
pleasure and joy in the *museo* of Pienza. As for the cope, who can
praise it enough or remember without regret that we made it in
England and cannot match it now? Indeed, there is nothing so
fine in England of England's own work; the only piece able to
match it being the cope at Ascoli, but this here is the finer of the
two. The Pienza cope represents in its exquisitely embroidered
figures, in the first two half-circles, the life of the Blessed Virgin,
beneath which, dividing this first from the second half-circle, are
set eight of her ancestors, including David and Solomon. The
Twelve Apostles divide the second from the third and last half-
circle of figures, which represents the life of S. Catherine of
Alexandria. The foundation of this magnificent vestment is linen,
but it is completely hidden by an embroidered field of gold; on
this are set the figures of various-coloured silks.

The cope, though it be the most splendid, is not the only relic
of Pio II we find in the *museo*. There, too, are his crosier and his
pyx, certain mitres, and other vestments and ornaments.

The pictures—a splendid, small collection gathered in a place
too small for them—are hung in the next room. Here is a poor
Madonna and Child with S. John Baptist, S. Biagio, S. Niccolò,
and S. Floriano by Vecchietta. Above is a beautiful lunette
of the Annunciation, while in the *predella* are three panels: the
Crucifixion in the midst, and on one side the Martyrdom of S.
Biagio, and on the other that most delightful story of how S.
Niccolò saved the three maidens—asleep here in their beds—from
harlotry.

Bartolo di Fredi comes next with a lovely Virgin of Mercy and
two angels: a most gracious picture. Then, of all things, here is
a Sassetta, a small triptych of the Madonna and Child with S. John
and some woman saint, and in the pinnacles God the Father and
angels; a rather disappointing work, much darkened.

A fine and even exquisite work by Matteo di Giovanni is the
last notable picture in the room. This is a Madonna and Child
with four saints; above, God the Father; below, three small *tondi*,
two saints and the Crucifixion. Two other works should be mentioned: one a diptych by an unknown master in which we see
S. Pio and S. Andrea on a gold ground; the other a triptych,

maybe by Bartolo di Fredi, with many scenes from the lives of Christ and the Blessed Virgin.

The great palace of Pienza, the Palazzo Piccolomini, fully comparable to any similar building in Florence or Siena, is well worth a visit; its court and *loggiata* are very charming, and the hexagonal well there, carved with the arms of Pius, is worthy of Rossellino, or is it Francesco di Giorgio? Within the palace are some magnificent old furniture and a fairly good collection of family portraits, among them the only known likeness, I think, of Pio II.

During my stay in Pienza I went up to Monticchiello, a wonderfully inaccessible *castello* about three or four miles away, which played an heroic part under Adriano Baglioni, the Sienese commander, when in 1553 it was besieged by the Imperialists under Don Garcia de Toledo. The fortress was dismantled by the Spaniards, but there are considerable remains of the towers and walls, the gate and the keep. Yet it was not this Rocca I had climbed up here to see, but the church of SS. Leonardo e Cristoforo which still possesses a masterpiece by Pietro Lorenzetti. The church is transitional Romanesque-Gothic in style with a fine portal. Within, over the first altar on the right is the masterpiece, a most lovely panel of the Virgin and Child, which reminded me of the famous fresco in the lower church of San Francesco in Assisi, not only because the Virgin and Child are looking each at the other with great intentness. This beautiful and tender, even passionate, picture by so famous a master of the fourteenth century was worth the fatigue of the way and should on no account remain unvisited by any one who finds himself in Pienza.

CHAPTER XXIV

SAN QUIRICO AND CASTIGLIONE D' ORCIA

I LEFT Pienza early one morning and went down to San Quirico d' Orcia. The road winds round the hills, till it descends to San Quirico on the Via Francigena in the Orcia valley. The little town consists of this one long street surrounded by perfect walls and it possesses two remarkable Romanesque churches. It was ceded in 1016 by Countess Willa, mother of Ugo, Margrave of Tuscany, to the monks of Abbadia San Salvatore, on Mont' Amiata, and the Emperor, Frederic I, set up there a *corte regia* with an imperial vicar. Later it came into the power of Siena, which in 1256 had provided it with a Podestà. It was a strong and important place on the road to Rome. Before the coming of the railway, travellers lunched there after leaving Buonconvento, the first stage out of Siena, proceeding thence to Radicofani to sleep. Forsyth in September 1802 dined here off an eagle.

"On reaching San Quirico," he writes, "I found the people just recovering from a consternation caused by a black spectre which had lately appeared in the air. Wild screams were heard: the very cattle caught the alarm. The profane pronounced the apparition to be a monk; the monks insisted it was the devil himself; and the curate was preparing to exorcise the parish, when at last the phantom descended in the shape of an eagle and carried off a kid. On returning for fresh prey it was shot by the peasants and roasted at our inn for supper."

Fifty years later Hawthorne passed through San Quirico on his way to Rome. He was struck by the "Piccolomini" Palace but thought nothing of the church which was "not particularly interesting". What interested him more was "a most wretched team of *vettura* horses which stopped at the door of our *albergo*; poor, lean, downcast creatures ... the harness fastened with ropes, the traces and reins with ropes, the carriage old and shabby. Out of this miserable equipage there alighted an ancient gentleman and lady, whom our waiter affirmed to be the Prefect of Florence and his wife."

The beautiful Romanesque church of San Quirico, the Collegiata which Hawthorne thought nothing of, stands at the entry to the town, with a magnificent façade and portico of the twelfth century supported on lions with beasts on the architrave. The portico on the right side has a canopy and is supported by caryatids standing on lions, I suppose of the thirteenth century, for the portico on the left side has an inscription dated 1298. Within, the church has been redecorated in the seventeenth century, but without, it is a noble example of a Romanesque building, with a fine bell-tower.

Over an altar on the right there is a very lovely altarpiece by Sano di Pietro, much like that at the Badia a Isola save that the Virgin and Child are accompanied by four angels and the figures at the sides are much less refined. These figures represent SS. John Baptist, Quiricus, Fortunatus, and John Evangelist. Above is a beautiful Ascension and Descent into Hades in the lunette. The *predella* is again rather rough, which is curious, as Sano is so often at his best in small pictures. It has scenes of the life of our Lady. The other Romanesque church is that of Santa Maria. It, too, has a fine portico, campanile, and semicircular apse.

The Palazzo Chigi behind the Collegiata and the Palazzo Pretorio opposite, are rather severe buildings for the seventeenth century. The Via Poliziano thence leads to the fine Porta dei Cappuccini.

San Quirico was known as *San Quirico in Osenna*, though no one seems to know why. It was Siena who fortified it in the fourteenth century. Its interest today lies in its Romanesque churches and in the ruined sixteenth-century park or garden called the Orti Leonini. The "Piccolomini" Palace too, opposite the Palazzo Pretorio which Hawthorne admired, is really the Palazzo Chigi, another Sienese papal family.

I left San Quirico and followed the Via Francigena on the way to Rome, over the bridge across the Orcia, and then immediately turned up on the right for the climb to Castiglione d' Orcia, wonderfully situated under Mont' Amiata, fifteen hundred feet high, a little forlorn fortress of a town which was able so effectively to hold the Roman road at the mouth of this difficult pass under Radicofani.

Castiglione d' Orcia was one of the many fortresses in this difficult and lonely country in the possession of the Aldobrandeschi of Santa Fiora on Mont' Amiata.[1] Santa Fiora itself, their capital

---

[1] For a description and the history of Santa Fiora, as for the whole of Mont' Amiata, see my *A Wayfarer in Unknown Tuscany*, with notes by William Heywood (third edition). There a complete history of the Aldobrandeschi is given, pp. 139–64.

and almost impregnable fortress, high up on the southern flank of Mont' Amiata, gave them no control of the Roman road which it must have been one of their chief necessities to obtain. The great castle of Radicofani, which certainly held it, they were never able to get possession of, for when the abbey of San Salvatore declined, it was already in the hands of Siena and the Holy See. The control of the Via Francigena, which enabled them to rob any caravan that came by, and practically to hold up the trade of Siena with the Eternal City, was given them by this little fortress of Castiglione d' Orcia and, as one might suppose, it was the first of their possessions to be wrested from them by the Sienese. In 1250 the Commune of Siena took the Rocca; but even then they had not done with it, for twenty years after the battle of Montaperto it formed a nest for the Sienese *fuorusciti*, and was only taken after a siege of forty days, and then by chance. It was not really till April 1300 that the Sienese made themselves masters of the place, when the Counts of Santa Fiora were compelled to renounce for ever their dominion here, and received a payment of 3,000 florins in compensation. In 1368, when Siena was ruled by the Dodici, Castiglione came into the hands of the Salimbeni, who built there the Rocca whose ruins we now see. Their rule lasted till 1418, when the place was once more incorporated within the dominion of the Republic. Over a hundred years later, in 1554, the Imperial army was able to enter without encountering any resistance; by then, doubtless, the fortress was practically useless.

One's chief delight in Castiglione d' Orcia today is certainly far from being its extraordinary position; for me at least, its wealth of pictures is something much more important. The three churches are full of fine things; even the *pieve* dedicated to SS. Stefano e Degno, though it has nothing else, possesses a beautiful picture of our Lady by Pietro Lorenzetti, that is not only a miracle picture, but also a beautiful and very interesting work of art. The Virgin holds her Divine Son on her left arm and loosely enfolds His feet with her right. She looks out of the picture as though at us, who have stayed in adoration. He gazes intently on His Mother. The picture, so far as the background is concerned, is in a poor state, the panel formidably split, but this does not impair the marvellous loveliness of the two divine figures.

Many years ago there used to be another picture in the church, an eikon of the Virgin and Child by some country follower of Segna. Where has it gone? There still remains the fifteenth-century Sienese fresco of the Madonna and Child and two angels with SS. Bernardino, Roch, Catherine, and Mary Magdalen, much damaged.

Other wonderful treasures are to be seen in Santa Maria Maddalena and San Simeone.

In Santa Maria Maddelana there is a charming panel picture of the Madonna and Child by Lippo Memmi, a thing so fair and devout that one might be accounted fortunate to see it alone at the price of a day's journey, yet in the same church there is a delightful, though damaged, work by Vecchietta—the Madonna and Child with four angels, an early work. In the sacristy is a damaged picture, probably by some follower of Pietro Lorenzetti, of the Madonna and Child.

Nor is this all, for not far away, in the Rocca, in the church of San Simeone, there is a fine Madonna of Mercy by Bartolo di Fredi, and a splendid panel picture of the Madonna and Child by Giovanni di Paolo. This is a Madonna dell' Umiltà. She is seated on a cushion on the floor minding her little Son, between two cherubs; below is the Annunciation and above the Crucifixion.

I left Castiglione d' Orcia with regret. It holds two pictures by Pietro Lorenzetti and Giovanni di Paolo which are among the loveliest of their works.

CHAPTER XXV

MONTALCINO AND BADIA SANT' ANTIMO

No better fate, no more happy destiny can await any traveller in Tuscany than that which leads him on a summer morning into Montalcino—one of the most lovely, one of the most pleasant, and one of the dearest places in a land where there is always something to be thankful for. Its perfections are so many and, gathered all together into an aerie for eagles, they must truly be unique. First, the people are of a sweetness and courtesy that are rare even in Italy; then the churches are charming and are full of pictures; then the country round about is delicious; and last, the inn is still a paradise of welcome and good living.

Of the beauty of the women I shall say little, and, indeed, nothing; of the very real courtesy of the people I would say much, but can say no more than that it reminded me that Montalcino is and always was Sienese, rather than Florentine, and that it was here the Republic made its last stand: and that, by the way, may have something to do with the really remarkable beauty of the maidens hereabout. Of the churches and their treasures, as of Montalcino itself, I will say more anon; but of the inn I have known so long I will speak at once.

The inns I once knew in half a hundred places in Italy—in San Gimignano, for instance, in Castel-Fiorentino, in Foligno, in Fivizzano, and Narni—are human places, where you will find friends, a soft bed, well-cooked food, a good wine, and a welcome. These places were treasured in the memory and not too easily published abroad, for an inn may be spoiled by its guests. Nevertheless, the inn at Montalcino was something apart. I will say that I have been happy there, and that there I lived like a king. At night I slept soft and clean, I ate well and punctually at the hours I had appointed, I was welcomed and I made friends, and from there I issued forth to see the magnificent town of Montalcino, tomb of the Sienese Republic; thither again I returned when I would, glad at heart, as to my own home.

You entered it out of the narrow street by a low door that brought you straight into a great odoriferous kitchen with an open hearth, where there were always many good folk at work at their victuals, and where, as I think properly, the host and his family dwelt. The place was no hole where they stewed messes in secret, but open to all; the floor was cold stone and you might spill wine upon it and do no hurt, and you might talk there with the company and rejoice in your fellow-men. The time to see it at its best was about noon on a market-day; but for me, I loved it most at evening, when the guests were few but rare of their kind, and when, if it were winter, you might be cosy by the fire and smoke and talk with your host, who was a travelled man, or with the Farmacista, who was a learned one and a graduate of a University, or with your hostess, who was all for comfort, or with some ancient of the village who remembered everything, or with some benighted friar whose important day's work had included the exorcizing of a witch, or with the young men of the village, who were full of their affairs, or very softly with Annunziatina the little daughter of the house. If you wanted character, here it was; if you wanted entertainment, here you might find it; if politics were your hobby, here you might get your fill of them; and if love your theme, you would hear many astonishing things and find an attentive listener. How can I praise you as I ought, O inn of the Lily.

As for the bedrooms of the inn, every one of them—there were but few—had a different and a perfect view. One looked, it may be, towards Buonconvento and one towards Pienza, but the fairest of all looked across the near valleys, over the olive gardens to the blue hills and Mont' Amiata, and that was the one for me.

Seeing, then, that all these things were as they were, it was no wonder that one found Montalcino delightful. And, indeed, who could find it anything else? It clings to the great hills high up like the nest of an eagle; it is set above the woods; across the olive gardens it looks to the desert; over the vineyards it looks to the mountains.

As for its history, it has much in common with Montepulciano, for it too was a bone of contention between Florence and Siena, but its end was more glorious.

Siena had enjoyed some years of splendour under the domination of the returned exile Pandolfo Petrucci "the Magnificent". Cesare Borgia expelled him in 1502. He was recalled in the following year but died in 1512, and his family did not last long, for he had not the gifts of a Medici, and presently Siena placed herself under the protection of the Emperor Charles V, who when he passed through in 1535 was received with great pomp. But the city was torn by faction and revolt and bad government. The Balia was reconstituted many times and finally, in 1548, by Don Diego de Mendoza the Imperial agent. In the following year Don Diego began to build a huge fortress, where the Lizza is today, to the distress and alarm of the whole city. It was as he laid the foundations of this monstrous engine of tyranny, that the ragged Augustinian friar Brandano used to stand on the hillside watching the builders and "chant aloud in wailing tones": *Nisi dominus aedificaverit domum* . . . "Except the Lord build the house their labour is but vain that build it." And when they stopped to listen he would chant louder still: *Nisi dominus custodierit civitatem* . . . "Except the Lord keep the city the watchman waketh but in vain." He was driven off, but returned again and again, and for some reason, possibly from superstition that this man might be a prophet, Don Diego would not have him killed. But it was all in vain, the building continued till certain of the citizens, among them Enea Piccolomini, appealed to the King of France, and with a French contingent, they forced their way into the city on 26 July, 1552. The people rose and drove the Spaniards into their own fortress, which they were forced to surrender, and they left Siena on August the fifth.

The government, such as it was, was now under French protection. But the Emperor was furious and Cosimo de' Medici in Florence conceived the idea of annexing Siena to his own dominion. He presently took the field, and his general, the Marquis of Marignano, seized the fort at Porta Camollia, which the Sienese men, women, and children had built with their own hands, and at Marciano in Val di Chiana defeated the Franco-Sienese forces commanded by the Florentine exile Pietro Strozzi. Siena was besieged, the heroic defence of the beloved city was begun. Everything was sacrificed by the citizens, but in April 1555 they were forced by their sufferings to surrender, and the Spanish troops entered the devoted city.

It was then many patriots with their women and children abandoned Siena and took refuge in Montalcino. For when the French on 21 April, 1555, passed out of the city of the Virgin by the Porta Romana, there went along with them a vast company of the citizens of Siena, who loved liberty more than they loved their own city, which they left finally ruined in the hands of Charles V. This remnant of the old Republic set out with their women and children, their goods and chattels, upon the long road that leads to Montalcino, which they determined to make the last refuge of the Sienese Republic. *"Ubi cives, ibi patria,"* said they, and so it was. Among that invincible company were to be found many of the noblest in the city—Tolomei, Piccolomini, Bandini, Spannocchi. Not all reached that last refuge: some, already weak with hunger after the siege, fell by the wayside; but the indomitable remnant marched on with Montluc, "toiling along after his troopers down the dusty Roman road, the father holding the daughter's hand, the mother carrying her baby, going forth into a dreary wilderness because they would not submit to the hated Spanish rule". "Never in my life," said Montluc, "have I seen a parting so piteous. . . . At the sight of their misery I could not keep back my tears, so great was my sorrow for a people which had shown itself willing to give up so much to save its liberty."[1] All in vain. The "Republic of Siena in Montalcino" only lasted for two years, and even during that time it was ruled by the French commander. In 1559 the Montalcinesi surrendered to Duke Cosimo, who then held practically all Tuscany, save the territory of Orbetello and the city of Lucca. Is it better to rule like Florence, or to reign like Siena?

Little remains in Montalcino to remind us of that forlorn and heroic hope; only the old fortress, half in ruins, and even there the arms of the Grand Duke are the most conspicuous ornament. Yet as one wanders about the city and out on to the wild heights above it, with the mighty panorama of mountain and valley about one, it is really the Republic of Siena one remembers, that unstable, inefficient but heroic government which so surely reflected the character of the Sienese, and which here, in this lovely hill town, has found a noble grave on the confines of its fatherland.

But history is not alone in having left us its memories to examine, and perhaps to weep over, in Montalcino. The town is full of artistic treasures of considerable beauty and importance. In the church of Sant' Agostino, for instance, the choir has been entirely covered with frescoes by Bartolo di Fredi, fragments of which remain, which a paternal government has uncovered from

---

[1] Montluc, *Commentaries* (Bordeaux, 1592), fol. 107.

whitewash. The old windows of the church, once simple and lovely, have been opened, and one notes the fine rose over the west door and the double cloisters. Stored away in these cloisters, too, is a very fine picture by Bartolo di Fredi of the Virgin and Child in half length.

Opposite Sant' Agostino, in the chapel of the Sacro Sacramento, on either side of the west door, is one of those fourteenth-century Annunciations, two great wooden figures, such as may be seen in Castel-Fiorentino and San Gimignano; and over an altar on the Epistle side of the chapel stands a picture of the Madonna of Mercy, very lovely in a white dress, attributed to Tamagni.

From Sant' Agostino one passes into the northern part of the town to the church of San Francesco, where, over the western door, is a terra-cotta of the Madonna and Child with S. Peter, S. John Baptist and two angels of Robbia ware, and in a niche in the south wall a figure of S. Sebastian of the same school. The cloisters here, too, are very fine, and from the piazza in front of the church a great view of Montalcino opens before one over the ancient olives.

Descending hence into the valley to regain the city, one comes, as one climbs again, to the little church of Santa Croce, where, over the sacristy door in the south wall, is an interesting picture of the Crucifixion by Girolamo Genga, with the influence of Signorelli and Pintoricchio strong upon it. Over the high altar stands a picture of the Madonna and Child with the two saints by Becca-fumi, a work from the master's hand usually called a school piece.

In the church of Sant' Antonio is a panel of the Virgin and Child by Segna; and in Santa Caterina, in the sacristy, a triptych of the school of Duccio, with the Virgin and Child in the midst, SS. Peter and Paul on either side, and in the pinnacled panels above, our Lord in the midst, with a saint on either side. This is a fine Ducciesque altarpiece.

The most delightful church of Montalcino, however, is set some way outside it on the road to Torrenieri, and there is what I take to be the finest picture in the city. The church belonged to a long since suppressed Franciscan convent of Osservanti, whose name it bears, and its great treasure is the picture of the Assumption by Girolamo di Benvenuto over the west door, which reminds one of his father's work at Asciano. Here, too, over the fourth altar, on the left, is a picture of S. Bernardino with two exquisite

angels by Sano di Pietro, and opposite to it a Pietà by some pupil
of Sodoma.

From the Osservanza there is a fine view of the *castello* of
Montalcino, which is certainly worth a visit.

On one's way back through the city one passes the Palazzo
Pubblico, where there is a small picture gallery containing the
ancient treasures of the churches. To take the pictures in order:
(1) The Madonna and Child in a garden of roses with angels, is
by Sano di Pietro. (2) The Madonna and Child is the masterpiece
of Tommè, a wonderful panel, the best thing he ever did. (3) The
Nativity is by Girolamo di Benvenuto. (4) The Coronation of the
Virgin is a masterpiece of Fredi. This is the centre panel only of
an altarpiece, the rest of which is in the gallery at Siena. (5) The
Blood of the Redeemer by Girolamo di Benvenuto—a curious
picture. Christ stands supporting the Cross between S. Angelo
and S. Egidio, the Precious Blood pouring from His side over a
wafer into a chalice. Above is God the Father and four angels.
(6) The Deposition. This is part of an altarpiece by Bartolo di
Fredi, signed and dated, the four saints (two panels) belong to it,
as do two panels of the Baptism and a scene from the life of S.
Philip of Montalcino here. In the background is the Cathedral of
Siena. (7) A Madonna and Child with two angels, a damaged but
interesting work by Tommè. (8) Scenes from the life of S. Filippo
of Montalcino. These two panels on either side the window probably belong to the Deposition altarpiece (No. 6). (9) The Madonna
and Child is a spoiled and very early Francesco di Giorgio according to Mr. Berenson.

On leaving the delightful little gallery, I often used to climb up
to the *fortezza*, where the Republic of Siena made its last stand.
It is wild and beautiful and mysterious and worth all the fatigue
of the way. Moreover, the road which leaves the city thus by the
hills will bring one in some eight miles to the forgotten abbey of
Sant' Antimo.

The abbey of Sant' Antimo was in the Middle Age one of the
greater Benedictine monasteries in Italy, and indeed it was the
most formidable ecclesiastical feud in Tuscany, with the exceptions
of the Badia San Salvatore on Mont' Amiata and the Badia San
Galgano in the Val di Merse. Moreover, it was, and still is even
in its ruin, one of the best examples in Italy of Romanesque
architecture, or rather of that kind of Romanesque peculiar to the

LA COLLEGIATA, San Quirico d' Orcia.

LA FORTEZZA, Montalcino

eleventh century. "It is precisely in these new ecclesiastical structures," writes Canestrelli—new, that is, as being the production of a
world awakened to a new youth by the passing of the millennium
which was supposed to bring the world to an end—"it is precisely in
these new ecclesiastical structures that we see the earliest examples of
that transitional style of architecture which continued to develop
itself through the eleventh, twelfth, and part of the thirteenth
centuries, and to which the name of Romanesque was justly given
because in the world of art its development was coeval and corre-
sponded with that of the *Romance* tongues in the world of literature."[1]
Whatever we may think of that explanation, we may note that
one of the most notable features of this new style was the substitution of vaulted stone roofs for the older wooden ones; now
though this was of slow growth, beginning with the covering of the
aisles when the nave was still roofed with wood, it became at last
universal, though the mixed style was long used in Italy even in
the twelfth century, when it seems the abbey of Sant' Antimo was
built.

As one sees it today even, the church of Sant' Antimo seems to
be perhaps the most beautiful interior in Tuscany, though the
cathedrals of Pisa and Lucca are maybe more firmly established
in our hearts. But in any case it is so fine that it is worth any
trouble to see, and it lies within an easy drive of Montalcino. The
country, too, is wild and beautiful to a degree, and all the way the
lovely shape and the mystery of Mont' Amiata guards the horizon.
So lonely and so wide is this stretch of almost unknown upland
that when returning in the gathering twilight one sees the few
lights of Montalcino one feels a distinct relief.

During my stay at Montalcino I went one day to Sant' Angelo
in Colle just above the railway to Grosseto. In the church of San
Michele there is a painting of the Virgin and Child very close to
Pietro Lorenzetti. The Child, as usual with that master, is on
the left arm of His Mother. His finger is in His mouth. His other
hand rests on the top of His tunic. Both figures have been crowned
with heavy metal diadems. This picture is in a poor condition.

[1] Cf. *Rassegna d'Arte Senese*, vol. XIII (1920).

CHAPTER XXVI

GROSSETO

S TROLLING about Montalcino one day, I thought I would
go down to Grosseto. It was many years since I had been
there, perhaps thirty, but I remembered very well my first
visit. I was with a friend, an art historian, and we had motored
up from Rome. My friend had with him an amazing acetylene
searchlight attached to which was a large box of batteries. He
was intent on examining the picture by Sassetta of the Madonna
and Child in the Cathedral. It was getting late when we arrived
and we made straight for the Duomo. We entered, the chauffeur
carrying the box of batteries. They were singing the Litany of the
Blessed Virgin before Benediction and the church was half full
of people. Nevertheless, my companion, disregarding all this,
found his way, the chauffeur with his burden following, to where
quite high up hung the picture. Then we switched on the
powerful light, and I suppose the Madonna of the Cherries was
never seen so well. *Delicta juventutis meae et ignorantias meas ne
memineris.*

Of course, we ought to have been kicked out of the church, but
we were not disturbed; the courteous Italian congregation no
doubt regarded us as barbarians who knew no better. I wonder
what would have happened had we done the same thing in an
English church, Salisbury Cathedral, for instance. But the
Protestants have left there no picture which would call for such
ruthless curiosity.

Grosseto proved to be not much more than an hour away by
train from Torrenieri, and very much changed I found it. It used
to be a small city within its medieval walls, but has now with the
exploitation of the pyrite mines and the revived agriculture of the
Maremma, spread into a large *borgo* or suburb all round the city,
but chiefly to the west, where the new Palazzo del Governo and
the new Post Office buildings are to be found and very impressive
they are.

Grosseto has a tragic if interesting history. In the Middle Age
it was a small *castello* on the great road between Pisa and Rome,

and really began to be of some importance when the Etruscan
Roselle was destroyed by the Saracens in 935, and when in 1138
Innocent II transferred the Bishopric from Roselle to Grosseto.
It then came into the hands of the noble family of the Aldobrandeschi, the lords of Santa Fiora on Mont' Amiata, and in their
hands it remained till the thirteenth century, when that family
was more or less disposed of by the Commune of Siena. The
struggle was a long one, and at one time the Abati family had
possession of the city, but Siena finally came into control in
1338, threw down the walls, and held Grosseto till the establishment of the Grand Duchy of Tuscany in the sixteenth century.
Under the Grand Dukes it flourished, and even more in the time
of the House of Lorraine, which drained the marshes and did
something, even much, to free the territory from the curse of the
anopheles mosquito and the malaria, by drainage and other beneficent works, as the great Cisternone in the Piazza Repubblica
bears witness. This work has been continued by United Italy, and
today Grosseto is said to be perfectly healthy and to enjoy one of
the best water supplies in Tuscany. This is no doubt true, but I
did not notice that the mosquitoes had become any less ferocious in
the thirty years since my last sojourn here.

Of course, my first visit was to the Cathedral, if only to make
an act of contrition for the previous outrage. But I could not find
the Sassetta and was presently told that it had been removed to
the new Museo d' Arte Sacra over the sacristy, and there later
I found it.

The Cathedral of San Lorenzo, the chief monument of the city,
dates from the twelfth century when the Bishopric was established
here, but it was rebuilt in 1294 by the Sienese architect Sozzo di
Rustichino in the Gothic style. Unfortunately it has been restored
many times, and the campanile is today a work of the twentieth
century. Though the façade was renewed in 1840 it retains something of its original Romanesque character. It has three portals,
and over the pilasters which support a frieze, are statues of the
symbols of the Evangelists perhaps by Sozzo or possibly earlier.
It is curious that the Angel which is the symbol of S. Matthew is
here an old bearded man. The right flank of the church and its
portal (not the lunette), with our Lord between the Evangelists,
seem to be certainly the work of Sozzo.

Within, the church is a Latin cross with three naves, and is mostly of the sixteenth century where it is not seventeenth-century Baroque or restored in modern times. There is a lunette of Christ in benediction with angels, of the thirteenth century, over the main portal, and the windows have glass, attributed to Benvenuto di Giovanni. The holy water stoup is of the sixteenth century, the large font is of the end of the fifteenth and is ascribed to Antonio di Ghino the goldsmith of Siena (1470), who also made the fine altar front with the Annunciation in the lunette, in the left transept, which he signed and dated 1474. This altar is that of the much venerated Madonna delle Grazie with its lovely picture of the Assumption of our Lady by Matteo di Giovanni. This is the central part only of a larger picture and is very like the Madonna by Domenico di Bartolo in the church of San Raimondo in Siena. Our Lady, seen in half-length with hands pointed, is surrounded by eight angels. The silver crown which has been placed on her head out of devotion rather spoils the beauty of the picture. In the presbytery is a fragment of a picture by Sano di Pietro—S. Anthony and S. Jerome.

I now made my way, led by the courteous *custode*, to the new Museo d' Arte Sacra over the sacristy, where pictures and works of art from all over the city have now been gathered. Here in the vestibule I found one of those great wooden painted Crucifixes which always attract me so much: this a Sienese work of the fourteenth century. In Sala I were some illuminated choir-books among some late pictures. In Sala II I found a small picture of the Virgin and Child ascribed to Andrea di Giusto; a Madonna and Child with SS. Jerome and Bernardino in half-length by Girolamo di Benvenuto, and above in a lunette, a Pietà with two saints, ascribed to Pietro di Domenico, but more likely by Pietro di Giovanni; a picture of the Madonna dell' Uccellino, possibly by the Ovile Master, and another picture of the Virgin and Child of the Sienese fourteenth century, here attributed to Simone Martini.

Then I came upon that unique panel of the Last Judgment, which used to be in the Cathedral. This is a strange work. I know nothing else like it in Italian painting. It is of the school of Guido da Siena. Above, Christ is seated in a *mandorla* enthroned on the rainbow, His arms outstretched, His hands and feet and side pierced with the sacred wounds. Four trumpet-sounding angels fill the four corners of the rectangular panel. Below is the Cross with the instruments of the Passion, supported by two angels, and under it are four scenes of the Judgment; on the right hand of the Christ the blessed issue from the tomb and are led by a friar up the stepped way into Paradise, welcomed by S. Peter; on the left hand are the damned in two scenes of resurrection and damnation.

I next came to a picture of the Madonna and Child by Segna di Bonaventura of considerable beauty, and then at last Sassetta's Madonna delle Ciliegie, which I had last seen under searchlight in the Cathedral. I regret its removal from the church, I regret the removal of the other pictures assembled here, though I can certainly see them better than I could in their proper places. It was easy, for instance, to see that the panel of the Sassetta is only a part of a larger picture and has been damaged in the process of cutting it down, but the tender charm of the picture remains in spite of injury. The Virgin sits impassive, the Child on her knees, His right hand reaches the clasp of His Mother's robe, while in His left is a cherry which He carries to His mouth. This is an exquisite picture of Sassetta's middle period, which I am glad to have seen once more. I cannot imagine what the background and sides of the picture may have been.

Two other churches are worth a visit, beside San Pietro, which is, I believe, the earliest of all: San Cristoforo, which retains some Sienese frescoes of the early fifteenth century, and San Francesco, which still possesses its wonderful thirteenth-century Crucifix, a majestic and important thing.

I was glad to have seen Grosseto again, but I shall not return. Whatever charm the place had of old is now overwhelmed by its modern prosperity, so that after two days and a night I was glad to get into the train and return to the uncommercialized unsophisticated happiness of Montalcino.

And all the way I was thinking selfishly: What a pity! I used to be fond of Grosseto, the Cathedral, the gardens on the ramparts, the Albergo Giappone. Why not leave things alone?

CHAPTER XXVII

SOL IN LEONE

IT was now very hot, even Montalcino was blazing, with Sol in Leone; the *cicale*, those "scalie harnest dragons", were shrieking among the olives.

This morning Annunziatina brought me my breakfast—coffee, bread, butter, honey. She is the daughter of the house and not so long ago, as it seems to me, I used to carry her as a baby to visit the pigs which she adored, and she would have a long and affectionate conversation of grunts with the old sow, her little body shaking with her efforts. Now she is almost a woman, tall and slim as a young poplar when in the spring it first puts forth its leaf and sways in the wind.

Yes, she brought me my breakfast and hoped I had well slept; and as she stooped to straighten the slip of carpet by the bed a peach fell out of her bosom on to the floor—the gift no doubt of some sweetheart or other, which she had hidden there and forgotten.

"*Fortunato lui!*" I said.

Swiftly she bent to pick up the fruit and without a word, covered with confusion, fled from the room.

It is July. The corn has long been reaped, the fire-flies have disappeared, the fields which in the too brief spring were emerald, then golden, are now pale with stubble, the grapes hang already in bunches on the vines. The *contadini* are now beating out the reaped corn with the flail, here in the courtyard, used as the *aia*, between the villa of the *padrone* and the peasants' house. I can see them as they go, Ulisse, Alfredo, Giulia and Emilio; while little two-year-old Giulietta sits beside me flat on the pavement, under the muscat vine, trained about the loggia on one side of the courtyard. As they toss the straw and the wind, such as it is, carries away the chaff, I have only to close my eyes to conjure up the "*mystica vannus Iacchi*" of Virgil.

In the *podere* the *cicale* are singing their endless song. High summer is here with its translucent mornings, its fiery heat, its blinding brilliance at midday, its exquisite evenings of gold, its nights of stars, its moonlight.

It is difficult to describe these days of high summer, when all the earth is subject to the sun, and the world is filled with an ecstasy of light. Only in the stillness the *cicale* sing ceaselessly, among the olives, a thing which the ancients used to enjoy and I too, perhaps because it proclaims the fullness of the summer glory and evokes memories of summers long gone by. But now . . . the grasshopper has become a burden.

And so I decided to go up into Mont' Amiata for a few weeks to Abbadia San Salvatore, that *castello* on the verge of the great forest of chestnuts that covers the mountain and its string of little towns, like the beads on a rosary, along the road that circles the mountain at about 3,000 feet. It is always fresh and cool up there and it would be delightful to see once more Ser Giovanni, the President of the mountain, and his sister, and to visit again the old and famous, but now ruined Badia where Ceolfric's codex of the Vulgate was preserved after he died on the way to bring it to the Pope in the eighth century; to see Santa Fiora, the ancient stronghold of the Aldobrandeschi, and Arcidosso where Davide Lazzaretti in the last century appeared, proclaiming himself to be the Messiah, till the *carabinieri* shot him as a revolutionary. And then there was Pian Castagnaio and Vivo, too, with its living waters.

So I set out and climbing for many hours, from the railway in the valley below Montalcino, up past Campigla d' Orcia, I arrived at Abbadia at evening.

The long summer days passed in a dream. It was not till late September that I left the mountain.[1]

[1] For all that concerns Mont' Amiata, see my *A Wayfarer in Unknown Tuscany* (third edition).

CHAPTER XXVIII

RADICOFANI

I CAME down from Mont' Amiata by way of Radicofani up-
reared like an heraldic beast, aloft, over the stony valley of the
Paglia to the east of the great mountain. On that wonderful
road, one by one, the beautiful cities began to shine about me—
Castiglione d' Orcia, Pienza, that lovely vanity, Montepulciano,
like a rose on the hills; till before me the scarped ruin of Radicofani soared like an eagle over the valley and the road to Rome, and
I found myself in the little *albergo* under the ruined fortress of
Ghino di Tacco.

Originally belonging to the monks of San Salvatore on Mont'
Amiata, the most splendidly situated of all the fortresses on the
Roman road, the Via Francigena, which passes under this Rocca,
Radicofani was divided in 1153, and half the *castello* given by the
Abbot to Pope Eugenius III and his successors. Later, the place
formed the last fortress of the Patrimony of S. Peter, or the last
fortress of the Sienese, as it happened, for both possessed it, the
one after the other, during many years. Finally it came to Siena,
and later, like all the rest of the Sienese *castelli*, it formed a part
of the Granducato of Tuscany.

Today Radicofani is a little naked village straggling round the
jagged hill under the fortress, with three churches, a fine clock-
tower, many old houses and a beautiful palace, evidently the
Palazzo del Governo, now a prison, covered with coats of arms;
while without the gates are a Capuchin convent, a pretty place
enough, among trees too, now secularized; and the old Posta,
"The Great Duke's Inn", where Richard Lassels on his way to
Rome in the seventeenth century tells us he dined. "From Siena,"
he says, "we went to *Bon Convento, Tornieri, S. Quirico*, an incon-
siderable place upon the rode, and so to Radicofano, a strong
Castle upon a high hill built by *Desiderius, King of the Longobards.*
This is the last place of the *Florentine State*, but not the least in
strength. Dineing here at the *Great Duke's Inn*, at the bottom of
the hill we went to lodge at *Acquapendente*, which is some twelve
miles off, and the first toune of the Pope's State."

Of the three churches within the walls, Sant' Antonio beside San Pietro in the little Piazza sopra Mura looking towards Rome contains nothing; but as though to make up for the emptiness of his brother, San Pietro has a wealth of beautiful things, the work of the Robbias, whom, as I suppose, the Sforza of Santa Fiora brought here, when, as their arms over the Palazzo del Governo go to show, they ruled in the place. Over the first altar to the right is a statue of S. Catherine made of that humble terra-cotta we know so well, and enamelled simply white—a touching and lovely piece of work one is surprised to find in this lonely place. But then, since all the guide-books have ignored Radicofani as they have ignored Mont' Amiata, one expects to find nothing there, whereas both Radicofani and Santa Fiora are as rich in della Robbia ware as any city in Tuscany, save Florence. Here in San Pietro opposite that statue of S. Catherine on the first altar to the left is a lovely altarpiece of blue and white with the Madonna in the midst and S. John Baptist on one side and S. Antonio Abate, with his pig, on the other. In the right transept is another splendid altarpiece of the Crucifixion, with S. Mary Magdalen kneeling at the foot of the Cross; and in the left transept yet another, the Madonna in the midst, with S. Catherine of Alexandria and S. Michael Archangel. In the little church of Sant' Agata, in the main street of Radicofani, one finds their work again, in the great altarpiece behind the high altar, of the Madonna between S. Francesco, S. Agata, S. Lorenzo, and S. Caterina. On the left wall of the nave, high up in a little cupboard, is hidden a curious and tiny model in plaster of Radicofani itself, with the Madonna above, protecting it, together with S. Agata and S. Emilio.

San Pietro, too, the parish church, has a treasure less tangible, certainly, a legend "of the judgement which befell a very great and cruel usurer of the town of Radicofani." Fra Filippo tells the tale in his *Ensamples*.

"There was," says he, "in the town of Radicofani, a wretched man; and albeit he became very old, it might be said of him as saith the proverb: 'Accursed is the child of a hundred years old.' All the days of his life this wretched man lent money upon usury, and never had he any sickness. And although he had many vices, especially was he covetous and avaricious and cruel, and an enemy of the poor, in far greater measure than the devil had known how to make him; and rather would he that the victuals and other

things which at any time remained over in his house should be
flung away than that they should be given to the poor; and never
was he seen to give alms, nor was he willing that any should be
given in his house. Now when his accursed days were ended, he
was smitten suddenly with an apoplexy; wherefore they laid him
upon his bed. Afterward two young men were sent for a venerable
physician of very holy life, who was a native of the town and dwelt
therein. And this befell between two and three hours after
nightfall. And when the physician had departed from his house
toward the house of the sick man, and had gone half way thither,
albeit the weather was clear and calm, and the heaven was full
of stars, and no cloud was to be seen in the sky, yet there came a
passing great thundering and lightning so that all men were
astonied; and, when he had reached the door of the house, there
followed another thunder clap with lightning twice as great as at
the first, and, in like manner, all men were stunned thereby. And
afterward, when he had entered the courtyard, and would have
gone into the chamber of the wretched sick man, there came a
third flash of lightning with a thundering so horrible that it stunned
whomsoever was in the chamber; and the physician and those who
were with him in the house fell to the ground, and all the windows
of the chamber where the sick man lay were broken and burst
open, and all the lights which were in the house were put out; and
they remained prostrate upon the ground for the space of a quarter
of an hour or more; and so terrified were they that none of them
dared to raise himself up. Afterward, at the last, they lighted a
lamp and went to the sick man and found him dead. And thus
the devil carried away his soul.

"Now, when I had already written the aforesaid ensample
divers times, according as it had been told me by the son of the
said physician, I afterward heard it from the lips of the physician
himself, the which was a man of credit, at least ninety years old,
of holy life, and a passing venerable person. He told me that there
came on a sudden so great rain and hail and tempest that it
seemed that all the town must be swallowed up; and all the house
trembled, and all the tiles of the roof thereof were beaten together;
and whoever was in the chamber swooned away, and in the
morning, all along the road which led from the house of the
dead usurer out of Radicofani, for seven miles, the ground was
covered with toads. And on one side of the road, and on the other,

the trees and vines and thickets were all broken and splintered. And neither before nor after in that mountain of Radicofani was there ever seen a single toad. Moreover, the physician told me that the priest of the town buried that usurer in the church for money; wherefore afterward, in the night-time, there were heard such knockings and such tempest and clamour in the church, that no man in all the town might sleep therefrom. Wherefore in the morning, the people of the town hastened to the church and dug up that wretched body, and buried it without the town in the most base and shameful place that they could find."

It is, however, to a more admirable villain that my thoughts continually turn, as I look up to the Rocca, that strange, fierce, almost grotesque fortress, ruined now, which under rain or sun dominates the whole country, and hangs there in the sky, even from Siena, like some threatening *stemma*, some fantastic coat of arms. The country folk tell you that Ghino di Tacco still haunts the valley of the Paglia, and here in his own mountain, certainly, the remembrance of the man whose victim Dante met in *Purgatorio* is never very far away:

Quivi era l'Aretin, che dalle braccia
fiere di Ghin di Tacco ebbe la morte.
(Canto vi, 13–14.)

But little, doubtless, remains of the fortress Ghino built on this mountain-top, whose scarped height overlooks not only the valley of the Paglia and the road to Rome, but the valley of Orcia, and the way to Siena, the pass over Cetona, too, and the roads to Chiusi and Umbria. As one climbs today up the rough, steep way, among the stones to where, sailing high in air, the ruined castle still leers across the world, it is the remnants of the Sienese and Papal stronghold one passes, and yet it is certainly not of them I was thinking, but of the cruel exploits of that ruined gentleman, turned highwayman, who slew Benincasa to avenge his father, and captured the Abbot of Cligni, and won thereby peace for a little, but fell at last under the daggers, perhaps of the Counts of Santa Fiora, who hated him, and whom he hated.

Ghino di Tacco is a characteristic figure of his time. There must have been many such in Italy when the Signorotti, having acquired their lordships rather than conquered them, as Aquarone[1]

[1] B. Aquarone: *Dante in Siena* (Città di Castello, 1889), pp. 85 et seq.

insists, and the opportunity for any personal enterprise of the sort
having passed away, many a patrician found himself almost starv-
ing and at the mercy of the crowd in the city where he lived or
had taken refuge. This seems to have been Ghino's case. There
are many theories of his birth, but Aquarone, following Tommasi
in this, comes to the conclusion that he was the son of Tacco
Monaceschi de' Pecorai da Torrita. However this may be, Ghino
was brought up as a boy to a wild and violent life till his family,
his father, his brother Turino, and himself, "disgusted with the
Republic", as Gigli says, were *cacciati da Siena*, expelled from Siena,
as Boccaccio tells us, one day in 1279. They became robbers, haunt-
ing the way between Siena and Asinalunga, till one day Siena
thought fit to attend to them with a force some six hundred strong.
They occupied Torrita. One day when Ghino was away on the
road, Tacco his father, and Turino his brother were taken by the
Sienese and imprisoned in Siena, and later tried before Messer
Benincasa di Laterina, in the Aretino, Vicar of the Podestà. They
were hanged; but Ghino was free, and, as Aquarone puts it, while
he was at large "the air of Siena no longer suited Messer Benincasa".
So he sought some other business, elsewhere, and having no little
reputation in jurisprudence, he became *Auditor Papae* and went to
Rome. Even there, as it proved, he was not safe. Ghino was not
to be denied. He had often looked up to the height of Radicofani
as he lurked in the valley, perhaps often hidden there to spy out
his prey, on a summer night, when the stars shine like jewels in
a monstrance round that spotless Host the moon. So, tired of rob-
bing on the road as a common highwayman, and hoping to make himself still a lord, he determined to secure himself in that place. Nor
was it long before it happened so, for with him to think was to act.
And once established there like a bird of prey, he sat all day looking
towards Rome. It was perhaps dawn when he set out with "some
four hundred of his brigands", as Gigli says, all on swift horses,
heartily ready. Through that dawn and the day and the night
they rode to Rome. They surprised a gate and held it. Then
Ghino, with a few followers, rode through the city on to the Capitol,
where he knew he would find Benincasa about his business. There
indeed, "in an upper room at audience", he found him, killed him
on the very judgment-seat, and taking his head, came away without hindrance. And re-mounting his horse, he rode in the midst
of his few followers through the city, leaving it by the same gate

through which he had come in, and so back to Radicofani, that he was then able to call his own.

Now it was with something of the same persistent violence, less sinister, but not less fearless, that this enemy of God, the Pope, and the Counts of Santa Fiora made his peace with Boniface VIII, as Boccaccio says, yet he came to die at last like a gentleman truly, and a lord, at bay, fighting, pierced by a hundred wounds.

"Ghino di Tacco," Boccaccio tells us in Elisa's story from the second novel on the last day of the *Decameron*—"Ghino di Tacco, a man both for his boldness and for his robberies sufficiently famous, being banished from Siena, and at enmity with the Counts of Santa Fiora, caused Radicofani to revolt from the rule of the Church of Rome, and establishing himself there, he and his band robbed throughout the neighbourhood. Now Boniface VIII being Pope in Rome, the Abbot of Cligni came to Court, and he was believed to be one of the richest Prelates in the world. His stay at Court having somewhat injured his digestion, he was advised by the doctors to go to the Baths of Siena, where he would be cured without doubt. Obtaining leave from the Pope, without caring for the fame of Ghino, he set out on his road with much pomp of harness and baggage, with many horses and a whole retinue of servants. Ghino di Tacco, hearing of his coming, set his snares, and without losing the meanest stable-boy, in a narrow place captured the Abbot, with all his household and his possessions.

"Then, he sent, well accompanied, to the Abbot one of the wiliest of his men, who on his behalf told him very politely that he must be pleased to dismount and to visit Ghino in the Castello. When the Abbot heard this he was furious, and replied that he wanted for nothing, that one like himself had nothing to do with Ghino; but that he would continue on his way, and he would like to see who would stop him. To whom the Ambassador, speaking humbly, said: 'Messere, you are come to a part where, save for the power of God, nothing makes us afraid, and where excommunications and interdicts are themselves excommunicated; and therefore it would be better to satisfy Ghino in this.' During this conversation the place had already been surrounded by brigands, so that the Abbot, seeing himself and those with him prisoners, very scornfully followed the Ambassador towards the Castello, and there went along with him all his people and all his harness.

"Dismounting there, as Ghino wished, he was placed alone in a

small room of the palace, rather dark and inconvenient, and all
his household, each according to his quality, was well lodged, and
as for the horses and the baggage, they were taken good care of,
no one touching anything. Later Ghino himself went to the Abbot
and said to him: 'Messere Ghino, whose guest you are, sends
praying you to be pleased to tell him where you are going, and on
what occasion.' The Abbot, who, like a wise man, had already
abated some of his haughtiness, told him where he was going, and
why. When Ghino heard this, he went off, determined to cure
him without any baths. Having ordered a great fire to be kept
constantly burning in the Abbot's room, which was small, he did
not re-visit him till the next morning, and then in the whitest
napkin he brought him two slices of bread, toasted, and a great
cup of vernaccia da Corniglia, the Abbot's own, and said to him:
'Messere, when Ghino was very young he studied in medicine, and
he says that there will never be a better medicine for your com-
plaint than that he will give you, of which these things which I
bring are the beginning; and therefore partake of them and be
comforted.' The Abbot, who had rather eat than be witty, though
still with a certain disdain, ate the bread and drank the vernaccia;
then he began to say many things, a little haughtily, asking many
things and advising many things, and especially he demanded that
he might see Ghino himself. Hearing this, Ghino took no notice
of much that he said, answered courteously the rest, and declaring
that Ghino would visit him very soon, departed, only returning
on the following day again with toasted bread and vernaccia; and
so he did many days, till he found the Abbot had eaten some dried
beans which he had purposely carried and left there; then on
behalf of Ghino he asked the Abbot how he was. The Abbot
replied: 'It appears to me that I should be well enough if I were
out of his hands; after that I should have no greater desire than to
eat, so thoroughly have his remedies cured me.'

"Ghino then had a beautiful room prepared with the Abbot's
own belongings, and caused a fine banquet to be set out, to which,
with many men of the Castello, were invited all the household of
the Abbot. The following morning he went to him and said:
'Messere, since you feel well, it is time you should quit this in-
firmary.' Then taking him by the hand, he led him into the room
he had prepared; and leaving him there with his own people he
went off to make sure the banquet should be magnificent. The

Abbot amused himself a little with his people, and gave them an account of his life, while they, on the other hand, told him how surpassing well they had been entertained by Ghino. But the hour for dining was come; the Abbot and the others were nobly enter-tained with excellent food and wines, though Ghino did not even then declare himself.

"When the Abbot had been treated in this fashion for some days, Ghino, having made them put all his goods into a great room, and all his horses, even to the last pony, into a court under it, went to the Abbot and asked him how he felt, and whether he thought himself well enough to go on horseback. And the Abbot replied that he felt well enough, and was indeed thoroughly cured, and that he would be perfectly well if he could only get out of Ghino's hands. Then Ghino brought him into the room where were all his goods and all his whole household, and causing him to look from a window at all his horses, he said: 'Messere Abate, you ought to know that it is not wickedness of heart which has caused Ghino di Tacco—for I am he—to become a highway robber and an enemy of the Court of Rome, but rather his position as a gentleman, driven from his own house, and the necessity to defend his life and nobility against many powerful enemies; but you appear to be an honourable lord, and as I have cured you of your illness, I do not intend to treat you as I should another who should fall into my hands, taking from him what might please me. On the contrary, I intend that, having considered my necessities, you should give me what you think is owing. Here is all that is yours: from that window you see your horses in the courtyard; take, therefore, either a part or the whole as it shall please you; from this hour you may go or stay, as you will.'

"The Abbot, astonished to hear such generous words from a highwayman, being much delighted, felt his anger and disdain suddenly dissolve into kindness, and in his heart grew a wish to become Ghino's friend. Running to him to embrace him, he said: 'I swear to God that to gain the friendship of such a one as I take you to be, I might well suffer a deeper injury than you have inflicted on me here. Cursed be the evil fortune which has led you to such a damnable life as this!' Then taking only a few necessities and some of his horses, he left the rest to Ghino, and returned to Rome.

"Now the Pope had heard of the Abbot's capture, and had been much distressed by it. When he saw him he asked him if the baths had benefited him; to which the Abbot smilingly answered: 'Holy Father, I found, before arriving at the baths, a physician who has thoroughly cured me.' Then he told him the story, and urged thereto by his generosity, asked a favour. The Pope, imagining that he would ask some other thing, freely granted him what he would ask. 'Holy Father,' said the Abbot, ' what I wish of you is, that you give a free pardon to Ghino di Tacco, my doctor, because, among all estimable people I have met, he is the most worthy, and the harm he does is to be imputed rather to bad fortune than to an evil heart. Change, then, this bad fortune by giving him something from which he can live according to his position, and I do not doubt but that in a little time he will pay you as he has paid me.' Hearing this the Pope, who had a great soul and loved valiant men, said he would do it willingly if, indeed, it was as he said. With this promise Ghino came to Court, where the Pope, soon convinced of his worth and reconciled to him, gave him a great priory with a hospital, and made a knight of him. There he remained the friend and servant of Holy Church and of the Abbot of Cligni as long as he lived."

Thus far Boccaccio, but Benvenuto da Imola tells us that the Pope created him Cavaliere di S. Giovanni, and that in his bene- fice he maintained *splendida vita*. As Knight of S. John, and the Pope's very good friend, he doubtless found it easier to deal with the Sienese Republic. Later Benvenuto tells us he retired to Fratta, perhaps his native village, a *castello* between Torrita and Sinalunga in Val di Chiana. However that may be, not long after his son Dino became Archbishop of Pisa. The Counts of Santa Fiora, however, would not pardon him nor give him peace. As great robbers as himself, it may be they resented his success, and especially his peace with the Church. One day as he went about in Sinalunga he was set upon by a number of armed men, Benvenuto tells us, and bravely defending himself, but in vain, he fell, pierced by a thousand wounds.

So much for Ghino. But though his ghost truly haunts, as I know, those gaunt ruins above Radicofani, it is hardly that fact which will interest the ordinary traveller, who has in the sweat of his brow climbed so far in the spring or autumn sunshine to see something more than an old ruin, howsoever bizarre and wonderful. And he is right. The great thing to be had at Radicofani is the view, so wide

THE VIRGIN AND CHILD OF THE CHERRIES, Sassetta.
Museo d' Arte Sacra, Grosseto

ULISSE, IL CONTADINO. *From a drawing by J. Kerr-Lawson*
in the possession of the Author

it is, so majestic, and so beautiful. Let me remind myself of it. Across the deep and bitter ravine to the west rises Mont' Amiata, an incredibly great and lovely thing, with Abbadia San Salvatore just visible on the verge of the woods. To the north lies the Sanese with its shining cities, with Siena itself visible at evening on the skirts of the farthest hills. To the east lies the splendid range of Cetona with its tiny scattered villages and lofty, sweeping outline, shutting out Umbria and her hills. And to the south? To the south lies the whole breadth of the Patrimony. No one who has once looked southward from Radicofani is ever likely to forget what he has seen. It is one of the great landscapes of the world. It almost gives you Rome. Evening is the hour when that world stretched at your feet is most lovely, and strangely enough most visible, for in the heat of the day a veil of mist hides it from the boldest sight. But at night, when far and far away across the hills, like a horn of pallid gold, like a silver sickle for some precious harvest, the moon hangs over the world, then little by little in her light that world at your feet becomes visible, at first never so faintly, as though still hidden in some impalpable but lovely veil. To the far right, to the south of Mont' Amiata, Castellazzara hangs over the precipice of Monte Civitella, like the nest of an eagle. Dimly in the lovely obscurity San Casciano rises behind Celle on the flanks of Monte Cetona. Somewhere lost in the southern valleys Piceno is hidden among the vines, Acquapendente behind her fantastic rocks. They in truth are rather felt than seen, only far away Lago di Bolsena shines like a jewel, Monte Cimino rises like a ghost beside Monte Venere, eternally separated the one from the other by the faint long saddle like a bow, against which Montefiascone rises like a lovely thought in the unbreakable silence, and the papal city of Viterbo lies like a white rose. Last of all in the farthest distance Monte Soracte, the holy mountain, guards the desert of the Campagna and the immortal thing which it has brought forth —the City of Rome.

CHAPTER XXIX

SARTEANO, CETONA, AND CHIUSI

THE road from Radicofani for Chiusi runs north-east quite round Ghino's stronghold across the upper valley of the Orcia, and after passing under the shadow of Monte Cetona it crosses that range of great hills and comes once more, though still at some height, into the Chiana valley at the quiet little town of Sarteano. The views all the way, and especially after crossing the shoulder of Cetona, are of an extraordinary loveliness. Far away stand the hills of Umbria, the great snow-capped mountains of the Central Apennine. Nearer, across the Chiana valley on the lower skirts of the great bastions that support the central range, lie innumerable little shining cities, among them Cortona, Castiglione Fiorentino, Passignano, and Magione with Trasimeno like a great shield at its feet. Nearer still, on their separate hill-tops ,where they stand like statues on their pedestals, are Montepulciano, Pienza, Chiusi, and Città della Pieve, while on this side the valley at one's feet lie Sarteano, Cetona, and an endless array of villages.

One writes down these beautiful names, one repeats them to oneself, but when that is done, what has been accomplished? Nothing or very little. Who can describe that world of hill and valley so happily peopled and with much that is most precious in our civilization? Who may rightly speak of the sky that covers so softly this landscape? Who can conjure up its sunshine or express the glory of its colouring, its majesty, its tenderness? Out of the fullness of the heart the mouth speaketh, but in vain to those who have never seen the sun, or for whom the sky is always as far off as it is in England.

Sarteano is clustered on a smiling hill under an ancient castle some five miles from Chiusi, and some fifteen from Radicofani. It is a populous little town with two parochial churches, one of which, SS. Lorenzo e Apollinare, is the Collegiata. Sarteano has been a fortified place at least since the eleventh century, when it was in the power of certain Orvietan Counts, who, according to Repetti, came of a branch of the Conti Senesi della Berardenga and della Scialenga, so omnipotent, as we have seen, between Asciano and

Montepulciano. About 1255 the Counts called Manenti, who held Sarteano, submitted to the Commune of Siena; but in 1264, when Charles of Anjou was in Rome, they rebelled and renewed their alliance with the Guelfs of Orvieto. Therefore the Sienese sent an expedition in the very next year to bring them to reason.

Nevertheless the Counts continued to hold Sarteano till the middle of the fourteenth century as feudatories of Siena, for they were a useful and a warlike race. They seem to have been ready to serve any master for the sake of war, and their almost artistic joy in the work they could do so well seems to be shown in the fact that they fought equally for Siena and for Florence. Such was the Count Manenti who, in 1292, with the title of Conestabile, led an army against Pisa for the Florentines, and such were his descendants who in 1325 officered the Guelf League in Val di Nievole against Castruccio Castracane, the greatest soldier of his time. Their valour seems to have filled even their doubtful descendants, for in 1339 we see a certain Neroccio, a natural son of one of the Counts, fighting in the Florentine army, and in 1344 a certain Count Manfredi held Pescia for the same Republic, while in 1353 one of them at the head of a Florentine expedition seized the territory of Cetona. They were a race of soldiers, and that they lasted so well might seem to prove that their rule in Sarteano had some virtue, and what we know of the liberties of the town confirms us in coming to such a conclusion. It seems that already in the fourteenth century the people of Sarteano were free: they appear to have remained so, till at the beginning of the fifteenth century, by a convention of that year, they came into the dominion of Siena: thereafter they paid tribute, and their story does not differ much from that of Lucignano. After 1401 they were compelled to elect a Sienese as Podestà every six months, and to pay him a salary of a thousand *lire*, as well as, among other things, to deliver up their *castello* to a *castellano*, elected every six months by the Commune of Siena, to make peace or war as that Commune should direct, and to hold as friends or enemies those whom she should choose, to offer Siena in the month of August a *palio* of scarlet of the value of 25 gold florins, and this for twelve years. The convention was renewed all through the fifteenth century, and thus Sarteano came into the Sienese dominion, as perhaps its most formidable fortress on the south-east frontier. In 1556 its fate was the same as that of its sisters, and its history closes when it entered the dominion of Cosimo I.

Charming as Sarteano is, with its old fortress and quiet country churches, it has but few works of art. In the Villa Bargagli is a collection of Etruscan antiquities of no great fame or interest. In San Francesco, rebuilt, alas! in 1723, there is a triptych of the Virgin and Child and the two SS. John by Giacomo di Mino del Pellicciaio, while in San Martino there is another picture by the same master, and a most delightful altarpiece by Andrea di Niccolò of the Virgin and Child enthroned between SS. Sebastian and Roch. Above, two cherubs hold a crown over our Lady's head. In the *predella* are half-figures of saints and in the pilasters three full-length small figures. The lovely Annunciation by Beccafumi should not be missed. It is too little known.

The Rocca, now a villa, is a fair example of a Sienese fortress rebuilt by Vecchietta. In the Misericordia church there is a fresco by Benvenuto di Giovanni, representing S. Bernardino of Siena and S. Anthony of Padua.

Sarteano lies but five miles from Chiusi by the direct road, but it is pleasanter to proceed thither, I think, by Cetona. The way lies south and east across the hills from Sarteano—a distance of not more than three miles. Almost at setting out I passed the Madonna di Belriguardo, an ancient public oratory of Sarteano, and then, descending the hills, presently came into the little town of Cetona, looking directly across the wide Chiana valley to Città della Pieve in Umbria.

Cetona is a languid little place lying in the shadow of its great ruined *castello*, girdled with cypresses, which crowns one of the last eastern spurs of the Cetona range. And just as at Lucignano I found a fortress of the Sienese guarding her confines where they ran with those of Arezzo and Florence, just as Radicofani was the last Rocca of Siena southward on the verge of the Patrimony, so here at Cetona stands the last castle of Siena on the confines of the territory of Orvieto and Perugia, part of the Papal States. Its business, according to Siena, was to hold the frontier on her behalf. This can never have been a very comfortable business in the thirteenth, fourteenth, and fifteenth centuries, when war was always about to break out, and raids and private expeditions were of daily occurrence. All these little frontier towns were continually changing hands, and one may believe that their policy was perforce something like that of the rival *condottieri*, who preferred war in much the same way as a learned man might prefer philosophy, and often with much less disastrous results.

Cetona must have known a hundred masters. What she was originally, how she rose, who called her into being, who knows? Many have given her an origin as ancient as that of Chiusi, and they may be right, but there is nothing to support any such theory. Indeed, little is known of Cetona till, in 1264, by a convention between Siena and the troops of Manfred, in the command of Conte Guido Morello, his Vicar in Tuscany against the Orvietans, the Conte was given leave to recover among other places both Sarteano and Cetona. That might seem to suggest that the Sienese had already certain rights in Cetona which might be "recovered"; but who can decide at this time of day as to the grounds of the claims of Siena over this small place?

It would be tedious to go into all the changes of fortune Cetona experienced during the next two centuries; sometimes she was held by the Sienese, sometimes by the Orvietans. She lay at the mercy of Albornoz in 1365, and in 1367 gave herself freely to Urban V, but in 1375 she was handed over to the Emperor, who gave her in feud to the Counts of Cervara, who held her till 1418, when Braccio da Montone, after defeating Carlo Malatesta of Rimini, general of the Perugians, took Cetona, destroyed the *castello*, and made the place over to the Sienese. Then, in 1455, came Jacopo di Niccolò Piccinino, the *condottiere* and adventurer, who set up there Puccino de' Puccini of Perugia, but the Sienese threw him out, and in 1458 rebuilt the fortress.

Cetona had felt every struggle of the fourteenth and fifteenth centuries, nor did she escape the disasters of the sixteenth. Both Duke Valentino, Cesare Borgia, and Francesco Maria della Rovere, Duke of Urbino, seized her in turn and departed on their way, the one to turn out Pandolfo Petrucci, the other to reinstate the *fuorusciti* in Siena. At that time the Cetonesi seem to have been faithful to Siena, nor was the Republic ungrateful. Thus encouraged, they proved to be the last to forgo their allegiance when the government of the Republic retired to Montalcino. They were overcome, however, by Mario Sforza of Santa Fiora in January 1556, and forced to enter the dominion of Cosimo I.

The ancient Rocca of Cetona, which has thus seen the whole history of Central Italy clang by up and down the valley of the

Chiana, was in 1650 restored and made habitable, and has for long been in the possession of the Terrosi family, who have turned it into a delicious *casino*, whence one overlooks the whole Val di Chiana. The town or village beneath it is still surrounded by an old wall with three gates, one of them leading to the Rocca. The finest building in the town, apart from the churches, is the Palazzo Terrosi, with its delightful *boschetti* and gardens and grotto of stalactites, which, by the kindness of the family, one is permitted to visit, together with a small collection of antiquities brought together there. None of the churches—the Collegiata, just within the *castello*, Sant' Angelo the Pieve, Santa Maria in Belvedere—has much to show; but in San Francesco, just outside the town, there are three Sienese pictures of some importance. Over the high altar there is a small picture of the Madonna by Sano di Pietro, and in the chapel of Sant' Egidio a Madonna and two saints by Matteo Balducci, the pupil of Pacchiarotto and the imitator of Pintoricchio, while in the cloister there is a fresco of the Madonna enthroned, by Benvenuto di Giovanni or Girolamo his son.

The road from Cetona to Chiusi descends first into the little valley of the Astrone, and then divides into two ways, either of which will bring one at last to Chiusi, for the way to the right turns into the great valley, and one soon finds oneself at Chiusi station, whence it is a walk of half an hour up into the city; the other crosses the hills by Poggio Montotto, and brings one out at last on the direct way from Sarteano, not a mile outside the city. It is this latter way I prefer, because it affords the better view; by it, I suppose, it is six miles from Cetona to Chiusi.

Few Italian cities, I suppose, can be more venerable than Chiusi, and as for the beautiful view thence, men must have loved it for some thousands of years. To the right rises Monte Cetona, like a vast pyramid shining in the sun, while to the left Città della Pieve hides among the woods of its dear hills. Between, the valley opens north and south, the wide and fruitful valley of the Chiana, through a quiet world of villages and homesteads and sweetly breaking hills. How softly the evening falls there, and how wonderful is the light over hill and valley and mountain! It is easy to tell one is here on the verge of Umbria; you have but to go down into the valley, and in something less than a hundred yards you find yourself in that mysterious country, "dim with valleys", which Perugino, the landscape painter, has shown us in all his pictures.

Well, Chiusi is, and has always been, the Mecca of the archaeo-
logist, yet I am sure he never found anything there half so lovely,
half so consoling as that view over the valley and the light on the
far hills. And whatever Chiusi may be or may come to be for the
world, a vast Etruscan Necropolis or a huge factory town and railway junction—God knows what they may make of her in the
years to come—for me she will ever remain what she was in those
too brief days in which I sat in the Leone d' Oro, and washed
my goat's cheese down with Montepulciano and smoked *sigari* on
the doorstep as I watched the evening procession of the maidens
and the beautiful ladies, who there, as in every other Italian town
and village, take their constitutional after the work of the day.
Chiusi is a place from which you may overlook grey olives and
green vineyards and golden corn, and beyond, a spell-bound lake,
and again the hills and then the mountains. I could watch just that
for ever. They came to me and spoke of Etruscan tombs, they
told me of an Etruscan museum. They were right, there are
Etruscan tombs at Chiusi, there is an Etruscan museum, but what
have I to do with the Etruscans or the Etruscans with me? My
world, the world I love, lies before my eyes. May I not look at it
and enjoy it a little before I must leave it, or it is spoiled for ever
by some fool who wants to make money and benefit his country,
as they say, by making it miserable and wretched?

All there is to know about Chiusi in the way of history, in the way
of Etruscan history, can be put into half a dozen or so fine words:

> Lars Porsena of Clusium,
>   By the Nine Gods he swore
> That the great house of Tarquin
>   Should suffer wrong no more.[1]

I have known that ever since I knew anything. This is the place.
If the ivory car of Lars Porsena were in the museum, or, better
still, in his tomb, I would certainly go to see it. Perhaps you did
not know that he had an ivory car? Oh, but he had, and he took
it to Rome, too. Doubtless it was utterly lost in the rout.

> Fast by the royal standard,
>   O'erlooking all the war,
> Lars Porsena of Clusium
>   Sat in his ivory car.

[1] Cf. also *Æneid*, X, 167.

The disastrous action of Lars Porsenna on behalf of Tarquinius Superbus, in the course of which false Sextus hoped to see brave Horatius drowned in the Tiber and was bitterly disappointed, is all the Etruscan history I know. I know nothing of the Etruscan League, save that it was composed of twelve cities; and I suspect that is all any one knows.

I returned to the evening in the valley. To the north-east one can see Cortona like some city of marble on the flank of those mysterious hills—

> Through corn and vines and flowers,
> From where Cortona lifts to heaven
> Her diadem of towers.

But Cortona lies on a hillside with a vast background of mountains, that always and from every point of view seem to overwhelm and to threaten her. She crouches there like a white dove. Yet the phrase is a good phrase—the lines are good lines—even now, when I have been in Cortona a hundred times, I have only to go away and to shut my eyes, and there she is, just as she used to be when I was a child, crowning the top of an incredible aerie, and lifting to heaven "her diadem of towers".

And now as to medieval Chiusi, if one would study that, if one would understand that, one must go to the Cathedral of Santa Mustiola, the mother-church of the city, which not only commemorates a gracious saint, but conserves, in so far as they have been conserved at all, the ancient memories of the Longobard rule here.

And first as to Santa Mustiola. Chiusi, if all be true, must have been already of immense antiquity when the Roman lady Mustiola came, during the Aurelian persecution in 275 to visit the Christian prisoners, as our Lord had ordained. Now the governor of Tuscany at that time was Tarcius, and he, seeing the merciful lady by chance, and loving her, as he said, tried to win her to his bed; and when she would not for anything, he had her beaten to death with a leaden scourge. Her tomb, formed out of an ancient column, is still to be seen in her cathedral, and on her *festa*, 3 July, it is even yet a mass of flowers.

When such incredible monsters as Tarcius were done with, at least for a time, the Goths thundered by Chiusi on their way to Rome; the place, in fact, became a sort of Gothic stronghold, and

so fit and useful was it as a base against the Eternal City that even
Totila—who, they tell you, destroyed everything—refrained when
he got Chiusi; indeed, the walls, so old that they were falling from
age when the Longobards came, were never thrown down.

The Longobards established a dukedom in Chiusi, as they did
in Spoleto, and we find a duke established there in the eighth
century, and that lasted till Charlemagne's day, disappearing for
ever in 776. After that Chiusi was ruled by an *esercitale*, and then
by a count. During these and the following centuries she seems
to have enjoyed considerable prosperity. Her true decadence
began in the eleventh century, when continual war at last brought
famine and pestilence. Then her immediate *contado* and the valley
of the Chiana became a pestilential swamp, that even till our
fathers' time made the whole country unhealthy. Something of
this we find expressed by Dante, who, considering that all must
pass away, says:

> Se tu riguardi Luni ed Urbisaglia
> come son ite, e come se ne vanno
> di retro ad esse Chiusi e Sinigaglia. . . .[1]

> If Luni thou regard and Urbisaglia,
> How they have passed away; and how are passing,
> Chiusi and Sinigaglia after them. . . .

No doubt the ruin was notorious, for Chiusi had been a city of
great splendour with two cathedrals, the superior and perhaps the
earlier being under the invocation of S. Secondiano, the other, of
course, under that of S. Mustiola. The *contado*, too, had been or
very considerable extent. Thus what we now call Castiglione del
Lago di Trasimeno was, before 1197, when it was taken and destroyed
by the Aretines, known as Castiglione di Chiusi. Then in 1214 it
seems that the Perugians were confirmed by Innocent III in jurisdiction over that part of the *contado* which was on their side of the
Chiana, and which was thereafter called Chiusi di Perugia. And
when in 1231 the Sienese gained their first victory in the *contado*
of Orvieto, it was Chiusi which suffered. In 1218 the Ghibellines
of Arezzo, captained by Farinata degli Uberti, occupied the place
after the defeat of Campaldino, but in the following year, as

[1] *Paradiso*, XVI.

Villani[1] records, they of Chiusi were routed and the Guelf refugees restored.

It was in the year 1332 that the Perugians first took Chiusi, which shortly after was retaken by the Orvietans, who ruled there till 1337, when Chiusi regained her liberty. She remained free till 1355, when Charles IV established a Vicar in the city. This rule in some sort lasted till 1380, when Siena began to rule there, which she more or less continued to do, though constantly deprived of the city, which was sold and resold all through the fifteenth century, till, indeed, in 1556 she opened her gates to Mario Sforza, Count of Santa Fiora, and with the rest of Tuscany was gathered into the dominion of Cosimo I.

Very little remains in Chiusi, apart from the city herself and the Etruscan tombs, most of the contents of which have been carried off to Florence, for the traveller to see. What there is will be found in the Duomo, a modernized but spaciously beautiful building containing many fragments of older erections, the nave being upheld by eighteen ancient columns of various quality and size. In the loggia in the Piazza are many Etruscan and Roman inscriptions. In the Cathedral are several pictures which should on no account be missed. In the left transept is a fine picture of the Nativity by Fungai, and in the sacristy a picture of the Madonna and Child with saints by Baldassare Peruzzi. Here, too is a beautiful illuminated Missal by Sano di Pietro.

This is really all there is to be had in the way of works of art in Chiusi, whose chief interest after all is in her Etruscan remains, in those vast cavernous tombs that honeycomb her hillside, and in the small museum full of vases, urns, *figurini*, and tear-bottles, which are constantly being found.

As one wanders through the place, quiet enough at any time of year, through the great empty piazza at the top of the town, from which there is so fine a view, past the beautiful red brick church of San Francesco, it is less of Chiusi than of the beautiful world in which she stands, scarcely more than an ancient grave-yard, that one thinks. History here is but a tale that is told. The reality is in the landscape, where to the west Cetona stands like some vast crater with Mont' Amiata looking over its shoulder; or where eastward lie the lakes like precious jewels, which only the passing clouds may trouble as they sail up from the sea to the

[1] *Cronica*, VII, p. 136.

Apennines and the Umbrian hills. Beside that marvellous and eternal beauty no tale of a dead civilization, of which we know nothing and can know nothing, is worth consideration for a moment. For here are the sun and the wind and the soft sky: let us rejoice in them; for too soon we also shall be of even less account than the Etruscans.

CHAPTER XXX

THE CHIANA AND THE WAY TO CORTONA

THE easiest way to reach Cortona from Chiusi is, of course, by train. By this route one passes quite along the western shore of Lago Trasimeno, past Castiglione del Lago in Umbria, coming into Tuscany again at Borghetto at the head of the lake. It is a journey full of beauty and delight, and may be done as well afoot as in the train. But for me that is not the way to Cortona, nor will it, in fact, reveal the true character of the country which lies between Chiusi and Cortona, the Val di Chiana with its great island of hills, the Poggi di Petrignano. To understand this strange and beautiful valley, so profoundly Umbrian in character, it is necessary to take the road, straight almost as a ruled line, across the narrow valley of the Tresa, east of Chiusi, so far as Strada, where it suddenly turns northward and winds slowly over the Poggi di Petrignano through Vaiano and Gioiella, through Pozzuolo, Santa Margherita, Petrignano, Centoia, and Selva, where it descends into the Chiana and makes straight across the wide and fertile vale for that wonderful rock-bound citadel, which is Cortona.

This road has many advantages for the traveller. It passes, for instance, close by Laviano, the birthplace (the house is still visible) of S. Margherita of Cortona, of whom I shall have something to say presently, and it affords a view of the whole country round about, thus revealing at once its character. Something certainly must be said of this valley, which was of old, indeed, more than a swamp, which the rival cities were so eager to dominate and to possess. Through it anciently in a multitude of little streams the river Chiana flowed, till it lost itself in the Paglia and so flowed into Tiber. Its condition during the period from the eleventh to the fourteenth century gradually grew worse; small lakes and vast swamps were formed by the ruin of the Etruscan and Roman system of drainage, which had rendered the river to some extent navigable probably as far as Chiusi, and the whole valley became a pestilential wilderness breathing malaria and death. Dante,

indeed, speaks of it as a hospital in the summer-time,[1] and Fazio
degli Uberti tells us:

> Quivi son volti pallidi e confusi,
> Perchè l' aere e la Chiana è lor nimica,
> Sicchè gli fanno idropici e rinfusi.

The early condition of the Chiana is brought picturesquely before
us in the old custom of Chiusi, whose civic magistrate, with a
great number of heralds and trumpeters, was rowed across the
swamp to the confines of Montepulciano, and in solemn ceremony,
in sign of possession, flung a ring into the waters—*desponsare Clanas*
—precisely as the Doge of Venice did in the Festa of the Bucintoro.[2]
And Pulci in his *Morgante* uses its name to express fever-
stricken and pestilential bogs. The district, that had thus become
a synonym for a dreary swamp, is now one of the most fertile in
Italy, and indeed not less healthy than the heights which sur-
round it. This wonderful change, which took more than two
centuries to effect, was achieved at last by filling up the swamp
with "alluvial deposits" and by a great system of drainage whereby
the Chiana, which originally flowed into the Tiber, was diverted
into the Arno. The attempt had been planned by the Romans,
who, according to Tacitus, only gave it up at the entreaty of the
Florentines, who feared their lands would be flooded. It is to the
Grand Dukes of Tuscany we really owe the great undertaking
which has turned a swamp that was a valuable hunting-ground,
with a great hunting-lodge at Bettolle, into this fertile district of
corn and wine and oil, where the great white oxen now draw
the plough and the girls sing in the vineyards, and the good land
yields a golden harvest. In these days when democracy so boasts
itself I think one should remember that.

The valley, so dreadful in the Middle Age, cannot, one might
think, have been so in ancient times, or certainly the Romans
would have dealt with it. Moreover, men do not as a rule choose
a swamp to fight in, and it was here, in the valley under Cortona
and along the northern side of the lake, Piano Sanguinoso—from
the blood that was spilt there—that Hannibal lured the Romans
out of Arezzo to follow him, and there he took them in ambush,

---

[1] Cf. *Inferno*, XXIX, 45.
[2] F. Petrucci: "I confini Senesi di Val di Chiana", *Bullettino Senese*, ann. ii (1895),
p. 289.

and after three hours of fighting utterly destroyed their army and killed their general, Flaminius. This on 21 June, 217 B.C.

It is, however, on something far more ancient and more venerable that one looks when, having crossed the valley, one enters Camucia and stands at the foot of the great hill where Cortona reigns.

CHAPTER XXXI

CORTONA AND SANTA MARGHERITA

I N one of those grand old-fashioned periods in which Dennis was wont to address his readers in the more solemn moments of his exploration of Etruria, on the eve of entering some once famous city or before discovering to them some extraordinary marvel of his beloved Etruscan art, he introduces us to Cortona. "Traveller, thou art approaching Cortona! Dost thou reverence age—that fullness of years which, as Pliny says, 'in man is venerable, in cities sacred'? Here is that which demands thy reverence. Here is a city, compared to which Rome is but of yesterday—to which most other cities of ancient renown are fresh and green. Thou mayst have wandered far and wide through Italy—nothing hast thou seen more venerable than Cortona. Ere the days of Hector and Achilles, ere Troy itself arose—Cortona was. On that bare and lofty height whose towered crest holds communion with the cloud, dwelt the heaven-born Dardanus, ere he left Italy to found the Trojan race; and on that mount reigned his father Corythus, and there he was laid in the tomb. Such is the ancient legend, and wherefore gainsay it? Away with doubts!—pay thy full tribute of homage—*acceptam parce movere fidem!* Hast thou respect to fallen greatness? Yon solemn city was once the proudest and mightiest in the land, the metropolis of Etruria and now—but enter its gates and look around."

Dear Dennis, companion of my boyhood, I have done thy bidding, and if I have forsaken what thou hast loved so eloquently for things that were hidden from thee—forgive me, master. It was thy hand led me hither, and in thy name I went. Also I did thy bidding. I "looked around", and it seemed to me that Corythus was little to me,[1] but Luca Signorelli very much, and as for heaven-born Dardanus, what was he after all beside Santa Margherita, Sister of the Seraphs, Lily of the Fields?

But before one can come either at heaven-born Dardanus or at S. Margherita it is necessary, as Dennis says, to come to Cortona, to enter its gates.

[1] *Æneid* III, 167. Aeneas is bidden, in his vision, by the Penates he had borne from Troy. "Corythum terrasque requirat Ausonias."

One may drive by the road that climbs the hillside to Cortona easily of course, but if one be young enough and keen enough, one should go by the pathway among the boulders, over the stones, straight up the hillside to the city, and by so doing realize what an unapproachable fortress Cortona is and on what tremendous ruins she is founded. But even when one has reached the Porta San Domenico and found the inn, one has still to see Cortona, a city of stone, and that entails climbing everywhere, and especially a long climb to the upper town, for Cortona hangs, as it were, down the mountain-side from the star which is her *fortezza*.

On the way up by road one passes the beautiful Renaissance church built by Francesco di Giorgio, the Madonna del Calcinaio full of light and space.

Nothing, I think, in all Tuscany will impress and astonish the traveller more than his walks, climbs rather, up and down Cortona through that maze of narrow precipitous streets between the sombre palaces of hewn stone founded on the naked rock, the cliffs and boulders that a hundred generations have been powerless to wear away.

One feels her ancientness at once, when one comes, even at Porta San Domenico, within sight of her walls, for though they be medieval or Renaissance they are based on the most ancient of all, and often, as about Porta Colonia, they have proved so lasting that all later ages have passed them by untouched, and one sees them as they were three thousand years or more ago. Only at the highest part of the town the old wall has disappeared that the *fortezza* might there be included in the city; yet it is just there, too, at Terra Pozza, outside the fortress, one comes upon a huge fragment of the old wall again, 120 feet in length, composed of enormous blocks of sandstone held together by weight and without cement or mortar. Here is something as formidably old as anything at Volterra or Fiesole, something that the Umbri may have built before the Pelasgi took Cortona, to be deprived in their turn by the Etruscans.

It will thus be seen that Cortona has much to offer, a wall of immense antiquity, streets narrow and precipitous, palaces and buildings of the Middle Age. Happily, too, she possesses many of those more human works which smile at us from the early Renaissance.

Just without the Porta San Domenico, in a delightful piazza,

BEATING OUT THE GRAIN IN THE AIA

ANGEL OF THE ANNUNCIATION (detail), Fra Angelico.
Museum, Cortona

there stands a church under the protection of that saint, a building of the fifteenth century. In the lunette over the entry is a fresco much damaged of the Virgin and Child between two Dominican saints, SS. Dominic and Thomas Aquinas, with two angels.

For Fra Angelico came here in 1409, when schism proclaimed Alexander V Pope, and the friars of San Domenico of Fiesole, rather than acknowledge this antipope, fled away, some to Cortona. Among them was a novice, Fra Giovanni, whom we call for love Beato Angelico. And here he painted several glorious works, two of which, happily still remaining to us, are now preserved in the church of the Gesù here in Cortona. Of all he did at San Domenico, in the church that remains, in the convent where he passed his novitiate, which has been destroyed, only one is left there for us, the lunette over the doorway, this half-ruined fresco of the Madonna and Child with saints.

But there are other pictures here. Within, over the altar on the right, is a Madonna and saints with the Bishop Sernini, for whom it was painted in 1515, by the great man Cortona bred for Italy— Luca Signorelli. It is one of his last pictures, now, unhappily, in very bad condition. The Madonna, in a beautiful red robe and green mantle, is enthroned with her little Son, her feet resting on the heads of cherubim, an angel on either side, while below stand S. Domenico and S. Peter Martyr. There is an altarpiece here by Lorenzo di Niccolò Gerini. This is a monumental work.

I have described these pictures as though they were still in the church, but owing to the war they were placed in the museum in the Baptistery, Il Gesù. A great misfortune befell the altarpiece by Sassetta which till the war of 1939–45 stood in San Domenico. It was placed in safety but was ruined by damp, one fears irremediably.

From San Domenico, the Via Nazionale within the gate leads straight to the Piazza before the Palazzo del Municipio. Thence the Via Guelfa runs to the left past a magnificent palace of the sixteenth century to the church of Sant' Agostino, where there is an altarpiece of the Madonna and Child with saints by Pietro da Cortona, a native painter of the sixteenth century. Turning to the right from the Piazza della Repubblica one soon comes to the Piazza Signorelli and the fine Palazzo Pretorio with its little museum of Etruscan antiquities—urns, vases, inscriptions, and so forth. Two objects here are of high importance: the painting of a

18

Muse, said to be of the second century, and the Etruscan Lampa-
dario of bronze of the fifth century B.C., the finest thing of this sort
ever to come to light, as this did in 1840.

From the Piazza Signorelli the Via Casali descends to the Duomo.
Built by Giulio da Sangallo, as it is said, in the end of the fifteenth
century, the Duomo was unhappily altered in the eighteenth
century, and has lost much of its beauty. It contains, however,
four works by Signorelli, all unhappily late works and none of them
in very good preservation, as well as a fine altarpiece of the
Madonna with angels by Pietro Lorenzetti. Signorelli's works are
all in the choir; they consist of a Deposition with *predella*, painted
in 1502; the Communion of the Apostles, painted in 1512; and two
pictures which are his only in part, an Immaculate Conception
and an Assumption of the Blessed Virgin. The most important
of these works is the first; it was not painted for the Duomo,
however, but for Santa Margherita. The fame of this picture, and
it was very famous, owes everything to Vasari, who, noting the
realism of the dead Christ, spread the legend he had heard, that
Signorelli painted it from the dead body of his own son. However
this may be, and Vasari as a little lad once met Signorelli, who
was his kinsman, we know that when the great painter lost his son
he would not part with him until he had made a drawing of the
young body, pathetic and beautiful, so that he might remind himself every day of a thing so frail which he had found so precious.

But the great treasure here is the picture by Pietro Lorenzetti.
This is an early work very noble and beautiful. The Madonna is
enthroned, her little Son on her left arm, mutually gazing one at
the other. Four angels are on guard about the throne.

Opposite the Duomo is the church of Il Gesù, the Baptistery
built in 1505, and here, in fact, are preserved the great treasures
of Cortona.

The finest of these is the exquisite Annunciation from San
Domenico, where under a delicate loggia, just without the house
at sunset, in the cool of the day, the Virgin has been reading, when
suddenly over the flowers Gabriel has come to her with his *Ave
Gratia Plena*, and she has crossed her white hands on her bosom,
and, the book still open on her knee, has leaned a little breathlessly
forward in humble acceptance. And indeed as the angel has said,
the Lord is with her, the Dove hovers softly over her bright head,
and God the Father Himself overhears His own message, passing

down under the arches. In the background, as though to show quite clearly what is happening, one sees as in a vision our first parents expelled from Paradise, that Eden to which Mary is about to win for us admission again. This is the most perfect of all the pictures by Angelico remaining to us. The *predella* shows scenes from the Virgin's life, and one scene, probably a substitution, of the life of S. Dominic.

The other work by Fra Angelico here, also comes from San Domenico. It is a triptych of the Madonna enthroned with her Divine Son between S. John Baptist, S. John Evangelist, S. Mary Magdalen, and S. Mark. Four guardian angels stand behind with tributes of flowers. In the pinnacles are our Lord crucified, the Blessed Virgin and S. John grieving, and in the *tondi* at the base is the Annunciation. In the *predella* are scenes from the life of S. Dominic.

Beside these two magnificent works hangs a *tondo* of the Madonna and four saints by Signorelli, a late and not very charming picture, possibly by his nephew Francesco.

There are here, however, two works by Signorelli himself, though not among his best. One represents the Institution of the Eucharist, the other the Immaculate Conception, painted about 1520 for the Confraternity of Jesus here in Cortona. This picture is almost as theological as Francia's altarpiece of the same subject painted earlier in Lucca.

From the Baptistery one makes ones way by Via Dardano to the Porta Colonia, where the view northward and east is fierce and desolate, and where the Etruscan wall still guards the city. Then returning through the city to set out for the *fortezza*, one can visit various churches on the way. In San Francesco, for instance, there is an Adoration of the Shepherds from the *bottega* of Signorelli. It is here Frate Elias was buried.[1] In San Niccolò are two beautiful things, a double altarpiece of the Madonna and Child with saints, on the reverse a dead Christ upheld by angels, by Signorelli, and a ruined fresco of a Madonna and saints on the left wall by the same painter. The altarpiece is of a rare beauty and originality, an important painting of the master's. The dead Christ half lies on

---

[1] It is about an hour's walk from Cortona to the beautiful Franciscan hermitage of Le Celle, very like the Carceri outside Assisi, but smaller. Here it was that S. Francis as recorded in the *Mirror of Perfection*, gave the cloak his friars had just given him, brand new as it was, to a beggar who had motherless children; and he made him promise not to part with it save at a fair price, so that the Brethren had to buy it back for the Saint. Frate Elias was sent to Le Celle when he was excommunicated.

the tomb, upheld by an archangel, while three others stand by in grief. Before Him kneel S. Jerome, and, on the other side, S. Francis and three other saints. The four archangels are very noble figures, and have much in common with Signorelli's work at Orvieto, while the S. Jerome is splendidly dramatic. The only figure that is disappointing is the dead Christ, which somehow in its over-expressive realism fails both in beauty and effect. The picture of the Madonna and saints on the reverse is not less fine. There we see our Lady enthroned with her little Son about to bless us, between S. Peter and S. Paul.

From San Niccolò it is still a long climb by a way cut out of the rock up to Santa Margherita, but no one, I think, can afford to miss going there, for though the church be modern the view thence is magnificent, and there is the shrine of S. Margaret, one of the most human of saints, a true daughter of S. Francis. And after gazing half in dread on the "still incorrupt" body of one who was so beautiful that she was called Lily of the Valleys, one continues on the way up to the *fortezza*, where all the world seems to lie at one's feet, where Cetona and Mont' Amiata guard the western horizon and the great valley of the Chiana stretches out for ever, dotted with villages and pleasant with vineyards and corn.

Somewhere among those island hills that lie in the great plain between this and Montepulciano, at the little village of Laviano, S. Margaret was born in the year 1247.[1] Her father was a husband-man, and of her mother we only know that she died when Margaret was but seven years old. Indeed, all that the child seems able to remember of her mother was her humility.

Margaret's misfortunes began when she was but nine years old, for then her father took a new wife who seems to have treated her with indifference, if not with harshness. Now for Margaret one thing was necessary above any other—to be loved. We can picture her miserable childhood, an alien in her father's house, unwanted, and even looked on with jealousy, for as she grew older her beauty astonished all who looked on her. Then when she was about seventeen a marvellous thing, as it must have seemed to her, befell. Suddenly the world was full of flowers. She was beloved. That she should give her love in return was just a matter of course. The suitor who came thus into her life was a young knight from

---

[1] An excellent Life of S. Margaret of Cortona, together with a translation of the essential parts of her legend, has been published by Fr. Cuthbert, O.S.F.C., under title *A Tuscan Penitent* (Burns and Oates).

Montepulciano. She never told his name; she gave him her whole heart. This youth, then, came to court her, probably secretly, and continually unsatisfied, besought her presently to flee from her unhappiness to his happiness, to go with him to his home in the city, promising her love, admiration, joy, and the whole world if she would come. He also promised her marriage.

So little Margaret, doubting nothing perhaps and certainly loving all, crept out of her father's house in the night and fled away across the dreary marshes, nearly drowned with her lover on the way, for the Chiana was in flood, till they came to the pleasant, smiling, seductive city of Montepulciano. And there with much joy she lived with him she loved for nine years: only he forgot to marry her. No doubt he was too busy with her in his arms; for we read that he gave her all her heart's desire, denying her only this one thing, that he should call her wife. Among other things he gave her was a little son. Then Margaret seems to have been ashamed: yet only in her heart, for she was used to unhappiness, and that happiness so great as that she had should be complete may well have seemed impossible. Her neighbours found her as lovely as ever, as gay, as witty, and as full of the desire of joy. One of them seems to have hinted to her one day that she should look to her soul; but she answered gaily and with spirit that one should have no fear for her, for she would yet be among the saints, and the whole world should come a pilgrim to her shrine, with staff and scrip and leathern bottle.

So she lived, so she met life, so she communed with her heart, till one summer evening, as she sat singing at the window awaiting her man's return, his hound came home without him and would do nothing but whine and run to and fro between her and the doorway. Then, suddenly cold at the heart, she followed him. And the brute led her to a lonely place not far from the road where was a wood, and there lay he who was her all—mangled and dead.

Presently she returned home with them who bore the body to her house. From that moment she was a changed woman. Her heart was broken, and all that had once been so precious seemed now nothing worth, since she had lost the best of all. Her actions and whole attitude towards life at this time prove her great love. She accused herself, her beauty, her love, to save her lover. She judged herself more harshly than even a prudish piety is able to do, and from that moment she determined to expiate her lover's

sin and her own by a life wholly devoted to God. She resolved
on bitter austerities, on humiliations past belief, on absolute poverty
and semi-starvation. First of all she returned to her lover's family
all he had given her, save some trinkets that were too precious to
be given to any but the poor; these she distributed among such as
were in distress, for they were her brethren and sisters. Then she
resolved to go back to her father's house and to suffer all things
with joy. With scarce enough to clothe her, she set out with her
little son, and when she came to the door she knocked for admittance timidly, like a beggar, and indeed without hope. Yet her
father would have received her gladly, but he could not answer
for his wife: the married woman turned her out, drove her from
the house.

Something of the tragedy of this time in Margaret's life has
found its way into the legend which from her own lips Fra Giunta
took down, and which Father Cuthbert has translated. For when
she was in despair and there was no one to protect her, then He
who, whether we will or no, is always near us, waiting till we need
Him, came—ah! as she was to learn, the best, true lover of all—to
take her into His keeping. He reminds her of this later, when she
might hear His voice:

"Remember, *poverella*, how, thy tempter being dead, thou didst
return to thy father at Laviano, with thy whole being filled with
sorrow, with thy tears and drawn face, clothed in a black robe and
utterly ashamed. And thy father, lacking fatherly pity and urged
on by thy stepmother, did drive thee from his home. Not knowing
what to do, and being without any adviser or helper, thou didst
sit down weeping under a fig-tree in his garden, and there thou
didst seek in Me a Guide, a Father, a Spouse and Lord; and with
a humble heart didst confess thine utter misery of soul and body.
Then lo! the serpent of old, seeing thee cast out by thy father,
sought to his own shame and thy destruction to make thy comeli-
ness and youth an inducement to presume upon My mercy; putting
it into thy heart that since thou wast now cast out thou mightest
excusably go on in sin, and that wheresoever thou shouldst come
or go thou wouldst not lack lovers amongst the great ones of the
world because of thine exceeding beauty."

That was spared her. For as she had called on our Lord, He
delivered her out of her distress, bidding her rise up from under

the fig-tree and go to the friars of S. Francis in Cortona, and they would know what she was to do.

Margaret, hearing that voice, did as she was bidden, and coming to Cortona, asked of two ladies whom she met on the way to the convent of San Francesco, but they—their names were Marinaria and Raneria, beautiful names—seeing her condition, took her and her little son home, and brought her to the friars, who gave her pity, kindness, and good counsel. Thus was begun the work of purification, of "expiation", which endured during the rest of her life.

Margaret came to Cortona in 1273, and she never left the city again but once, and that was to go to Montepulciano publicly to proclaim her sin before the city in the Duomo. This Fra Giunta reluctantly gave her leave to do, and truly in order to save her from a worse humiliation, which she would have inflicted on herself: for she desired to go thither naked, with a rope round her neck, led by a hired woman proclaiming her sin through the streets.

In Cortona she earned her bread by nursing the sick; and presently leaving the house of Marinaria and Raneria, which seemed too soft, she went to live in a hut in a lonelier place. There she began to live wholly upon alms, begging her bread day by day, refusing money, and only accepting the refuse from the tables of those, who themselves can have been scarcely other than poor. They refused to see in her a mere beggar, and gave her more than the refuse, but this she gave to the poor, and took for herself and her son only what remained over. Thus, though she was hard on her own child,[1] as the result of her sin perhaps, she was called the "mother of the poor".

Thus three years passed away. But though Margaret's whole life had suffered a revolution, a purification if you will, fundamentally she was the same nature. She had always longed for love, for the outward manifestation of it, and in her new love of Christ, which had come to her "in that passionate way of hers", she desired it also by way of assurance. And it was in that Voice which had spoken with her in the garden under the fig-tree that she found this, while to prove to all her sincerity she entered the Third Order of S. Francis. Yet it was the Voice that she lived to

---

[1] "She told the boy on one occasion that in serving the poor she knew she was serving Christ, because she was moved by the spirit, whereas in serving him she was not sure but that she was obeying the impulse of the flesh." The lad became a Frate, and appears to have died a martyr's death.

hear: "My child," it would say, and "*Poverella*"—poor little one. And so began a wonderful interior and mystical life in which Christ held familiar conversation with her and discovered to her many mysteries. This is not the place to discuss the mystical experiences of Margaret. It will suffice to refer the reader to the beautiful legend written by Fra Giunta, her "unworthy staff", which Father Cuthbert has translated with so much sympathy.

To return to her life of action. For if as a contemplative and ecstatic she was great, she was by no means a mere recluse. That tending of the sick presently organized itself, her cottage became a hospital, and out of it grew the great Spedale of Cortona, the Spedale di Santa Maria della Misericordia, opened in 1286. The sisters who served it were all, like Margaret, Franciscan Tertiaries, and the people of Cortona, remembering S. Francis, called them *Le Poverelle*.

But even this organization had not exhausted all Margaret's power for good. She was the great peacemaker of Tuscany at that period. Already in 1277 she had fearlessly warned the warlike Bishop of Arezzo, Guglielmo Ubertini Pazzi, to amend his ways and cease from strife, and two years later, in 1279, by her prayers she saved the Cortonesi from invasion. In 1289, she again warned Bishop Guglielmo, but this time he would not hear her, and two days later he fell in battle.

Yet for all her influence in the great things of this world, it was as a comforter, as the mother of her people, as a nurse, that she was most beloved. "If a child were sick the parents would come to Margaret that she might lay her hands upon it and bring back health. Those who were strongly tempted to sin would come laying bare their temptation, and seeking in her prayers and words of counsel the moral strength they lacked. If a mother despaired of a son's salvation because of his evil life, she came begging Margaret to send him some bread from her table, believing that if the son but tasted bread sanctified by Margaret's presence he would be converted. . . . It was useless for Margaret to plead that she was a sinner like themselves, and that because of her sins her very touch would soil them. The people disbelieved her protestations and believed the more in the efficacy of her intervention."

Yet even she did not escape scandal. Evil-doers cast suspicion upon her relations with Fra Giunta, her confessor, and for this cause, much to the regret of the friar, who looked to have her body after death, she removed from her house near San Francesco to the spot under the *fortezza* where now her church stands, but which was then occupied by the ruined and deserted church of San Basilio. Fra Giunta at the time of the scandal, in which the friars were not blameless, had been sent away to Siena. It was, however, in his arms that, seven years later, Margaret came to die on 22 February, 1297; and immediately all Cortona proclaimed her a saint, but she was not formally canonized till May 1728.

It is strange that Cortona should have held almost at that same time two such different Franciscans as Frate Elias and S. Margaret—the one a great statesman who abhorred poverty, the other a poor woman who loved it. Elias built here in the city a vast palace full of every sort of splendour that later became the Vescovado, Margaret built the hospital and restored the church which, after being rebuilt, was to bear her name. And it is she who is the victor, not he, for all his power and wealth and greatness of mind. He is forgotten by all save a few historians, while her name is still familiarly dear on the lips of peasants and children, who invoke her, their all-powerful friend, as we may hear any day in the fields or the byways about her home:

> O Lily of our fields,
> O Violet of humility,
> O little Sister of the Seraphs,
>   Ora pro nobis.

INDEX

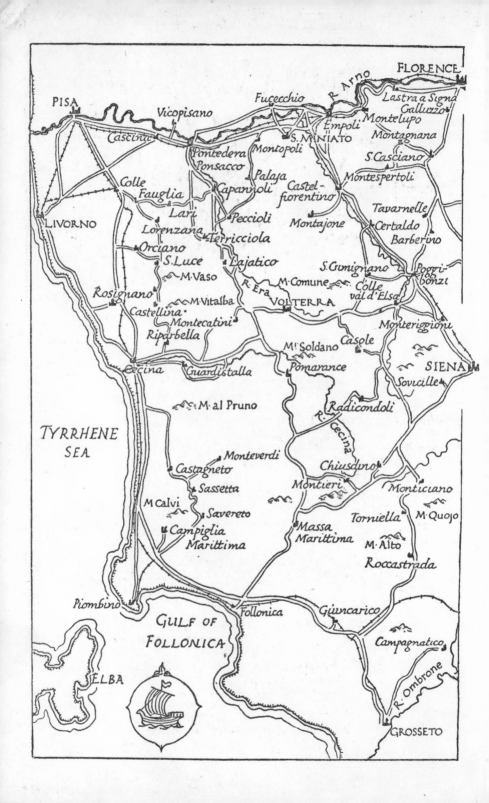